SAMMY MILLER
MOTORCYCLE LEGEND

First in the Field

Sammy Miller, Trials Rider Extraordinary

Duckhams

The oil with the perfect body

SAMMY MILLER
MOTORCYCLE LEGEND

MICK WALKER

DB
PUBLISHING

First published in Great Britain in 2010 by
The Derby Books Publishing Company Limited
3 The Parker Centre, Derby, DE21 4SZ.

This paperback edition published in Great Britain in 2014 by DB Publishing,
an imprint of JMD Media Ltd

ISBN 978-1-78091-213-4

Contents

4

Every so often a unique snapshot of times gone by is discovered in a dusty vault or in shoeboxes in an attic by an enthusiastic amateur photographer. They are living history. Each and every one of us cannot resist the temptation as we marvel at the quality of the images, to let our mind drift back to the good old days and wonder what it was really like.

We at Mortons Motorcycle Media, market-leading publishers of classic and vintage titles, own one of the largest photographic archives of its kind in the world. It is a treasure trove of millions of motorcycle and related images, many of which have never seen the light of day since they were filed away in the dark-room almost 100 years ago.

Perhaps the biggest gem of all is our collection of glass plates – almost two tons of them to be precise! They represent a largely hitherto unseen look into our motorcycling heritage from the turn of the century. Many of the plates are priceless and capture an era long gone when the pace of life was much slower and traffic jams were unheard of.

We are delighted to be associated with well-known author Mick Walker in the production of this book and hope you enjoy the images from our archive.

Terry Clark,
Managing Director,
Mortons Media Group Ltd

MORTONS
Media Group Ltd

Preface

Sammy Miller: Motorcycle Legend is the eighth in a series intended to cover the world's leading motorcycle competitors.

The most successful trials rider of all time – with more than 1,200 victories – Sammy would have been a legend for this alone. However, this is only one facet of a truly remarkable career which has spanned well over half a century (and is still continuing), embracing road racing, scrambling, sand racing, grass-track racing and, of course, trials. Then there has been Sammy Miller as businessman, designer and development engineer. If all this was not enough, there is also the Sammy Miller Motorcycle Museum and Trust. Founded from a private collection in 1983, the museum has continued to grow in size and importance; it has now been placed into a trust to leave behind a legacy for future generations.

Words alone can not amply describe just how much Sammy has devoted to the sport, giving his whole working life to motorcycling in general. Perhaps it is the museum which is the testament to the fact that Sammy was not simply a brilliant rider, but also a very skilled engineer and restorer, ambassador and custodian of motorcycle history. It is all these qualities which have led me to realise just how significant his career has been.

I would like to thank all those who have helped in some way to produce this book with either photographs or information, sometimes both. These include my Austrian friend and Grand Prix photographer Wolfgang Gruber, Jeff Smith, Nick Jefferies, Bill Lawless, John Surtees, Murray Walker, the late Ralph Venables, Tommy Robb, Dan Shorey, Vic Bates, the late Terry Hill, Bob Stanley, Bill Gibson, Amanda Frend, Lynette Goodman and, most of all, Sammy and Rosemary Miller.

I sincerely trust that you, the reader, will gain as much pleasure from *Sammy Miller: Motorcycle Legend* as I have in compiling it. But the front-cover picture is not my choice, if it had it would have been Ariel GOV 132.

Mick Walker
Wisbech, Cambridgeshire

Chapter 1

Early Days

S.H. (Samuel Hamilton) Miller – more simply Sammy to millions of motorcycle fans around the world – was born in Belfast, Northern Ireland, on 11 November 1933. The youngest of three children (brother Fred and sister Mabel), the Miller family resided in the northern part of the Ulster capital in Inver Avenue, just off the Antrim Road. Sammy's parents, Alexander and Jean, owned a painting and decorating business.

A Love of Racing

Together with his father, from the age of 12 Sammy attended numerous sporting events featuring cars and motorcycles. His father had owned a large number of both four and two-wheeled vehicles, and his enthusiasm soon rubbed off on young Sammy.

Sammy's father and sister Mabel in the late 1930s; the motorcycle is a side-valve Ariel single, with hand-change gearbox.

Racing of any kind always guaranteed large crowds in Ireland, notably the Ulster Grand Prix, which was then staged over the famous Clady course to the north-west of Belfast. Clady was most notable for its seven-mile (11.25km) straight, where riders would become airborne flat out in top gear.

Soon the Miller household was full of names such as Stanley Woods, Artie Bell, Ernie Lyons and the McCandless brothers. As Sammy was later to recall: 'Most of the events we visited were pure road racing, but we also took in the occasional grass-track or trial.' And it was the latter event which left what Jeff Clew described in his 1976 biography *Sammy Miller, The Will To Win* as: 'An indelible impression on Sam. For once he could actually brush shoulders with the competitors and not just view them as untouchable gods over a hedge or stone wall as they passed.'

Sammy's first motorcycle, a 1929 twin-port 197cc Villiers-powered Francis-Barnett, purchased for £10 from Comber, near Belfast, in 1948.

The Coming of War

With the outbreak of World War Two at the beginning of September 1939, everything changed. Eventually, the Miller family closed their home for the duration, moving to Templepatrick, a small town some eight miles (12.9km) to the north-west of Belfast.

Obviously, moving from a city to the countryside was a major shock to the system for Sammy, then six years old. At first he found things hard, as he had to change school and find new friends. Country life did have its benefits, however, as for the first time he was able to appreciate the animal kingdom – something he treasures to this very day. Indeed, he has a genuine love of the diversity of animals to be found in the grounds of his museum complex.

The Francis-Barnett

Sammy's motorcycling career began in 1948, at 15 years of age, after saving up £10 to purchase, in his own words: 'a really old 1929 197cc Francis-Barnett [twin-port] two-stroke. It wasn't very reliable but it got me around to the races and taught me a lot about how to keep a motorcycle running. It wasn't any good for competition riding, though, and as I was dying to race, I swapped it for a 150cc four-stroke New Imperial.'

The 150cc New Imperial with unit construction four-stroke engine, with which Sammy won his first grass-track race at Downpatrick towards the end of the 1951 season. Beaten by Sammy in that 200cc scratch race was Austin Carson who, like Sammy, took up road racing but unfortunately was killed in Sweden racing a 350 Norton. This was a big blow for Sammy.

Although Sammy's mother eventually came around, to begin with she was not too keen on him becoming a motorcyclist. For example, he had to coerce an aunt who lived five miles (8km) away at Glengormley to let him keep the Francis-Barnett there, which meant that whenever he wanted to ride it he was forced to take a tram journey.

When Charles Deane asked him in 1978 'Surely you didn't race that?' Sammy replied: 'Of course I did. I tuned it a little and took it to the road races and grass-track meetings. In fact, I won my first grass-track race at Downpatrick, organised by the Temple MCC at the end of the 1951 season, on that old machine. Trouble was that it was always breaking piston rings and I was constantly having to strip and rebuild it.' Earlier that year Sammy had competed in his first grass-track event at Mullusk.

The Ill-fated Moto Guzzi

The following year, in 1952, Sammy decided to upgrade: 'Well, grass-track was only really a stop-gap. I wanted to go road racing and I bought a partly-dismantled 250cc Moto Guzzi Airone. It was only a 1937 roadster model, but I thought I could tune it for racing. Unfortunately it didn't work and the bike proved too slow for road racing. Anyway, I sold this to somebody in England and decided that if I was going to go road racing, I had to do it properly.'

Trials versus Road Racing

We now arrive at a trials versus road racing situation – one which was to dominate Sammy's competitive career until it was resolved, finally, during mid-1958.

The first clash of interests, so to speak, was between Sammy's home-built SHS (Samuel Hamilton Special), a 197cc Villiers-powered trials mount and a 1949 AJS 7R racer. Essentially, the former commenced with the purchase of a 1933 250cc Matchless four-stroke single from a breaker's yard for the princely sum of £3. The engine was, as Sammy says, 'beyond repair', so it and the separate gearbox were removed, to be replaced by a new 197cc Villiers 8E engine, at the cost of £32 10s, including shipment from England.

In a foretaste of things to come, and undaunted by such a demanding project, Sammy set about the construction of his trials special himself. The first task was to cut out the required engine plates needed to fit the Villiers unit into the Matchless frame. And he was to spend several evenings fashioning these plates from scratch – there being no existing template for such a conversion.

As anyone who has built a special will know, the engine has to be located in such a way that the chainline is absolutely correct. As Sammy admits, it was very much a case of trial and error, and he was also later to confess that he was 'So ignorant of material specification at the time that on one occasion I was sold a spring steel sheet.' Which, of course, was totally unsuitable for the job at hand. As for the welding, a fellow motorcyclist, Billy Spence, helped with this task, and in due course the SHS was finally completed. The SHS showed the age of its Matchless components by sporting not only a rigid frame, but also girder front forks; later the latter assembly was ditched in favour of more modern teles. Sammy constructed the SHS over the summer of 1953.

While the SHS was being readied, Sammy, with the help of his father, purchased a 1949 AJS 7R from former TT rider Charlie Gray, who had decided to retire from road racing. Unlike the SHS, the AJS was a purpose-built racing motorcycle (see boxed section within this chapter) and was therefore a completely different proposition compared to the diminutive two-stroke machine.

It was also at about this time that Sammy left Cloakies, a glass manufacturer, which he had joined after leaving Belfast High School. There he worked in the stained glass department as part of the drawing and laying out department. Sammy recalls: 'I left Cloakies because I hadn't enough time to practise and compete, it was a 48-hour week.' After leaving Cloakies he entered the family painting and decorating business.

It is also worth pointing out that during the early 1950s the trials and road racing seasons were (unlike today) clearly divided, making it possible to concentrate on one discipline at a time. The road racing season began on Easter Monday and the trials season on 1 October.

Riding the SHS

Sammy's first-ever trials event came at the Shane Cup event near Randlestown, Northern Ireland, and took place on the first Saturday in October 1953. This is how Sammy described the event many years ago: 'Without the luxury of transport, I set off on the morning of the event to ride to the Shane Cup Trial some 50 miles [80km] away. The route took me onto the famous seven-mile [11.25km] straight on the old Ulster Grand Prix circuit,

Sammy with his home-built SHS (Samuel Hamilton Special) after completing it in the summer of 1953. Essentially the SHS was a 1933 Matchless chassis with a new 197cc Villiers engine.

Later, the girder forks of the SHS were ditched in favour of more modern teles.

but it felt like a good 14 miles [22.5km] on the little undergeared SHS.' He continued: 'I always like to arrive in good time, but for this event I was there before the organizer! After a mediocre ride which did not please me at all, a quick burn-up home and I was off to the usual cinema show with my pals to forget all about it. When the show was over we rushed out to get the evening sports paper, and there it was in black and white: I had won the novice award and finished ninth overall. I must have jumped about 10ft in the air!'

Seven days later our man had his next event, at the Lead Mines in Conlig, County Down. And as Sammy recalls: 'With more midnight oil being burned I was all set to try and climb up a few places from ninth.'

Again, Sammy was pleasantly surprised by his performance, winning the semi-experts' award. Now he was in the Experts Class with the Kirks (Alfie and John), Terry Hill, Billy Hutton and the rest of Ulster's leading trials stars.

After some eight trials came the McCrum Cup event, held at Wolf Hill, near Belfast. 'All the sections were relatively easy except for two,' says

Sammy. 'One was a difficult climb over rocks in a deep gully with very steep banks. When I arrived all the experts had departed, a fortunate circumstance, as there were four laps and I did not want my line to be copied. My line was to drop off one bank and "wall-of-death" it up the other, missing the rocks and hoping to have enough speed to make the exit. It worked and SHS had the only clean on the first lap!'

'I footed hard through the other difficult sections like most of the riders and cleaned all the easier ones. This went on for four laps. Then my advantage weakened; all the experts were on to my line and cleaning the section. It was such a relief to hear on the radio that I had won by three marks from the then Irish Champion, John Kirk.'

Even so, Sammy wondered whether he could beat the English works riders on their own ground. 'Could I even hope to win the Hurst Cup Trial [staged during February in Ulster] when there was a formidable invasion of works teams: BSA, Triumph, Francis-Barnett, James, AJS and DOT?'

Sammy's First Hurst Cup Trial
After spectating at many Hurst Cup Trials, at last Sammy had a machine and was thus able to enter this famous event. As he was to recall in his book *Sammy Miller on Trials* (first published in 1969): 'I was very "raw" at the time and spent every minute practising before the event, with the result that I was worn out and the machine below par for the actual event.'

All went well on the first lap of the Clandeboyne Estate course, but on the second, at the notorious Tower section, a steep climb over rocks and tree roots, there was, said Sammy: 'A deadly sound with terrible vibrations.' This was the result of the gearbox sprocket having lost most of the tops of its teeth! The only solution was to pull the final drive chain 'tight as a banjo string' and press on. This solved the problem – providing the banjo string was kept in tension. Next the rear chainguard got damaged by the rear chain and was torn off. After struggling on for a further two laps, the front mudguard was the next victim and Sammy's mechanical ability was being called into question.

This is how Sammy summed up the final part of the 1954 Hurst Cup Trial: 'With the loss of some bolts the seat was just dangling on. I came up to the finish to see the chequered flag, but not for me. There was another lap to struggle round and the SHS was slowly deteriorating. But we made the finish. Although slow on time, I was the best Irishman on observation.'

Sammy was later to comment: 'It is a very true saying that many a good event is won in the workshop. Machine care is of the utmost importance both for performance and machine life.' And machine 'fitness for purpose' is just as important as the skill of the rider. In fact, without the former, the latter will not be able to give of his best. Certainly, in Sammy Miller's case, his rise to the top in the trials world was very much a case of a totally dedicated rider and expertly prepared machinery. And that 1954 Hurst Cup Trial lesson was instrumental in setting Sammy on a course which aimed at perfection in the machine preparation stakes; something he has followed through to this very day, as witnessed by the outstanding workmanship which is to be found on all the exhibits in his museum.

The 1954 Scottish Six Days

The limit set by the organisers for the 1954 Scottish Six Days Trials was 180 – with number 72 being allocated to S.H. Miller (197cc SHS) – out of 176 entries received. The total distance to be covered in the six days totalled 952 miles (1,532km), and, as was then customary, the trial would start in Edinburgh (on Monday 6 May).

In the Scottish, marks were lost under three main headings: reliability, performance on hills, and machine condition. With the exception of the

Sammy taking part in his first Scottish Six Days aboard the SHS in May 1954. And a brilliant debut it was too, as he not only gained a Special First Class Award, but also won the Ben Nevis Quaich award for the best newcomer.

third day, each day's route included one or more check points; marks being deducted for late starting in the morning and for arriving before or after the specified time margins at the checks. Because a few very difficult sections had seen the entire entry penalised the previous year, certain 'more-difficult-than-average sections' – known as 'star hills' – saw the marking system modified to provide a more precise assessment of performance. On all other hills repeated footing or a single dab entailed a loss of three marks and failure resulted in a loss of five marks. At each day's machine-examination note was taken of the faults, and marks were deducted accordingly.

Snow Storms

For a month previously the weather in Scotland had been mild and dry; however, the weekend prior to the start of the Scottish all this changed, with Arctic-like weather conditions, including freezing temperatures, heavy rain and snow in the Highlands.

As was customary in those far-off days, Sammy rode the SHS to the docks in Belfast, then embarked for Glasgow by ferry, carrying his possessions in a haversack strapped to the machine's fuel tank. On arrival at Glasgow, he wheeled the SHS off the boat and rode the 40 miles (64.4km) to the Scottish capital.

After the problems experienced in the Hurst Cup Trial, Sammy had made sure that the machine was in tip-top order – well, as far as was possible with such an ancient chassis.

The first day of the Scottish saw the run from Edinburgh to Fort William, a total of 184 miles (296km), which included some observed hills.

Although he had prepared the SHS well, the same could not be said of his own well-being. That first day Sammy was frozen to the skin and literally crying as he motored northward in the intense cold. Even so, he stuck to the task and eventually arrived in Fort William with the other riders. But the extreme weather had taken its toll, as only three riders remained unpenalised at the end of that first day (G.E. Fisher, 122cc Francis-Burnett; P.T. Stirland, 197cc James; L.A. Ratcliffe, 347cc Matchless). Five others had lost only three marks; these were P.H. Alves (199cc Triumph), J.H. Wade (197cc Francis-Burnett), W. Nicholson (348cc BSA), G.O. McLaughlan (490cc Norton) – plus Sammy and the SHS!

Behind these were famous names such as Hugh Viney, Geoff Duke, Brian Martin, Johnny Giles and many more established stars.

Sammy continued to impress for the remainder of the week. Not only did he gain a Special First Class Award (with the loss of 67 marks), but he also won the Ben Nevis Quaich award for best newcomer.

A Road Racing Debut

A mere 10 days after the finish of the Scottish Six Days, Sammy was back in Ulster competing in his very first road race. And what a debut it was too, on 19 May 1954. *The Motor Cycle* commented: 'The grass-track and trials rider, S.H. Miller, who gained a special first-class award in the Scottish Six Days Trial, won the Cookstown 100, a handicap event on the Cookstown-Drum-Orritor course on Wednesday of last week.' The report continued: 'His number was 51 in a field of 59, and he received a handicap allowance of 5½ minutes. Riding a 348cc AJS, he averaged 73.98mph [119km/h] – one of the fastest winning speeds ever recorded in the series.'

A youthful Sammy with the 197cc Norman, which replaced the SHS, during spring 1954.

From the start the young Miller moved steadily through the field to take the lead just before beginning the last lap of the 100-mile (162km) event. Charlie Gray, who manned Sammy's pit, described the youngster's performance as 'Almost a record in consistency for the event, for his lap times scarcely varied.'

Cookstown 100 Handicap – 19 May 1954

1st	S.H. Miller	(348cc AJS)
2nd	R. Ferguson	(348cc AJS)
3rd	G.A. Coulter	(248cc New Imperial)
4th	N. Crossett	(348cc AJS)
5th	W.J. Spratt	(348cc Velocette)
6th	J. Haynes	(348cc AJS)

The Skerries 100

As he was a novice, Sammy could not ride in events such as the North West 200 or Ulster Grand Prix during 1954, so his next road race that year was south of the border in the Skerries 100, organised by the Dublin & District Motor Cycle Club, held on 3 July. And, as with the Cookstown races, the Skerries was a handicap event.

Receiving the plaudits of the crowd after his victorious Cookstown 100 ride. His father is to Sammy's right.

A shower of rain fell during the start but the roads dried rapidly and conditions quickly improved. As in his first road race, in the Skerries Sammy once again put in an excellent performance, eventually finishing runner-up to V.J. Bracken (349cc Triumph), an AA patrolman on the Dublin-Belfast road. Bracken's handicap was four laps, against Sammy's one lap and two minutes – their average race speeds being 57.05mph (91.79km/h) and 72.93mph (117.34km/h) respectively.

Skerries 100 Handicap – 3 July 1954

1st   V.J. Bracken (349cc Triumph)
2nd   S.H. Miller (348cc AJS)
3rd   A. Carson (348cc BSA)
4th   J.A. Dickson (348cc AJS)
5th   R.J. Callow (248cc Excelsior)
6th   W.A. Martin (249cc Triumph)

Third Time Unlucky

Two weeks after the Skerries came the Mid-Antrim 150, run over the 10.4-mile (16.7km) Ballygarvie circuit. Although there were three sharp bends, a feature of this course were the long straight sections which encouraged sustained high speeds. But it was the sweeping right-hander at Quarrytown on the fourth lap which was to cause Sammy unforeseen problems. Jeff Clew takes up the story: 'While stowing himself away for the attempt [for the lead], he [Sammy] unknowingly flicked open the oil filler cap with his leg as he lined up for the corner at the end of the straight that led into it. Oil spilled on to the rear tyre, and as he laid the bike over, the back wheel slid, then stepped out. Remembering his push bike days and the need to stay aboard until the very last moment, even when all seemed lost, he opened the throttle and tried to ride the bend speedway style.'

And Sammy might have achieved success, but for the fact that the 7R's front wheel encountered one of the huge roots of an Irish thorn hedge

Sammy (53) leading a Gold Star rider during the Temple 100 on 31 July 1954; it was his last race on the AJS 7R.

which lined the side of the road. This signalled the end of his attempt to stay aboard and resulted in him going one way, the bike the other. As Sammy recently related: 'The travelling marshal who stopped to see if I was alright was the local NSU importer, Terry Hill, who had been watching my progress and wasn't put off by my accident.' This was to result in the young Miller being offered a ride on the new NSU 250cc Sportmax racer which Terry was bringing over from Germany for the 1955 season. In truth, this offer was truly incredible and one has to ask, who else has been offered a fully sponsored ride after only three races – especially immediately after crashing out at high speed?

But, for Sammy, the major concern at that time was what he was going to say to his family, in particular his mother. Luckily, the rest of the family had departed on holiday. And in the meantime he was able to make progress with both his own injuries, and the damage sustained to the AJS.

Immediately after the crash he was badly bruised, but just before Sammy's mother and father returned from holiday his friends took him to the cinema to give him a little extra time to recover from his injuries before he dare mention Terry Hill's offer. The motorcycle was more of a problem. However, while he was out of action, friends came to his aid, not only stripping the bike, but also sending all the damaged components off for repair or replacement. As a sign of just how serious the crash had been, the frame had to be replaced.

The AJS is Back in Action
Sammy and the AJS were back in action at the Temple 100, held at Broadmills, County Down, on 31 July 1954.

The Temple club's annual road race had first been staged way back in 1921. The initial 100-miler (162km) handicap arrived in 1933 and finally came to an end in 1966. But by now the handicappers had given Sammy a much harder task compared to the first three events, putting him with the fastest six riders or so. When this bunch were given the green light, a battle developed between Sammy and Bertie Mann, the latter riding a five-hundred BSA Gold Star.

Prior to the meeting Sammy had had a special high-profile camshaft fitted, but this proved to be his undoing, as it placed an additional burden on the vernier coupling, which subsequently broke, severing the drive to the offending camshaft.

As things transpired, the Temple outing was the swansong for the 7R, certainly as far as road racing was concerned. And, in anticipation of

Terry Hill's sponsored NSU ride, it was sold. Before this happened, however, the 7R often doubled up as Sammy's road-going transport, suitably equipped with a baffled megaphone and 'bobby dodgers' (cycle lamps) to meet the requirements for use on the public highway.

Changing the SHS for a Norman

Meanwhile, following the 1954 Scottish Six Days, the SHS had been pensioned off and a brand-new Norman trials mount purchased. Again powered by a 197cc Villiers engine, the machine (which Sammy says was the only new bike he purchased for many, many years) had been built at the company's factory in Ashford, Kent.

On the Norman he not only competed in trials, but also gained enough points during the summer of 1954 to win that year's Irish Grass Track Championship. When there were no grass events, the Norman doubled up as a sand racer, on the beaches of Magilligan, near Portrush on the northern coast of Ulster. Sammy also added the national Sand Racing Championship title to his grass racing crown.

The SHS was retired and Sammy obtained a brand new Norman trials mount. Here Sammy leads Bertie Mann (James) on the Norman at a grass-track event in the summer of 1954.

The James

The Norman that had replaced the SHS was itself pensioned off well before the end of the 1954–55 trials season. It gave way to a second-hand James Commando.

Like the SHS and Norman, the James employed a 197cc Villiers engine and had a rigid frame. Of all the British lightweight two-stroke trials mounts, the James Commando had been the most successful, thanks in no small part to the efforts of Bill Lomas (later a double 350cc World Champion with the Italian Moto Guzzi factory).

Sammy competed on the James for some 18 months, and it was to prove a useful stepping stone from the Norman and his being invited to ride as a member of the Ariel works team (see Chapter 4).

In the Ulster edition of the *Sunday Express* newspaper dated 7 November 1954, in the 'Irish Sport' section, journalist James Forrest had this to say in an article entitled 'Miller is Rider of the Year': 'Way back in February I told you that Sammy Miller could become the star motorcyclist of the 1954 season. Sammy has done me proud. He made my prophecy a reality. He won the Cookstown 100 in May, his first road race, and then decided to concentrate on reliability trials. He took the first three major trials of the year [in Ulster] and to such purpose that he is practically a certainty for the Irish team in next year's International Six Days Trial. Indeed, the only people who did not regard him as a certainty for this year's team were the selectors.'

The Norman was replaced well before the end of the 1954–55 season with a second-hand James Commando. Like the SHS and Norman, the James employed a 197cc Villiers engine. Sammy was to compete on the James for some 18 months, gaining considerable success on the way.

During the trials seasons of 1954–55 and 1955–56 the partnership of Sammy and his James Commando proved a potent combination. As proof of this, in one season alone he amassed over 20 premier events to his credit, including the Iveagh Trial, the Kelly Trophy Trial, the Larkin Cup, the McCrum Cup and many others. The highlight of the 1954–55 season was the 250cc award in the Hurst Cup Trial (run in February 1955). Organised by the Knock Motor Cycle Club, this annual event was the only trial in Ireland to secure entries from the leading British works teams. And it was an event which, in future years, Sammy would make his own.

The 1955 Hurst
The 1955 running of the Hurst event was marked by a light covering of snow on most of the six-mile (9.65km) lap, which had to be circulated six times in all – with each circuit having no fewer than 16 observed sections.

Johnny Draper, riding a factory-entered 499cc BSA Gold Star, was the eventual winner, from an entry which included star names such as Gordon Jackson, Brian Martin and Ted Usher. But for Irish eyes at least, Sammy and his James were the combination to watch.

The 1955 Scottish Six Days
After his successful debut 12 months earlier, Sammy might have been quietly confident of doing even better in the 1955 Scottish Six Days, but a frame breakage on the James during the second day forced his early retirement from the event. However, otherwise he continued to put in excellent performances on the Birmingham-made two-stroke, including retaining his grip on the Irish Trials Championship title. These successes were scored both sides of the border. For example, Sammy won the Dublin & District Motor Cycle Club's Mander Cup Trial for the second year in succession, finishing 20 marks ahead of J.C. Dawson (BSA), with 343 marks. It should be noted that the Irish method of scoring at this time was for marks gained, as against marks lost on the British mainland.

A Surprise Offer
As the 1955–56 trials season was coming to an end, with only the Scottish to come in May 1956, Sammy's competitive riding very much split between trials on the James and road racing with the NSU Sportmax provided by Terry Hill (see the following chapter). But the big surprise in spring 1956 was the offer, from a major English factory (via Terry Hill), of a four-stroke trials mount; an event which was to ultimately change Sammy's entire life more than he could ever have imagined at the time.

Chapter 2

Terry Hill

Sammy and sponsor Terry Hill with the NSU Sportmax two-fifty, which the Ulsterman rode from spring 1955 through to 1958 with considerable success (this is a 1957 shot).

As we know from the previous chapter, Terry Hill, a well-known competitor in trials and road races, owner of the Belfast-based Hills Garages and Ulster importer for the German NSU factory, had already offered one of the forthcoming Sportmax 250cc racers to Sammy. This came after Terry had been impressed by the youngster's performances on the ex-Charlie Gray AJS 7R during the 1954 season.

An early meeting with the NSU front brake still in place. It was soon replaced by a Manx Norton assembly.

The Dock Strike

The batch of Sportmax machines (which were all hand-built in NSU's race shop) was not ready until the spring of 1955. The Hill machine was then caught up in the threatened British dock strike during early May that year. It had been hoped that Sammy would make his debut on the NSU during the North West 200 in mid-May. However, this was not to be. Instead, the motorcycle was stuck in a Customs shed at Harwich, where it had been since it arrived from Hamburg a week earlier. Unfortunately, the bike did not come under the heading of 'perishable goods', and it was only these that the Customs officials would deal with in view of the threatened strike.

In the week prior to the North West meeting, all efforts to persuade the Customs authorities to release the NSU proved unsuccessful. As a final and urgent appeal was made the day before practising was due to get underway, a van stood by at Harwich ready to rush the bike to London Airport (Heathrow) to be flown to Ulster. But the Customs man would not be moved, simply saying: 'We are rushing to clear perishable goods. They must be given priority, and there are tons of them. The bike cannot be released. We have our instructions.'

As for Terry Hill, all he could say was: 'This is a bitter blow to me.'

The Cookstown 100 at the end of May, the first of the annual Irish 100-mile (162km) races, was also missed due to the machine not being released by Customs.

Artie Bell

Besides Terry Hill, it was Artie Bell, the former Norton works rider, who was to play a pivotal role in Sammy Miller's early competitive riding career.

Born in Belfast on 6 September 1914, Artie had begun to attract factory interest while racing a 350cc Velocette during 1939. Then came the war and racing activities, together with other peacetime pursuits, were replaced by military priorities.

Artie Bell with his wife after winning the Ulster 100 Victory Year road race at Lisburn, Co. Down, on 22 September 1945.

During the war years Artie, together with his friend Rex McCandless, was engaged in aircraft work at the Short Brothers factory in Belfast. There they became engaged in heated and lengthy debate over just what was needed to constitute the ideal motorcycle. McCandless was of the opinion that with ever-increasing power output from the engine it was frame design which had been lagging behind. Artie had to agree, pointing out that as racing motorcycles existed in 1939, the big weakness was that the rear of the machine was apt to attempt to take over control from the rider. In other words, as *Motor Cycling* put it: 'The tail was prone to wag the dog.'

By 1942 McCandless, with the help of Artie Bell, had produced a prototype machine using modified suspension units from a Citroën car, which was powered by a Triumph twin-cylinder engine inclined in the frame at 45 degrees.

By the cessation of hostilities McCandless had all but perfected his theories, so in the immediate post-war era both he and Bell were to benefit both in competition and commercially.

The first major post-war racing event in Ireland was the Ulster Grand Prix on Saturday 17 August 1946, and although like the vast majority of the field that day Artie Bell did not finish, he did have the satisfaction of setting the fastest lap at almost 89mph (143km/h). Other results that year were also excellent, so much so that 1947 saw him invited to join the Norton racing team.

Meanwhile, the frame of the McCandless springing won much acclaim on both sides of the Irish Sea, and during the latter part of 1946 and into 1947 enquiries by the score were received by the Bell-McCandless partnership. Satisfied customers of the relatively simple and inexpensive swinging-arm conversion generated even more customers. Eventually, due to a combination of increased demand and Artie Bell's racing career, the conversion kit business was sold off to Feridax, the Birmingham wholesalers.

Artie Bell played a vital role in the development of Sammy Miller's early riding career. He is seen here between Sammy's father and Sammy (astride the 350 Manx Norton).

In 1948 Artie Bell won the Senior TT in the Isle of Man – then the blue riband event of the motorcycle racing calendar. Next, in 1949, the first year of the FIM World Championships, Artie finished runner-up (to world champion Les Graham riding an AJS Porcupine) in the 500cc Ulster Grand Prix, and also finished the season fifth in the Championship table. He was also third in that year's Junior TT. But Norton were handicapped by their heavy and ill-handling 'Garden Gate' plunger-framed machines.

And so to the 1950 season and the Rex McCandless-designed Featherbed frame, which the factory team were to use that year. This innovation completely changed Norton's fortunes, and at the season opener, the TT, Artie was victorious in the Junior (and setting a new class lap record), while Geoff Duke took the Senior – with Artie runner-up.

The second round of the Championship series was the Belgian Grand Prix, held over the famous 8.8-mile (14km) Francorchamps – Malmedy – Stavelot circuit in the Ardennes, in the eastern part of Belgium, near the German border. After finishing runner-up to Velocette-mounted Bob Foster in the 350cc event, all eyes turned to the main race of the day – the 14-lap 500cc event. There were no fewer than 12 full factory entries – Norton plus AJS, Velocette, Gilera and MV Agusta.

The following is an extract from *The Motor Cycle*: 'Bandirola [Gilera] in front brought the average above 100mph [161km/h] for the two laps, unaware of the tragedy that occurred a foot or so behind his back wheel. On a corner about a mile from the end of the second lap, he eased slightly to the discomfort of Graham inches away, Graham crash-braked and was thrown; Bell took to the bank to avoid the spinning AJS and was seriously injured.'

Even though he received the best possible treatment, the Belgian accident meant that Artie Bell lost the use of his right arm and was never to race again.

However, Artie retained an active interest in motorcycle sport, particularly racing, and, in the author's opinion, was something of a mentor to the young Sammy Miller. There is absolutely no doubt that Artie could see Sammy's potential, while Sammy for his part respected the man immensely.

Later Artie became the Honda distributor for Northern Ireland.

Shortly before his sudden death on 5 August 1972, Artie Bell moved to a new home at Boardmills, on the Temple 100 circuit. He left a wife, and a son and daughter.

Sammy Miller still reveres Artie to the present day, saying: 'He was my hero as a schoolboy. I liked his way of thinking, and he was a very articulate guy who could explain a point clearly. He was really involved, even when he was one of the top men for Norton. I can remember him coming to a grass-track meeting in Dunmurry at the end of one season to race with the local lads, with knobblies and a straight-through exhaust on his Manx Norton. You'd never get the prima donnas doing that today, tucked away from people in their motor homes.'

The Leinster 200

So the international Leinster 200 at Wicklow in Southern Ireland was the setting for Sammy's debut on the NSU, this taking place on Saturday 18 June 1955.

In the 250cc event Sammy finished runner-up behind Jackie Wood, the latter having taken over the NSU that Reg Armstrong had originally been down to ride. Both Wood and Sammy beat the existing class lap record set the previous year by Arthur Wheeler (Moto Guzzi). In addition, Sammy won the C.W. Taylor Trophy (best Irish rider). It is also worth mentioning that the 500cc scratch race was won by Reg Armstrong riding a works four-cylinder Gilera.

Victory in the Skerries 100

Sammy gained his first victory on Terry Hill's NSU Sportmax in the Dublin Club's annual Skerries 100 on 2 July 1955; he was also 12th in the Handicap event. Both the race and lap records for the 250cc class were smashed – the

Irishman Reg Armstrong rode a four-cylinder 500cc Gilera in the Leinster 200 on 18 June 1955 (the photograph was taken at that year's Senior TT, where he had finished runner-up to Geoff Duke on a sister machine).

former by Sammy at 73.07mph (117.56km/h) and the latter by Harry Lindsay (also riding an NSU Sportmax) with a speed of 74.30mph (119.54km/h). After Lindsay had crashed, breaking a footrest and bending the streamlining of his machine, Sammy won 'easily' (*The Motor Cycle*).

Skerries 100 – 250cc – 2 July 1955
1st   S.H. Miller (NSU)
2nd   J.E. Herron (Norton)
3rd   S. Hodgins (Excelsior)

A Norton Victory
Later that same month, on 17 July 1955, Sammy took part in the Munster 100 held over the Carrigohane road circuit, near Cork. As there was no 250cc class at this event, Sammy had made an entry on his recently-acquired three-fifty Manx Norton – purchased with the proceeds from the sale of his AJS 7R. His main opposition was to come from Dubliner Joe Woods on another Manx. Right from the fall of the flag these two were at it, hammer and tongs. This is how *The Motor Cycle* described their scrap:

'The larger entry was in the 350cc event, which resulted in a grand tussle between Norton riders J. Woods and S.H. Miller, who were never more than a second apart all through the race. Woods led at first, but his weaving to shake off the slipstreaming Miller incurred the displeasure of officials; although Woods was given the black flag three times he failed to stop, but he ceased his weaving tactics.' *The Motor Cycle* report continued: 'After Miller had led for four laps, Woods resumed the lead for the last six laps and crossed the finishing line with 0.2 sec to spare. He was excluded from the results for ignoring the black flag, and his protest to the stewards was turned down, Miller being awarded first place.' This is a standing joke to this very day – when Sammy meets Joey he mentions the black flag and Joey shakes his fist at him, but the friendship and respect remains to this day. At the time Sammy was furious with his Irish pit crew who failed to give him the last-lap signal as he was ready to pass Joe on the last lap. Sammy also had the satisfaction of setting the fastest lap, at 85.88mph (138.18km/h).

Our man also came home third in the Handicap – his race average being a new record for the course.

Munster 100 – 350cc – 17 July 1955
1st   S.H. Miller (Norton)
2nd   A. Carson (BSA)
3rd   H. Morrogh (AJS)

Sammy and Dubliner Joe Woods battling on 350 Manx Nortons during the Munster 100 on 17 July 1955. Woods was black flagged and later disqualified, leaving victory to Sammy.

Upon his return to Northern Ireland following the Munster, Sammy's Norton was impounded by customs officials. The problem centred around the fact that when he took his machine south into Eire by train and later made the return journey, there had been no request for customs papers. So, when eventually asked to produce the documents they were unstamped and the bike was immediately impounded. In fact, not only was it impounded but Sammy was also accused of illegally importing it! The situation remained deadlocked for several weeks, until, eventually, Sammy's father convinced the officials that his son's story was true and they agreed to release the bike.

An Ulster GP Debut

Sammy Miller made his debut in the Ulster Grand Prix on Saturday 13 August 1955, riding Terry Hill's 247cc NSU Sportmax. And what a debut it was. The meeting was held in brilliantly sunny conditions, and as *The Motor Cycle* reported: 'Vast crowds – Saturday's attendance was estimated at

100,000 – lined the circuit to see what turned out to be some of the finest racing ever witnessed in Northern Ireland.'

The 7.4-mile (11.9km) Dundrod road circuit had a great selection of going from fast, straight sections to tight bends and everything in between. Before the commencement of the 250cc race there was much speculation about its outcome, with Bill Lomas (MV Agusta) holding a single-point advantage over the German NSU rider, Hermann Müller, in the World Championship points table. In fact, besides Lomas there were three other works MV Agusta entries: Luigi Taveri, Remo Venturi and Umberto Masetti. Certainly, nobody could have predicted what the actual outcome would be. In fact, it was a trio of NSUs which streaked into an early lead: John Surtees heading Sammy Miller, with Müller third.

At the end of the first lap Surtees led from Sammy, while Lomas was now third. In describing the third lap, *The Motor Cycle* said: 'Miller, who was competing in his first major meeting, was riding like a veteran and perceptibly increasing his advantage over Lomas.' And Sammy maintained his position to the finish. When one considers it was Sammy's international debut – and that he beat some of the world's finest and most experienced racing stars – his performance that August day could only be described as brilliant.

The first three finishers of the 250cc Ulster Grand Prix, held at Dundrod on 13 August 1955. Sammy, making his debut in the event, was runner-up to John Surtees, while MV works rider Umberto Masetti was third.

John Surtees

John Surtees and Sammy Miller have known each other since they both raced NSU Sportmax machines during the mid-1950s. And, in fact, Sammy chose John to officially open his museum in 1980.

Born in the pretty village of Tatsfield on the Kent-Surrey border, a couple of miles south of Biggin Hill Airfield, on 11 February 1934, John

John Surtees, with Sammy in the background, after the pair finished first and second respectively in the 1955 250cc Ulster Grand Prix at Dundrod on NSU machines.

Surtees succeeded Geoff Duke as the dominant force in Grand Prix racing.

John's first motorcycle race came as a 14-year-old when his father Jack recruited his services as a passenger. The pairing actually won the event, but were subsequently disqualified because of John's age. His first solo victory came at 17, at the tree-lined Aberdare Park in South Wales. He was riding a 499cc Vincent Grey Flash single, which the young Surtees had constructed while serving his apprenticeship at the firm's Stevenage works.

Except for a 1953 TT practice crash while riding an EMC 125, John would have been a Norton works rider that year. As it was, Norton retired from fielding full Grand Prix 'specials' at the end of 1954; however, John, together with John Hartle and Jack Brett, was signed to race works development Manx models for the 1955 season. He responded by having an excellent season, the highlight of which was winning the British Championship title.

He then signed for the Italian MV Agusta team to race its four-cylinder models during the 1956 season. In doing this, John was following in the footsteps of Geoff Duke (although Duke had gone from Norton to Gilera). John made his MV debut at Crystal Palace near his south London home in April 1956, winning in style. Then he went on to win the 500cc World Championship title – despite suffering a fall in Germany at the Solitude circuit. Even though he had broken his right arm, which effectively kept him out of racing until the following year, John had already amassed enough points to carry off the title.

Although he could only finish third behind the Gileras of Libero Liberati and Bob McIntyre in the 1957 500cc title race, John had the honour of giving MV its first-ever victory with the smaller 350 four-cylinder model at the Belgian Grand Prix in July 1956.

Then came the golden years, with a trio of double 350 and 500cc titles, when John won just about everything in 1958, 1959 and 1960. Having nothing else to prove in the two-wheel world, Surtees moved to four wheels, first as a driver for Ken Tyrell, then as a member of the Lotus Formula 1 squad. In 1962 came a switch to a Lola, plus drives in a Ferrari 250 GTO in sports car races.

Next came a move into the full Ferrari team, competing in the 1963 and 1964 Formula 1 series. And in the latter year he won the World Title – thus becoming the only man to achieve the feat of taking the premier Championship crowns on both two and four wheels.

After Ferrari came a spell with Honda, whom he joined for the 1967 season, and finally BRM in 1969. John then founded his own team, with drivers including Mike Hailwood. Team Surtees was disbanded towards the end of the 1970s, its F1 'position' being acquired by Frank Williams.

From the early 1980s John was to be seen with both cars and motorcycles at countless historic meetings all around the world; his immaculate style and ultra-fast lap times impressing everyone who was privileged enough to see the great man in action again.

250cc Ulster Grand Prix – Dundrod – 13 August 1955 – 13 laps – 96.32 miles
1st   J. Surtees (NSU)
2nd   S.H. Muller (NSU)
3rd   U. Masetti (MV Agusta)
4th   W.A. Lomas (MV Agusta)
5th   C.C. Sandford (Moto Guzzi)
6th   H.P. Müller (NSU)

Getting Ready for Monza

Later that month Sammy took part in the Ards Motor Cycle Club's meeting at Kirkistown airfield, competing in two races prior to rushing off for the evening boat en route to Monza for the following Sunday's Italian Grand Prix. The chance to ride in Italy was as a direct result of his performance in the Ulster GP.

At Kirkistown he had an easy victory in the 350cc event. His chief opposition came from Ralph Rensen (Norton). Despite the smaller engine displacement of Terry Hill's NSU Sportmax, Sammy had soon established a clear lead from Rensen, eventually winning by seven seconds, with the third-placed R. Ferguson (AJS) a further 32 seconds adrift.

The Italian GP at Monza on 4 September 1955, with Sammy (66) leading the field. He was later slowed by a misfire, but still managed an excellent third place.

On the rostrum at Monza in September 1955, 250cc race winner Carlo Ubbiali (MV – centre), second Hans Baltisberger (NSU) and Sammy (NSU).

In the other event, the Handicap, Sammy was given the scratch mark – the deficit being too great to make up in the time available.

Monza

As at Dundrod, Sammy stunned pundits with his performance at Monza. Riding a fully streamlined Sportmax, he once again showed his potential by at one time actually leading the race, before the Ulsterman's engine began to misfire, slowing his progress. Showing the extreme determination which has been a feature of his life, he coaxed the sick machine home to the finisher's flag. At the end, after 22 laps and 78.56 miles (126.40km), he was a mere 16 seconds behind the winner Carlo Ubbiali (MV Agusta) and sandwiched between them was the German NSU star Hans Baltisberger.

Simply studying the result below proves what an outstanding ride the young Ulsterman had achieved with a less-than-perfect machine.

250cc Italian GP – Monza – 4 September 1955 – 22 laps – 78.56 miles

1st   C. Ubbiali (MV Agusta)
2nd   H. Baltisberger (NSU)
3rd   S.H. Miller (NSU)
4th   H.P. Müller (NSU)
5th   W.A. Lomas (MV Agusta)
6th   U. Masetti (MV Agusta)

On their way home from Italy, Sammy and his sponsor Terry Hill not only visited the NSU factory at Neckarsulm, but also took in a round of the German National Championship series, staged at Hannover. Once again, Sammy showed his ability by leading fellow NSU riders Müller (by now the 250cc World Champion) and Baltisberger, although he was eventually forced to retire from the race with electrical problems. This was the same problem as at Monza; after many laps the frame expanded due to the heat and the electrical ion wiring was pulled apart as it was taped too much against the frame.

After Monza, Sammy and Terry Hill not only visited the NSU works at Neckarsulm, but also took in a round of the German National Championship at Hannover.

Sammy prior to the start of the 250cc race at Hannover with his fully-streamlined Terry Hill NSU Sportmax.

The start of the 250cc German Championship race at Hannover in September 1955. Most of the bikes are NSUs, but there were also a smattering of Adler and DKW machines. Sammy is number 128 on the front row.

Sammy showed his potential at Hannover by leading fellow NSU riders Hermann Müller (that year's World Champion) and Hans Baltisberger, before being forced to retire from the race with electrical problems.

Winding Up the 1955 Season at Aintree

Previously, Sammy had not raced on the British mainland, but all this changed on Saturday 24 September 1955, when he took part in the international Aintree meeting near Liverpool. The circuit, first used exactly 12 months previously, measured three miles (4.8km) to the lap and ran side-by-side with the world-famous Grand National racecourse. Completed in May 1954 at a cost said to be in excess of £100,000 (many millions in today's values), there was stand accommodation for 20,000 spectators, while the total capacity for the circuit was quoted to be in the region of 200,000. Almost all the top stars of the day were there, including Geoff Duke, John Surtees, John Hartle, Bob McIntyre, Jack Brett, Cecil Sandford and sidecar men including Cyril Smith, Walter Schneider and Willi Faust.

Sammy's first race was the 15-lap 250cc event, which he led from start to finish in commanding fashion, with a fastest lap of 75.52mph (121.51km/h), which was also a new class record.

When one realises that the opposition included the likes of Cecil Sandford, Maurice Cann, Arthur Wheeler and Percy Tait, this victory was a clear sign that Sammy's recent GP successes were no flash in the pan.

250cc Aintree – 24 September 1955 – 15 laps – 45 miles
1st   S.H. Miller (NSU)
2nd   C.C. Sandford (Moto Guzzi)
3rd   M. Cann (Moto Guzzi)
4th   A.F. Wheeler (Moto Guzzi)
5th   P.H. Tait (Beasley Velocette)
6th   G. Monty (GMV)

The Handicap Race

The final race of an action-packed day at Aintree was the 30-lap solo Handicap event. And once again it was Sammy and the fully-faired Terry Hill NSU Sportmax who impressed. In fact, he led for the first 22 laps, and early on the semi-works Nortons of Surtees and Hartle were second and third. Then the real struggle became clear; the NSU, then the two Nortons, and far down in ninth position after 10 laps, the 500cc World Champion Geoff Duke on his four-cylinder Gilera. Eventually, first Surtees and towards the very end Duke both caught and passed the flying Ulsterman. And thus Sammy crossed the line in third spot, still a magnificent effort.

Solo Handicap – Aintree – 24 September 1955 – 30 laps – 90 miles

1st	J. Surtees	(348cc Norton)
2nd	G.E. Duke	(499cc Gilera)
3rd	S.H. Miller	(247cc NSU)
4th	J. Hartle	(348cc Norton)
5th	R. McIntyre	(499cc Norton)
6th	G.A. Murphy	(348cc AJS)

After returning from his Continental foray, Sammy took part in his first British mainland race meeting at Aintree on 24 September 1955. After winning the 250cc event, he is seen here during the 30-lap, 90-mile Handicap event later that day, leading a Manx Norton rider.

And so Sammy's 1955 racing season came to a close. It was one he had begun as an almost unknown, certainly outside his native Ireland, but he had finished very much a rising star of the tarmac world.

Sammy pictured with the silverware he had won during the 1955 season.

NSU Sportmax

Sammy Miller readily admits to having a soft spot for the NSU Sportmax, and an example of the German machine today resides in Sammy's museum, as one of the star exhibits.

The prototype of what was to emerge as the Sportmax was first seen at the end of 1953 at the Spanish Grand Prix. Thereafter, development continued apace both on track and in the test shop. There were several race tests during the 1954 season, at events including Hockenheim, the Swiss and Italian Grand Prix, plus some more minor outings. Riders included Georg Braun and Kurt Knopf.

All these early development bikes were essentially similar to the production version – which was to go on sale to selected riders during the spring of 1955. A major difference, however, was that of the front brake, these development models having an assembly of much smaller diameter. There were, of course, other differences, but these were much less noticeable.

Dipl. Ing. Karl Kleinbach was responsible for the Sportmax development programme, but there has always been controversy about how many genuine Sportmax machines were actually built by the factory. NSU publicity officer Arthur Westrup stated 17, while other well-informed sources suggest as many as 34. In addition, a number of other examples were constructed later from spare parts, when the race shop was sold to the Herz family during the late 1950s. Finally, there were a large number of converted Max, Special Max and Supermax production roadsters – some of these being crude to say the least – they not only employed non-racing components, but also, in some cases, poorly-made replica Sportmax tanks and seats.

The genuine Sportmax, or type 251RS (250 one-cylinder Renn Sport), had a displacement of 247cc (69 x 66mm) and a compression ratio of 9.8:1, giving a power output of 28bhp at 9,000rpm (NSU

The 1955 NSU Sportmax in factory fresh trim – at the time the finest 250cc racing motorcycle available to private entrants in the world.

Sportmax engine assembly with full unit construction, dry clutch, four-speed close-ratio gearbox and dry sump lubrication.

quoted safe engine revolutions to be 9,500rpm). The Sportmax piston was a forged 3-ring Mahle assembly. The special steel connecting rod employed a roller big-end bearing, while the single overhead camshaft was operated by what NSU referred to as the 'Ultramax' system. Instead of the conventional method of either chain, gears, bevel shafts or belt, in the Sportmax's case this was a pair of long rods with eccentric discs, both immensely strong – but expensive to manufacture. Carburation was courtesy of an Amal GP instrument with a remotely-mounted float chamber.

The distinctive 4.84 imperial gallon (22 litre) fuel tank was in hand-beaten aluminium. Both wheels were 18-inch diameter, with 2.75 front and 3.00 rear section tyres. With a dry weight of 246lb (112kg), maximum speed was 124mph (200km/h) and there was a wide variety of gearbox and rear-wheel sprockets available for changing the gearing. Compared to the 1954 prototype machines, the 1955 production version featured an increase in front-brake drum diameter from 7in (180mm) to 8.3in (210mm).

The Sportmax proved even more successful than NSU could ever have
dreamed. During the 1955 Grand Prix racing calendar, not only did H.P.
(Hermann Paul) Müller (then 46 years old) become the 250cc World
Champion, but in that year's Ulster Grand Prix John Surtees also scored
his first GP win, and Sammy Miller finished a brilliant second, the two
NSU riders beating all the official works entries.

Over the next few years many other riders went on to achieve
success with the Sportmax, including Tommy Robb, Mike Hailwood,
Hans Baltisberger, Pierre Monneret, Horst Kassner, Jack Murgatroyd
and Eric Hinton.

The Winter Months

Sammy then returned to the trials scene, and during the winter months of
1955 and 1956 was occupied riding his 197cc Villiers-powered James
Commando. This period has already been fully documented in Chapter 1,
but suffice to say that Terry Hill and Artie Bell were both heavily involved
in helping shape the young Miller's two-wheel career at this time.

A Winter Visit to the Isle of Man

The advantage of having the support and expertise of Terry Hill and Artie
Bell is best illustrated by the fact that during the early new year of 1956
Sammy crossed the Irish Sea to the Isle of Man with the purpose of learning
the 10.79-mile (17.36km) Clypse circuit, over which he was to make his Isle
of Man debut in June that year.

Sammy stayed in the Isle of Man some 10 days, taking with him a three-
fifty BSA loaned by Terry Hill. Being Sammy, he planned on covering five
laps in the morning followed by a further five laps in the afternoon – over
100 miles (161km) a day!

Wintertime in Douglas was totally different to that of the holiday season
in the summer months – as was the weather. Not only was it much colder
and wetter, but also the daylight hours were much shorter. Back in 1976 Jeff
Clew described just how dedicated Sammy was to his task of course learning
by saying that he: 'Made the most of the long winter evenings by taking his
landlady's daughter to the pictures and it was assumed that some kind of
romance was in the offing. Maybe the landlady's daughter liked to think this
was so, for she could not have known that Sammy's mind was on one thing
only – learning and memorising the Clypse circuit! Even in the cinema it was
foremost in his mind; he had visited the Isle of Man for a set purpose and
nothing was going to deter him.'

As for the course-learning BSA, this was left on the Island, awaiting
Sammy's return as a competitor during the practice period in late May.

At a waterlogged
Silverstone on 14 April
1956 Sammy finished
runner-up to John Surtees
(MV Agusta) in both 250cc
races.

'Waterlogged Silverstone'

So read the headline from *The Motor Cycle* dated 19 April 1956. The report began: 'Last Saturday's Silverstone programme listed sufficient talent to give promise of lap records in all classes. Alas, any hopes of such excitement were dashed by the waterlogged state of the track and the wretched drizzle which persisted throughout the meeting.'

But the most interesting extract from *The Motor Cycle's* Silverstone race report, as regards this particular book, was the following: 'Though Surtees won the first race of the day (a five-lap contest for two-fifties) after a brilliant start on his 203cc MV Agusta [John now being a factory MV rider], many observers were impressed by the fact that S.H. Miller (NSU), who got away badly, reduced the Londoner's lead from a quarter-mile on the first lap to 80 yards at the finish. Perhaps the Irishman could have extended Surtees had the NSU fired up more promptly?' Then, in the later 13-lap Championship race for 250cc machines, the same two riders dominated the proceedings.

The Silverstone meeting proved two things as far as Sammy Miller's racing career was concerned. First, that he had carried on in a similar vein to how he had finished the previous season. And, secondly, that he was just as capable in the wet as he was in the dry. In fact, Sammy was later to admit that he actually enjoyed wet conditions.

250cc Silverstone – 14 April 1956 – 13 laps – 39 miles
1st   J. Surtees (MV Agusta)
2nd   S.H. Miller (NSU)
3rd   C.C. Sandford (Norton)
4th   G. Monty (GMS)

Sammy then took a break from the hard stuff to partake of the muddy stuff in the shape of the Scottish Six Days. As fully described in Chapter 4, this was to be his first-ever outing on the now legendary Ariel HT5 trials mount, GOV 132. Later (autumn 1957) Sammy moved from his native Belfast to Birmingham, to be nearer his then employers, Ariel Motors. But in the spring of 1956 he was still very much based in Belfast near his sponsor (in road racing) Terry Hill.

A Victorious North West Debut
As has already been related, Sammy had been unable to race in the North West 200 in 1955 due to the brand-new German NSU Sportmax being held up in the Customs shed at the port of Harwich, thanks to a threatened dock strike.

With the exception of the Ulster Grand Prix, the North West 200 was by far the biggest road race in Ulster. The race had begun back in 1929 and continues to the present day, being run over the well-known triangular, anti-clockwise Portstewart-Coleraine-Portrush circuit, which for many years

Making a victorious debut in the North West 200 on Terry Hill's NSU on 12 May 1956.

During the early stages the Australian Eric Hinton led the 1956 North West 200 250cc class, with Sammy, as shown here, in close attendance.

measured 11.1 miles (17.9km) to the lap. The course has been altered and improved in detail over the years, and up to 1959 (and thus applicable to Sammy Miller's racing career) there was one single 200-mile (322km) race, but from 1960 onwards there have been a number of separate events.

As for the 1956 '200', with a minute between the classes, 25 riders got away in the 500cc event, 33 in the 350cc and eight in the 250cc class. As far as the results are concerned, the 500s completed 18 laps, the 350s 17 and the 250s 16.

Throughout the week there had been speculation that the former Norton, NSU and Gilera works star Reg Armstrong would turn out on an NSU Sportmax – an identical machine to Sammy's Terry Hill bike – but at the last minute Armstrong was substituted by Eric Hinton, a member of the famous Australian motorcycle racing dynasty. *The Motor Cycle* stated, however, that Hill was 'quite confident' that his man would win.

And so it proved, as not only did Sammy at last take part in the North West, but he also emerged victorious and set a new 250cc race record at an average speed of 87.67mph (141.06km/h).

The race had begun with Hinton in the lead, but only just, and after two laps Sammy was tucked so closely behind him 'that the pair could hardly be separated' (*The Motor Cycle*). And so the race unfolded, with the two NSUs

After both Hinton and Sammy had repeatedly broken the lap record, the Australian faded and Sammy finished a full 31 seconds in front at the flag.

consistently breaking the existing lap record. And although it was Hinton who eventually did the fastest lap (at 91.13mph – 146.62km/h), his performance faded after this, with Sammy finishing a full 31 seconds ahead of the Australian at the finish.

250cc North West 200 – 12 May 1956 – 16 laps – 177.6 miles
1st   S.H. Miller (NSU)
2nd   E. Hinton (NSU)
3rd   J.E. Herron (Norton)

Another Aintree Victory

After the North West, Sammy easily won the 250cc scratch race at the annual Cookstown 100 meeting on Wednesday 16 May, during which he set a new class record of 78.78mph (126.75km/h).

Then, only three days later on 19 May, Sammy was back at Aintree for the 1956 international meeting. And once again he showed he was a true master of the Liverpool course. But although the Ulsterman won the 15-lap 250cc race from Michael O'Rourke (MV Agusta) and Geoff Monty (GMS), it was the main race of the day, the Aintree 90 Solo Handicap for *The Motor Cycle* Trophy, in which he really excelled.

Terry Hill

As Sammy Miller would be the first to admit, Belfast's Terry Hill played a major part in Sammy's road-racing career.

Terry Hill was not only one of Ireland's leading sponsors, but also a skilled engineer and no mean rider in earlier days. As Jim Reynolds recalled shortly after Terry Hill's death in December 1999, he: 'Made his mark as a rider while serving his time as an apprentice at Thornycroft Engineering. His talent was soon recognised and he hurried into the Ulster team as a substitute for the 1936 ISDT in Germany. He didn't finish on that debut ride, but in 1938 he was team captain, riding a 350cc International Norton.'

Terry Hill was also a talented road-racer, his first victory coming in the mid-1930s in the Cookstown 100 aboard a Levis. After finishing 12th in the 1936 Ulster Grand Prix on the same machine, he was sponsored by Chambers Engineering with a pukka racing 350cc International Norton for 1937, finishing eighth in the Ulster; the first non-works machine home.

The following year, 1938, Terry won the 350cc class of the North West 200 riding the same Norton. These successes, combined with his ISDT performance, came to the attention of the Birmingham-based BSA factory, who contracted him to ride one of the new Gold Stars in the 500cc class of the 1939 North West. However, after leading the race, he was forced to retire with a holed piston.

Terry Hill pictured just before the start of the 1956 North West 200, which Sammy won on the fully-faired NSU Sportmax.

Then came the war, which, as it did for many other riders, halted Terry's riding career. At first he worked in Shorts aircraft plant. But later in the conflict he was head-hunted by Thorneycroft to fit 1,000 horsepower diesel engines into tank landing craft. An old stable was converted on Belfast's Holywood Road and this was the start of the Hill's Engineering concern. As Terry was to recall later: 'By the end of the war we had a thousand men working for us and we'd moved to Warren Point.'

With the war at its end Terry, together with Harry McDermott and David Woods, opened an engineering workshop, specialising in reconditioning engines. In the same period Terry returned to riding works BSAs, both in Ulster and on the British mainland, in off-road events.

In 1949 Terry won a gold medal in the ISDT, which was staged in Wales that year. He also made his mark in one-day trials with BSA. But Terry's days as a factory-sponsored rider came to an abrupt end in the 1952 ISDT (staged in Italy). In his own words: 'I was following Hugh Viney on the AJS and Charlie Rogers on the Royal Enfield, sitting behind quite happily on my 500 Gold Star. An Italian had come off and the whole place was covered in dust. We were doing about 60mph and Hugh, Charlie and I went over the edge. I hit a big rock and broke my jaw in three places and the eighth vertebrae in my spine. I was in hospital for 10 days.'

However, Terry did continue riding BSAs, on a private basis, at the same time building up a successful garage business which had grown from the engineering operation.

Coming home from a holiday on the Continent, Terry was impressed by an NSU Quickly moped he saw. He purchased an example from the factory. It was the start of a most profitable relationship between the German concern and the Ulsterman. Terry commented: 'We were spoilt with NSU. People were lining up to buy them – we had them sold before we got them off the boat.' He continued: 'We imported them for 10 years and brought in 1,000 a year. I was offered the franchise for all of England and Ireland, but I thought it was too much bother and didn't take them on.'

Then in 1955 he was offered a brand new, just-released Sportmax racer, together with a spare engine, by Peter Bolton, then head of NSU Great Britain. And so began a new career as a sponsor. His first rider was Billy Spence; however, as we know from the main text, Spence was soon replaced by Sammy Miller. When interviewed by Jim Reynolds, Terry said: 'I was very impressed with the way he rode. Then I saw him in a scramble and he was superb. I thought he was the man for the NSU.'

It was to be the beginning of a hugely successful partnership. During his time with Terry Hill's NSU, Sammy went from being a local Ulster racing man to a top international level star, often beating the best there was. And during 1955 and 1956 the Miller/Hill Sportmax built up a reputation as the combination to beat.

Terry built a second NSU from spares and let a young Tommy Robb into the saddle. When Sammy was signed by the Italian FB Mondial factory to ride in the 1957 World Championship series, Robb was promoted to number one in the Hill squad.

Terry Hill continued his association with the dirt bike world, both in scrambles and trials. For example, in 1960 he was involved with the Bianchi factory when it built a scrambler, while he was still competing in trials, and eventually in the mid-1960s switched to Bultacos – following the lead set by his former sponsored rider, Sammy Miller.

Terry Hill passed away during Christmas week 1999, and a mere two days later was followed by his wife Betty. Even today, the name Terry Hill is revered in his native Ulster homeland, as 'Belfast's Mr Motorcycle'.

This race saw the 10 fastest competitors from each of the solo races starting in groups. As several riders had qualified on two machines there were only 25 starters. First away were the 250s – with Sammy to the fore. As he passed the stands for the second time the 350s were dispatched, and, one lap later, the 500 men led by Geoff Duke (Gilera four). With a third of the race over, Duke was lying 12th and gaining 12 seconds a lap on the

A mere seven days after his 1956 North West success, Sammy made a triumphant return to Aintree, near Liverpool, where he won the 250cc scratch race and set a new class lap record of 78.78mph (126.75km/h).

leader, Sammy. And so it went on, only to be resolved during the final lap, with Geoff Duke emerging the victor by a mere four seconds. Sammy was runner-up, and Frank Fox (499cc Norton) third.

It was also at the Aintree meeting that Sammy was approached by none other than Joe Craig, the Norton works team manager. However, although Sammy was honoured to have been offered a ride by one of his boyhood heroes, he politely turned down the chance. Although he had told Joe Craig that he did not feel he had enough experience, Sammy had realised that the 1955 Norton squad were mounted on unfaired production Manx models rather than specialised works bikes and he (correctly) considered that as a Norton rider he would have to ride 'over the limit' to get anywhere. This was something he was not prepared to do.

The Isle of Man TT

Without doubt the highlight of Sammy's 1956 racing season was his first visit to the Isle of Man TT, even though he was to experience a mechanical problem which caused his retirement in the 250cc race (his sole event).

At that time the Sidecar, 125 and 250cc races were staged over the 10.79-mile (17.36km) Clypse course, not the much longer 37.73-mile (60.70km) Mountain circuit.

Though demanding a high degree of riding skill, the Clypse circuit had few high-speed stretches of any great distance. Instead, the characteristics of the circuit put the emphasis on machine handleability, brakes and acceleration.

Sammy pictured with the Hill NSU during TT practice week on the Isle of Man, 1956. This previously unseen photograph is from the author's archives.

Making his TT debut, Sammy led the Lightweight (250cc) race for almost half the nine-lap, 97.11 mile (156.24km/h) race distance, before being forced to retire, after first being slowed with a sick engine, then calling it a day when the motor locked up.

Entered on Terry Hill's NSU, Sammy's 1956 TT number was 23. The entry included not only factory machines from MV Agusta and FB Mondial, several other NSUs (notably Hans Baltisberger, Horst Kassner and Eric Hinton), but also Nortons, EMCs, BSAs, Moto Guzzis and CZs, plus a number of specials such as JEL, GMV and RDS (Reg Dearden Velocette).

Conditions for the 1956 Lightweight (250cc) TT race were 'as wretched as could be imagined,' but this did not seem to affect Sammy at all, just the reverse in fact. For almost half the nine-lap, 97.11-mile (156.24km) distance the young Irishman led the field (from a massed start, unlike the Mountain circuit), before first being slowed by a sick engine and finally being forced to retire on lap six when the NSU's big-end seized. The race was eventually won by Carlo Ubbiali on a works MV Agusta, with Roberto Columbo on another of the Italian machines runner-up. Hans Baltisberger was the first NSU home in third spot.

Although he had been unable to finish the race, Sammy's debut TT ride had further shown the racing world his potential at even the highest level.

A Leinster Victory

Twelve months earlier the Leinster 200 meeting had seen Sammy's debut on the Terry Hill NSU. However, by late June 1956, he was a big-name aboard the German-made machine, with a string of successes behind him.

Also, the 1956 Leinster was notable for the conditions which prevailed. Although the race began on dry roads, this did not last for long before drizzle and fog descended on the Wicklow course. The 16-lap, 133.5-mile (214.8km) race began with a simultaneous massed start for the three classes (250, 350 and 500cc).

Before the conditions deteriorated, Sammy had raised the 250cc lap record to 83.40mph (134.19km/h) and was the leading rider of both the 250s and 350s.

Besides victory in his class (over Jackie Woods on another Sportmax), Sammy took third place in the Hutchinson Trophy Handicap, even though he had fallen after hitting a patch of oil and remounted to rejoin the race.

The Skerries 100 on 7 July 1956 saw Sammy score another 250cc class victory – this time over Harry Lindsay (NSU), but neither rider was to finish in the top 15 riders of the Handicap. Once again Sammy set a new 250cc class lap record, this time with a speed of 75.84mph (122.02km/h).

On a New Circuit

Moved from its traditional surroundings to a new and slightly faster course in Mid Down, the Temple 100 meeting was staged on Saturday 28 July 1956. Unusually, the top four finishers in each class (except 200cc, who had a handicap race of their own) were excluded from the Handicap result. This meant that although Sammy completed his by now usual 250cc class victory, he had no chance of a Handicap win.

The Ulster Grand Prix

The 250cc race of the Ulster Grand Prix was run on Thursday afternoon, 9 August 1956. Many thought that on his home ground Sammy and the Terry Hill NSU would provide a strong challenge to the reigning World Champion, Carlo Ubbiali (MV Agusta). But it was Ubbiali's teammate Luigi Taveri who did the winning after the former's carburettor float needle stuck only a few miles from certain victory. Sammy finished runner-up for the second year, while Arthur Wheeler (Moto Guzzi) came home third, after Bob Brown (NSU) was forced to retire. Incidentally, the sixth-place man, M. Bula, was actually Maurice Bula, later to become a well-known GP photographer and author.

250cc Ulster GP – Dundrod – 9 August 1956 – 13 laps – 96.32 miles

1st   L. Taveri (MV Agusta)

2nd   S.H. Miller (NSU)

3rd   A.F. Wheeler (Moto Guzzi)

4th   P.R. Coleman (NSU)

5th   W.J. Maddrick (Moto Guzzi)

6th   M. Bula (Moto Guzzi)

The 250cc race at the Ulster GP was run on a Thursday afternoon, 9 August. For the second year running Sammy finished runner-up, this time to Luigi Taveri (MV Agusta). In this photograph Sammy (15) leads Bob Brown; the latter was destined to retire his NSU later in the race.

The Italian Grand Prix

What a difference a year makes. The 1955 Italian Grand Prix had seen John Surtees and Sammy head the 250cc race at Monza, but on Sunday 9 September 1956, against a horde of works or works-supported Italian factory entries, the best Sammy could do was finish top privateer (even though he was slowed by a misfire caused by a loose electrical cable) in sixth, a lap behind winner Carlo Ubbiali's MV. But Ubbiali's victory had been a hard-fought one, as Enrico Lorenzetti (Moto Guzzi) had led the race until the last two circuits of the 3.57-mile (5.74km) Monza circuit, the second fastest at that time in the World Championship calendar.

250cc Italian GP – Monza – 9 September 1956 – 22 laps – 78.6 miles
1st   C. Ubbiali (MV Agusta)
2nd   E. Lorenzetti (Moto Guzzi)
3rd   R. Venturi (MV Agusta)
4th   L. Taveri (MV Agusta)
5th   A. Montanari (Moto Guzzi)
6th   S.H. Miller (NSU)

A lovely period photograph of Sammy surrounded by admirers with the Hill NSU during spring 1957. This view shows machine details to advantage, including the Norton front brake.

Then it was back to trials action, albeit this time as a member of the Irish Vase A team, riding a 346cc Royal Enfield Bullet in the ISDT (Sammy's first), held in Bavaria. A broken frame put him out of the running while in line for a Gold Medal on the fifth day. Even though he now had the use of the Ariel HT5 for one-day trials, 1956 was very much a year of success in racing above all else. He also took part in several other races including a new one for the calendar, the Killinchy 150 held over the Dundrod circuit.

1957

Sammy's 1957 racing season got underway at Lurgan Park – a short, tree-lined course – on Easter Saturday, 20 April. Riding Terry Hill's NSU he won not only the 250cc Handicap race, but also the 350cc scratch event. Quite simply no one could match him that day.

Then it was over to the mainland to take part in the national road races at Oulton Park on Easter Monday. It was Sammy's first-ever visit to the Cheshire circuit, and in the end the best he could achieve in his only race of the day was fourth in the 250cc race on the NSU.

250cc Oulton Park – 22 April – 6 laps – 16.2 miles
1st   C.C. Sandford (FB Mondial)
2nd   J. Hartle (REG)
3rd   T.S. Shepherd (MV Agusta)
4th   S.H. Miller (NSU)

The Big Surprise

Next, while Sammy was away riding in the Scottish Six Days on his Ariel HT5 (see Chapter 4), the TT entry list was published on 16 May. Previously two entries had been made by Terry Hill, both on NSUs for Sammy and his teammate David Andrews. However, in Sammy's case, instead of NSU now read FB Mondial. And although Terry Hill was still listed as Sammy's entrant, he was now down to ride not only one of the Italian machines in the Lightweight (250cc) event, but also another FB Mondial in the Ultra Lightweight (125cc) race.

As fully detailed in Chapter 3, the man responsible for this was none other than Artie Bell. So Sammy was about to become a fully-fledged works racer for the first time, thus moving him into a higher league, the top flight in fact. However, the Mondials were only for World Championship events, and thus Sammy continued to ride the NSU under the Terry Hill banner for the remainder of the 1957 season, and he continued to do so into 1958.

Another North West Victory

For the first time ever, the Portstewart-Coleraine-Portrush circuit, venue of the North West 200 meeting, was lapped at 100mph (161km/h), on Saturday 18 May 1957. The man who achieved this feat was the 500cc class winner and ex-Norton works star Jack Brett. Bob Anderson also broke the 350cc record while winning his class, and Sammy shook off all opposition to 'romp home as he pleased' (*The Motor Cycle*). In fact, Sammy's victory was absolute – having lapped every other 250cc machine by half distance!

The 1957 North West 200 race winners, left to right: Jack Brett (Norton 500), Bob Anderson (Norton 350) and Sammy (NSU 250).

250cc North West 200 – 18 May 1957 – 16 laps – 177.1 miles
1st   S.H. Miller (NSU)
2nd   F. Purslow (NSU)
3rd   W.G. Kirby (Velocette)

Cookstown 100
Run on Wednesday 22 May 1957, the annual Cookstown 100 road races saw all lap records broken, including the 250cc class by Sammy at 80.57mph (129.63km/h) on his way to yet another NSU victory.

Next came the TT fortnight, and as we know Sammy rode factory FB Mondial machines, this phase of his career being covered in detail in the following chapter entitled 'Works Road Racer'.

Because of his new commitments on the Grand Prix scene, Sammy was unable to take part in domestic meetings which clashed with Championship rounds. Even so, he was still to compete in several British and Irish meetings that year.

The Leinster
After the TT, Sammy took the Hill NSU to Southern Ireland for the Leinster 100. As *The Motor Cycle* said in its 20 June 1957 issue: 'Tradition returned to the Wicklow circuit last Saturday with the reversion to handicap form of the Leinster "200" road race; there were but 20 starters yet fine racing resulted, with a terrific finish in which 17 riders crossed the line within six minutes.' The report continued: 'High spot of the day was the 170-mile [273.5km] duel between NSU-mounted Sammy Miller and Bob Brown, in the course of which Miller's previous two-fifty lap record was smashed on

no fewer than 21 of the 24 laps. The record was ultimately pushed up to 88.05mph [141.67km/h] by Miller, after Brown had five times set up new figures.' Sammy won both the Open and Class Handicaps.

Open Handicap – Leinster 200 – 15 June 1957 – 24 laps
1st   S.H. Miller (247cc NSU)
2nd   R. Farlow (348cc BSA)
3rd   A.F. Wheeler (248cc Moto Guzzi)
4th   J.W. Fawkes (348cc AJS)
5th   S. Murray (348cc AJS)
6th   G.A. Murphy (349cc AJS)

Yet Another Victory
Precisely a week after the Leinster came the Killinchy 150 over the Dundrod circuit on 22 June 1957. This time the handicappers were on Sammy's case, resulting in his being out of the top six; however, the 250cc scratch race was to see yet another Miller victory – and a fastest lap of 86.68mph (139.46km/h). This meeting also saw the arrival of Tommy Robb into the Terry Hill NSU squad, with Tommy putting up some 'lively lapping' (*The Motor Cycle*).

250cc Scratch Killinchy 150 – 22 June 1957
1st   S.H. Miller (NSU)
2nd   T. Robb (NSU)
3rd   S. Hodgins (Velocette)

Then Sammy was away in Europe contesting the Dutch TT and Belgian GP on Mondial machinery, which meant he missed his annual visit to the Skerries 100 in Southern Ireland.

The Temple 100
Held for the second year in succession over the triangular 5.5-mile (8.8km) circuit at Saintfield, County Down (though with a new start and finish at Lisbane Road crossroads), the Temple Club's 100-mile handicap was run on 27 July 1957. For once Sammy did not win the 250cc class, instead that honour went to his new teammate Tommy Robb. But the two men shared a new class lap record of 78.26mph (125.92km/h). This was no fewer than 10 seconds better than the previous record and a superior time to that put up by Ralph Rensen (Norton) in the 350cc class.

Then it was back to Grand Prix action on the Mondials; first the Ulster in mid-August, followed by the Italian round at Monza on Sunday 1 September.

End-of-Season British Meetings

With the 1957 GP season over, Sammy took in a couple of mainland meetings on the Terry Hill NSU. The first of these was the Hutchinson 100 at Silverstone on Saturday 21 September. Although grey skies greeted the many thousands of spectators who flocked to this, probably the biggest of all British meetings except for the Isle of Man TT, there was virtually no rain during the racing period.

It was notable that Sammy's Mondial teammate Cecil Sandford had the use of both 125 and 250 works machinery for these end-of-season events, whereas Sammy did not. With entries for the 250cc event which included John Surtees and Cecil Sandford on works bikes, Sammy had to be content with fourth position, but at least he did not get lapped, a fate which befell riders such as Percy Tait, Florian Camathias, Arthur Wheeler, Tom Thorp and Jack Murgatroyd.

250cc Silverstone – 21 September 1957 – 15 laps – 54 miles

1st	J. Surtees (MV Agusta)
2nd	C.C. Sandford (FB Mondial)
3rd	D.V. Chadwick (MV Agusta)
4th	S.H. Miller (NSU)
5th	G. Monty (GMS)
6th	H. Kassner (NSU)

The Motor Cycle called it: 'Duck's Day at Aintree.' Right from the off when low, heavy clouds swept over the exposed Aintree circuit as riders prepared to come to the line for the first race, the clouds broke to give cold, stinging rain; from then on there was simply no respite. In the 12-lap 250cc race, Sammy finished third to John Surtees (MV Agusta) and Cecil Sandford (FB Mondial) – again, both these machines were full works entries.

250cc Aintree – 28 September 1957 – 12 laps – 36 miles

1st	J. Surtees (MV Agusta)
2nd	C.C. Sandford (FB Mondial)
3rd	S.H. Miller (NSU)
4th	D.V. Chadwick (MV Agusta)
5th	T. Robb (NSU)
6th	H. Kassner (NSU)

Ulster Grand Prix

Notable motorcycle enthusiast and Ulster Member of Parliament, the late Thomas Moles, assisted in pushing through parliament the first Road Races Act, which made it legal for the Clady course to be closed to the public for the inaugural Ulster Grand Prix on 14 October 1922. That initial race had a total of 75 entries.

In 1926 the 500cc race was won by Graham Walker (father of Murray) on a Sunbeam. He also went on to win the 1928 Senior event on a Rudge.

For 1936 the FIM (*Federation Internationale Motorcycliste*) gave Ulster the title of Grand Prix of Europe, an honour which was to be repeated in 1948. When the World Championships arrived for the 1949 season, the Ulster GP was included among the calendar, a position the event held right up to 1971. But, sadly, the worsening political situation in Northern Ireland forced the promoters to cancel the 1972 event, and with the lobby against the danger of pure road racing gaining momentum all the time, Championship status was destined never to return.

Nevertheless, together with the Isle of Man TT and the North West 200, the Ulster Grand Prix is still considered to be one of the greatest of the three true 'road' races still in existence.

From 1922 until 1939 the event was staged over the legendary 20.5-mile (32.98km) Clady Circuit, including the notoriously bumpy seven-mile (11.26km) straight. At this time it ran across part of the grass runway at the Royal Air Force Station, Aldergrove.

Alterations to this section of the circuit during World War Two resulted in a new, shorter post-war Clady circuit measuring 16.5 miles (26.5km) to a lap, used from 1947 until 1952. In 1953 the event was transferred to the nearby Dundrod road course, this being some 7.401 miles (11.908km) in length.

During the 1920s the top names of the Ulster GP included Graham Walker, Wal Handley, Alex Bennett, Charlie Dodson and Joe Craig (the latter would win greater fame as Norton's race supremo from the late 1920s until his retirement in the mid-1950s).

In the 1930s a new set of names appeared in the Ulster's entry lists, including Stanley Woods, Jimmy Guthrie, Jimmy Simpson, Walter Rusk, Jock West and Dorino Serafini.

The late 1940s and 1950s witnessed greats such as Freddie Frith, Les Graham, Artie Bell, Geoff Duke, Carlo Ubbiali and John Surtees. As the 1950s turned into the 1960s yet more names arrived on the scene, notably Bob McIntyre, Alastair King, Gary Hocking and Mike Hailwood. By the mid-1960s these had been joined by Jim Redman, Phil Read, Bill Ivy and Giacomo Agostini.

In August 1939, on the very eve of war, Walter Rusk set the first 100mph (161km/h) lap in Grand Prix history (riding a supercharged AJS V-four). In more modern times the Ulster Grand Prix produced some superb races, and even after it had lost its World Championship status still attracted the likes of Tom Herron, Ron Haslam, John Williams and

South African Jon Ekerold in the 1970s, while the 1980s saw the emergence of stars like Mick Grant, Brian Read, Wayne Gardner, Steve Hislop and Carl Fogarty. But Joey Dunlop (24 victories) and Philip McCallan (14 victories) head the winners' listings.

As is fully explained in the following chapter, FB Mondial, together with Gilera and Moto Guzzi, pulled out of racing, and although Sammy visited the Italian factory during the close season of 1957–58 he was to have no success in getting Mondial to change their mind.

For the 1958 Grand Prix season Sammy eventually signed up with Ducati in the 125cc class and CZ in the 250cc.

A500 Manx from Ernie Earles

Birmingham engineer Ernie Earles sold Sammy a 500 Manx Norton over the close season. *Motor Cycle News* dated 12 March 1958 carried the following advertisement in its classified section: 'Exchange 1957 500 S/S Norton engine, works overhauled, for 1957–58 350 Norton engine – Miller, 20 Bibsworth Avenue, Birmingham 13.' Sammy said 'Nothing came of this and I eventually sold the Earles 500 Manx on.'

Sammy poses with the Terry Hill NSU Sportmax prior to the start of the 1958 racing season.

Riding NSU and Norton Machinery in 1958

Even though Sammy was riding for Ducati and CZ, he could still compete in domestic meetings on the Terry Hill NSU and his own three-fifty Manx Norton when not riding the works machines.

This policy saw Sammy once again taking part in the international status North West 200 in his native Ulster. As *The Motor Cycle* race report dated 22 May 1958 commented: 'Greatest excitement came in the 250cc race. Terry Hill of Belfast had three fleet NSUs in the race ridden by Ulstermen Sammy Miller, Tommy Robb and D.G. Andrews. But they faced stern opposition in Mike Hailwood, also riding an NSU Sportmax, and Bob Anderson (GMV).'

As the field rocketed away from the start line, it was Anderson (winner of the 350cc class the previous year and the 500cc class in 1956) who immediately tore into the lead, obviously keen to make it a hat-trick of victories. But on the fourth lap his engine failed. That left Robb at the head of the pack, but he had to ride on the very ragged edge as he knew that Hailwood and Sammy were not far behind.

The 250cc race at the North West 200 in May 1958 resulted in one of the closest-ever finishes seen at this legendary event, with Sammy beating none other than Mike Hailwood – both mounted on dolphin-faired NSUs.

After his sensational 250cc victory, Sammy lines up with the other 1958 North West winners, Jack Brett (500) and Alastair King (350).

After setting a new lap record of 90.04mph (144.87km/h), Tommy pushed his luck a shade too far, falling off on the fifth lap at Black Hill. Mike Hailwood, who was close behind, missed Robb's fallen machine by inches! Mike now assumed the lead, with Sammy next. This is where experience told, because our man played a waiting game right up to the very last corner, with the finish almost in sight. And this is precisely what Sammy had planned – passing the surprised Hailwood to cross the line as the victor – his third successive North West victory. As *Motor Cycle News* reported: 'Only once before, in 1949, has such a close finish been seen at Portstewart and on that occasion it was between Freddie Frith and Harold Daniell.'

250cc North West 200 – 17 May 1958 – 16 laps – 177.6 miles

1st   S.H. Miller (NSU)

2nd   S.M.B. Hailwood (NSU)

3rd   T. Robb (NSU)

4th   D.G. Andrews (NSU)

5th   R. Grey (Moto Guzzi)

6th   H. Stanford (Norton)

On the Wednesday prior to the North West, Sammy had taken part in the Cookstown 100 on his three-fifty Manx Norton. The 350cc scratch class boasted a number of good riders, including Ralph Rensen and Fron Purslow. And soon a battle royal developed between Rensen and Sammy, the two riders locked together at the front of the field. On the sixth lap Sammy was only 'a few feet' (*The Motor Cycle*) behind when Rensen skidded on some molten tar and crashed. Somehow Sammy avoided the mêlée, but later crashed himself at the same spot. Meanwhile, Rensen had remounted and went on to win, while Sammy's machine was put out of action.

Sammy with his three-fifty Norton, which he had purchased back in 1955 to replace the AJS 7R.

During spring 1958 Sammy's main rival for 350cc race honours in Ireland was Englishman Ralph Rensen (seen here on one of his Nortons in that year's Isle of Man TT).

Another Rensen Battle

On Saturday 14 June 1958, battle resumed between the two Manx Norton riders, the venue this time being the Leinster 200 – held that year over the new four-mile (6.4km) Dunboyne circuit that had replaced the well-known Wicklow course. As one newspaper report stated: 'Sammy Miller and Ralph Rensen were evenly matched on 348cc Nortons. They started off together from the 2½ minute mark and justified the handicapper's estimate by staying locked in combat for the whole 37 laps, with never more than a second between them and swapping places several times.' The report continued: 'Rensen put the 350cc lap record up to 83.72mph [134.70km/h] on the 20th lap, but Miller hung on and waited for the last lap. Then he made his challenge, got by and lapped at a new record speed of 83.92mph [135.02km/h] to reach the line four-fifths of a second ahead of Rensen.'

In the Leinster 200 Handicap Sammy was seventh, Ralph Rensen eighth.

Leinster 200 – 350cc Scratch – 14 June 1958
1st   S.H. Miller (Norton)
2nd   R.B. Rensen (Norton)
3rd   R.A. Coulter (BSA)

As is recorded in the next chapter, Sammy's final Grand Prix was to be the Dutch TT at Assen on Saturday 28 June 1958, in which he retired at his pit at the very start of the 250cc race, the first of the day with his CZ. Then he came home seventh in his final race, the 125cc on the Ducati. When asked by Charles Deane in 1967: 'Do you regret giving up road racing for trials riding and which do you enjoy more?' Sammy replied: 'No, I don't regret giving up road racing as I prefer trials riding to any other motorcycle sport. You can practice any time you feel like it, you don't need a special track and the machinery you use is easier to maintain, less costly and less sophisticated. Personally, I find practising for trials the most satisfying part of motorcycling; I really enjoy it.'

As for his NSU sponsor, Terry Hill, when interviewed by Peter Howdle for *Motor Cycle News* in July 1969, Terry said: 'If Sammy Miller had gone on putting as much effort into racing as he has into trials he would have been another Hailwood.'

Chapter 3

Works Road Racer

With some excellent Grand Prix results behind him on Terry Hill's two-fifty NSU Sportmax, it was perhaps not unexpected that Sammy should have been seen as a future signing for a major factory. Certainly, back in 1955 Joe Craig, the Norton team boss, had offered him a ride, which, as we know, Sammy politely turned down, realising that the Norton single was no longer competitive at the very highest level.

Artie Bell Intervenes

While Sammy was competing in the 1957 Scottish Six Days Trial, a complete list of entries for that year's Isle of Man TT races was published on 16 May. Although originally entered by Terry Hill on the NSU, the list now showed Sammy (still entered by the Hill Equipe) on an Italian FB Mondial in the Lightweight 250cc event, and also a completely new entry, on a Mondial, in the Ultra Lightweight (125cc) race. The 250cc machine was notable for its seven-speed gearbox and fully enclosed streamlining.

So what was going on? Well, the man responsible for these startling developments was none other than Sammy's old hero, the former Norton works star Artie Bell.

Although it was many years since Artie had been forced to hang up his leathers following a serious crash during the 500cc Belgian GP in 1950, he still retained a great interest in the sport and, more importantly as far as this story is concerned, valuable contacts throughout the racing world.

In the normal course of events Sammy would have been left to make the choice himself of either staying with Terry Hill and the NSU, or quitting and joining a factory team. But in this case Artie Bell's intervention meant that Sammy was able to ride FB Mondials in the World Championship events, while at non-Championship races he could continue campaigning the Hill-NSU.

Of course, it had also been Artie Bell who had encouraged Sammy right from his earliest days – from when the youngster and his two school friends had visited him at his Woodstock Road, Belfast, showroom.

Sammy pictured during 1957 TT practice on one of the factory FB Mondial machines.

Jeff Clew correctly summed up the situation regarding Sammy's works rides with the Italian factory, saying: 'It was therefore all the more fitting that Artie should understand Sammy's predicament and take the initiative to get him a ride on works Mondials, retaining the sponsorship link with Terry Hill. A very diplomatic way out of a difficult situation. But this was Artie at his best.'

TT Practice Begins

Although Sammy's debut as a Mondial teamster began at the TT, this was not the first round of the 1957 World Championship series; this had begun, for both the 125 and 250cc classes, at Hockenheim in West Germany. Here the top placed Mondials had been ridden by Tarquinio Provini (second – 125cc) and Cecil Sandford (third – 250cc).

The first TT practice session in which Sammy was involved with the Mondial team was on the 125cc model, which began at 6pm on Wednesday 29 May 1957. He was fourth fastest – a very creditable start to his Mondial career – in 9 minutes 21 seconds (69.24mph).

Then, after the 125s had been flagged off at 7pm, the first of the 250s got underway. As was the usual practice at the time, both the Lightweight events, plus the Sidecars, were held over the shorter 10.79-mile (17.36km) Clypse course. And the six fastest 250s were Sammy in 8 min 32.8 sec (75.75mph), Tarquinio Provini (Mondial), Carlo Ubbiali (MV Agusta),

Englishman Cecil Sandford was one of Sammy's teammates in the Mondial team. Highly experienced, Cecil had been the 1953 125cc World Champion on an MV Agusta.

Dave Chadwick (MV Agusta), Cecil Sandford (Mondial) and Bob Anderson (GMS).

Other riders out in that session included John Hartle, Bob McIntyre, Bob Brown and many more well-known names.

The *TT Special* said Sammy was: 'Very, very fast.' And as the practice period continued, Mondial's new signing was usually either at or near the top of the leaderboard; his racing numbers being 14 (125) and 4 (250).

Sammy's Greatest Race – and Heartbreak

10am on 5 June saw the start of the 1957 Lightweight (250cc) TT – arguably Sammy's greatest race, and certainly his biggest disappointment.

The 1957 Lightweight (250cc) was to prove a dramatic race. Here, early in the race, Cecil Sandford leads Sammy, both riding fully streamlined works dohc FB Mondials.

Right from the start of the 10-lap, 107.90-mile (173.61km) race Sammy showed he meant business by streaking into an immediate lead. However, at Craig-ny-Baa Cecil Sandford had taken over. From then on until midway through the final lap Sammy sat right on Sandford's rear wheel. At his pit

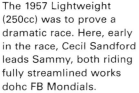

On the last section of the course and within sight of the finish, Sammy crashed. Here he crosses the finish line, exhausted, to the acclaim of everyone there that day in June 1957.

Sammy had received a signal. What was it? The answer soon came because at Cronk-y-Garroo Sammy had taken the lead. As *The Motor Cycle* reported: 'Miller was in front – so it was the "faster" signal that his pit had given. At Hall Corner he continued to lead and by the time the Manx Arms had been reached he had streaked away on his own. Only a few seconds later the bulb over his number on the scoreboard signalled Miller's arrival at Signpost, and the crowds in the stands rose to give an appropriate welcome to the brilliant young rider from Belfast roaring home for his first TT win.'

Sadly, the crowds had risen a shade too early. And Sammy's luck was about to dramatically run out. At Governor's Bridge, almost within sight of a magnificent victory, Sammy spilled and the lucky star passed to Sandford – who was as surprised as anyone to take the win.

As for Sammy, even worse luck was to come, for in spite of a desperate attempt to restart the Mondial, it refused to fire up. Instead the young Ulsterman was forced to push the machine almost half a mile uphill to the finishing line. This took some 15 minutes, during which time Luigi Taveri, Roberto Columbo and the Czech rider Frantisek Bartos roared past the stricken Mondial.

The winner of the 1957 Lightweight TT, Cecil Sandford; even he had to admit that luck was on his side, as he would not have won had not Sammy fallen.

The National Press

Sammy's misfortune even reached the national press. Typical was the *Daily Express*, which began by saying: 'You cannot measure the courage of racing motorcyclists – these men with nerves of steel. But if you could, the name Sammy Miller would be way out ahead in that field tonight. He is the gallant, pale-faced, sandy-haired Ulsterman who had today's Lightweight International TT in his pocket – only to come hurtling off his Italian Mondial just half a mile from the finish.'

After a sandwich, a glass of milk and bandages to a badly grazed knee and arm Sammy set off that same day for another 107-mile (172km) race on his smaller Mondial, in which he finished fourth. After the two races, officials around the course declared: 'No TT rider has shown greater grit or courage in the 50 years the races have been held.'

Sammy's View

That evening Sammy told reporters: 'At speed you haven't time to think about yourself. The second race did me a lot of good. Anyway, I shouldn't have come off in the first one – so it served me right if I had any pain.'

Lightweight (250cc) TT – 10 laps – 107 miles – 5 June 1957
1st   C.C. Sandford (FB Mondial)
2nd   L. Taveri (MV Agusta)
3rd   R. Columbo (MV Agusta)
4th   F. Bartos (CZ)
5th   S.H. Miller (FB Mondial)
6th   D. Chadwick (MV Agusta)

Ultra Lightweight (125cc) TT – 10 laps – 107 miles – 5 June 1957
1st   T. Provini (FB Mondial)
2nd   C. Ubbiali (MV Agusta)
3rd   L. Taveri (MV Agusta)
4th   S.H. Miller (FB Mondial)
5th   C.C. Sandford (FB Mondial)
6th   R. Columbo (MV Agusta)

The first three finishers of the 1957 Lightweight TT. Left to right: winner Cecil Sandford (FB Mondial, 29), runner-up Luigi Taveri (MV, 3) and third Roberto Columbo (MV, 2).

Dutch TT

Some three weeks after the TT came the Dutch round of the Championship trail. This was staged over the 4.79-mile (7.70km) Van Drenthe circuit at Assen in the northern area of Holland, a circuit which Sammy had never even seen before. Certainly he did not disgrace himself, with a third-place finish in the 250cc race and a sixth on his smaller Mondial.

250cc Dutch TT – 14 laps – 67.02 miles – 29 June 1957

125cc Dutch TT – 14 laps – 67.02 miles – 29 June 1957
1st   T. Provini (FB Mondial)
2nd   R. Columbo (MV Agusta)
3rd   L. Taveri (MV Agusta)
4th   C.C. Sandford (FB Mondial)
5th   F. Libanori (MV Agusta)
6th   S.H. Miller (FB Mondial)

250cc Dutch TT – 17 laps – 81.38 miles – 29 June 1957
1st   T. Provini (FB Mondial)
2nd   C.C. Sandford (FB Mondial)
3rd   S.H. Miller (FB Mondial)
4th   F. Libanori (MV Agusta)
5th   F. Stastny (Jawa)
6th   A.F. Wheeler (Moto Guzzi)

Belgian Grand Prix

A mere eight days after the Dutch TT came the Belgian Grand Prix at Spa Francorchamps. In the 125cc event Sammy was well placed before being forced out at Malmedy on the second lap. But he fared much, much better in the 250cc race. And although he was to finish a superb second to John Hartle, who had been drafted onto the MV Agusta team on a new twin-cylinder model, during practice Sammy's Mondial was found to be well down on speed compared to teammate Provini's machine. This was the first time that Sammy had cause to think that he was being provided with inferior equipment. This situation was eventually to lead to disillusionment about road racing in general. In fact, Provini would have won, had he not retired with lack of sparks on the final lap; his machine was many miles-per-hour faster than the Ulsterman's.

250cc Belgian Grand Prix – 91 laps – 78.66 miles – 7 July 1957
1st   J. Hartle (MV Agusta)
2nd   S.H. Miller (FB Mondial)
3rd   C.C. Sandford (FB Mondial)

4th   A.F. Wheeler (Moto Guzzi)
5th   F. Bartos (CZ)
6th   G. Beer (Adler)

No Real Luck in Ulster

Much could have been expected of Sammy at his home Grand Prix, the Ulster at Dundrod. Because of the Suez Crisis and the effect of fuel rationing in Great Britain, the meeting, normally a two-day affair, was condensed into a single day – with the Sidecar race cancelled.

In the 125 event Sammy's Mondial seemed well down on speed and he was some six minutes down on the winner, Luigi Taveri (MV Agusta) at the finish, in fifth position.

At the start of the 250cc event, Cecil Sandford led from his Mondial teammates Tarquinio Provini and Sammy. But Sandford was the only one of the trio to finish, Provini retiring with engine trouble on lap five and Sammy's engine going bang on lap 10. With this victory Sandford became the 1957 250cc world champion.

125cc Ulster Grand Prix – 10 laps – 74.16 miles – 10 August 1957
1st   L. Taveri (MV Agusta)
2nd   T. Provini (FB Mondial)
3rd   R. Venturi (MV Agusta)
4th   D.V. Chadwick (MV Agusta)
5th   S.H. Miller (FB Mondial)
5th   W.M. Webster (MV Agusta)

Better Luck at Monza

Wall-to-wall sunshine at Monza brought the 1957 Championship season to a close. In the 125cc event there were works teams from not only FB Mondial, but also MV Agusta, Ducati and the East German MZ factory.

The initial leader was Luigi Taveri, followed by his MV teammates Venturi and Carlo Ubbiali. However, Sammy's Mondial teamsters Tarquinio Provini and Cecil Sandford were soon forced into retirement. As the race wore on, Ubbiali moved into second place, while Sammy followed him through, pushing Venturi back to fourth. Both Ubbiali and Sammy then passed Taveri. And so it remained to the flag, a truly brilliant result for our man.

125cc Italian Grand Prix – 18 laps – 64.31 miles – 10 September 1957
1st   C. Ubbiali (MV Agusta)
2nd   S.H. Miller (FB Mondial)

3rd   L. Taveri (MV Agusta)
4th   F. Libanori (MV Agusta)
5th   G. Salo (FB Mondial)
6th   E. Degner (MZ)

The 250cc event saw the MV and Mondial teams joined by Emilio Mendogni on a works Moto Morini and the former class champion Enrico Lorenzetti and Alano Montanari on ex-works Moto Guzzis to add spice to the proceedings.

However, for several of the leading contenders, including Sammy, it was to be a race of problems.

Carlo Ubbiali led the field away, followed by Sandford, Lorenzetti and Mendogni. Lying fifth was Provini, on the first of the Mondials. The latter quickly overhauled Mendogni, Lorenzetti and Sandford, finally taking the lead when Ubbiali was forced to call it a day after experiencing ignition gremlins.

With Provini established in the lead, MV's Venturi moved through the pack to take the runner-up position. Next both Mendogni and Taveri struck mechanical woes and were sidelined. Sammy was now in a secure fourth position; however, this state of affairs was not to last and his engine too went sick. Being forced to nurse his machine home over the final circuit, Sammy was caught and passed by fellow Mondial man Cecil Sandford.

250cc Italian Grand Prix – 22 laps – 78.6 miles – 10 September 1957
1st   T. Provini (FB Mondial)
2nd   R. Venturi (MV Agusta)
3rd   E. Lorenzetti (Moto Guzzi)
4th   C.C. Sandford (FB Mondial)
5th   S.H. Miller (FB Mondial)
6th   A. Montanari (Moto Guzzi)

The Championship Tables
Sammy was only able to contest five of the six rounds, as he had not joined FB Mondial until the second round, at the TT. Bearing that in mind, third place (behind Cecil Sandford and Tarquinio Provini) was an excellent result in the 250cc title race, which was backed up by a fourth in the 125cc table (behind Provini, Luigi Taveri and Carlo Ubbiali).

Both these results were solid performances in what were, after all, Sammy's first experiences of Grand Prix racing as a works team member.

The Withdrawal

Even as early as the Italian GP at Monza, rumours were circulating concerning a planned withdrawal from racing by several Italian factories – including FB Mondial. As the Grand Prix season ended everyone held their breath and waited for the truth to emerge.

The news was not long in coming. At the end of September the shattering announcement was made that Gilera, Moto Guzzi and FB Mondial would not be racing in 1958.

Dr Gerado Bonelli, director general of Moto Guzzi, made the official announcement at a press banquet (forever after known in Italy as 'The Last Supper') in the presence of representatives from Gilera and FB Mondial. In today's Moto GP scene it would be akin to Yamaha, Honda and Ducati all quitting together – just think about that!

Various reasons for the decision were given, including the fact that all three companies had: 'Demonstrated the undeniable technical excellence of their products and that recently there had been no foreign opposition.' Added to that had been an outbreak in Italy of an anti-racing lobby, fuelled by the popular press and the restrictions introduced by the authorities following the Mille Miglia car tragedy (in which a car had run off the road, killing several spectators). But the real reason, and one that could not be given at the time, was that motorcycling itself was in trouble. It was the beginning of an era in which customers would turn away from two wheels in favour of small cars in ever-increasing numbers.

So where did this leave Sammy?

To Ride For Ducati

After failing to persuade FB Mondial to loan him machines for 1958, Sammy began to look at other possibilities. The first to emerge came in mid-February, with the announcement that he would be riding Ducatis in the 125cc class in the TT and other meetings counting towards the World Championship.

CZ

CZ (Ceska Zboiouka) did not commence motorcycle production until 1932, even though the company was formed in 1918, initially to manufacture armaments. It was Jaroslav Walter who really got the company into racing – which goes some way to explaining why the post-war CZ racing story involves exclusively four-strokes, rather than the two-strokes, which the Czech concern used for both its standard production roadsters and the vast majority of its various motocross and enduro bikes.

In 1938, Walter, one of the two sons of the founder of the Walter marque, created an extremely modern 248cc ohv road racing engine and in 1939 an ohc version, which after the war scored a string of racing successes. In 1947 a new 348cc ohc racing single was added, which (together with the original 248cc model) was taken on board by CZ when Jaroslav Walter joined the much larger Stakonice factory the following year.

The period 1951–53 had seen the larger-engined machine win several races in Austria, although it did not have the power or roadholding abilities of the latest Featherbed-framed Manx Norton.

But 1955 was to be the year when CZ really entered the international racing arena, with brand machinery in the 125 and 250cc classes, and a team of three domestic riders: Bartos (team leader), Parus and Kostir. The new squad made its debut at the Swedish Grand Prix that year, gaining a brilliant second place in the 125cc event. The 125 CZ produced 14.5bhp, the 250 model 24bhp.

Both engines used double overhead camshafts, with full unit construction and five-speed, close-ratio gearboxes; there was also wet sump lubrication. In addition, both the designs shared the same full-cradle duplex frame layout. While the smaller mount used telescopic front forks, the two-fifty CZ featured a fork of leading link design with external hydraulic dampers. Full-width alloy brake hubs were employed, with a larger diameter front assembly on the 250.

The following year, 1956, saw the CZ team turn up at the Austrian Grand Prix in early May, with Bartos taking victory in the 250cc race. But the first event counting towards World Championship points was the Isle of Man TT the following month. There were three CZ entries – the first for 21 years from a Czech manufacturer – in the shape of two for Bartos (125 and 250) and Parus on a 125. All three CZs were fully streamlined, with aluminium dustbin fairings and large capacity hand-beaten fuel tanks in the same material.

In the 125cc race Parus finished sixth, averaging 59.82mph (96.25km/h) for the nine laps of the shorter Clypse course. Bartos, though, failed to complete one lap in the same race. He made amends

Frantasek Bartos aboard one of the Czech double-overhead-camshaft single-cylinder machines during the 1957 Isle of Man TT.

The CZ dohc single-cylinder racing model was produced in both 125 and 250cc guises. The larger model, as raced by Sammy Miller for part of the 1958 season, is shown here.

for this by coming home fifth in the 250 event (again nine laps), at an average speed of 63.28mph (101.81km/h). The team then went to the Dutch TT at Assen, where the third teamster, Kostir, scored his first Championship points by finishing sixth on the 250; Bartos was also sixth in the 125cc race.

The Isle of Man TT celebrated its Golden Jubilee in 1957 and CZ sent a team of four riders – the original trio plus Franta Stastny (later to gain fame riding Jawa bikes). They had two entries in the 125cc event – Bartos and Parus. But only Bartos took part, finishing a creditable seventh, with only the rapid works MVs and FB Mondials in front.

In the 250cc class Bartos did even better, coming home fourth in a race won by Cecil Sandford (World Champion that year) on an FB Mondial. Bartos actually finished in front of Sammy Miller (on another works Mondial), after our man had to push in after suffering a crash on the final corner of the final lap when leading the race. Meanwhile, Kostir came home seventh and Stastny 12th, enabling the Czech riders to take home the team prize. As for the Continental Grand Prix circus, the 1957 highlight for CZ came in Belgium, where Bartos again proved his worth by finishing fourth in the 125 and fifth in the 250.

As detailed in the main chapter, in 1958 Sammy Miller signed to race the Czech machines, and in doing so he created a piece of history by becoming the first British rider for a Czech factory in the Isle of Man since Jawa designer/rider George Patchett's days back in the 1930s.

After Sammy retired from GP racing to concentrate on trials in mid-1958, CZ confined their racing activities to within the Czech borders until the early 1960s. They then had a presence at the top level for the remainder of the decade, finally quitting the sport in 1972.

However, CZ won international fame with their two-stroke off-road bikes, gaining world titles (motocross) and gold medals (ISDT) from the mid-1960s onwards.

The CZ double-overhead camshaft engine. One of the 125cc units is shown here.

Austrian Grand Prix

The Austrian Grand Prix was a non-Championship meeting held over a 3.167-mile (5.1km) autobahn circuit at Salzburg. As *Motor Cycle News* described: 'Although the autobahn forms the two main straights the circuit is by no means an easy one and use is made of approach roads and a flyover to give a number of bends and no less than three hairpins!'

It was here that Sammy made his CZ debut. After winning the 125cc event, MV World Champion Carlo Ubbiali was soon back on the grid for the 250cc race. This time one of his challengers was Sammy and the CZ. From the flag the Italian 'rocketed away' (*MCN*), with our man making a poor getaway due to clutch drag. By the end of the first lap the works MV was well ahead and Sammy had come through a strong entry of NSUs to take second place, with the Australian Jack Forrest third on one of the German bikes.

As *MCN* reported in its 7 May 1958 issue: 'Clearly the CZ – a hack machine that was being used at Salzburg to test a new six-speed gearbox – could not match the MV and Sammy was content to let Ubbiali go and to build up a big lead over his pursuers, who were led by Helmut Hallmeier (NSU) after Forrest had retired on the fifth lap with machine trouble.'

250cc Austrian Grand Prix – 15 laps – 47.5 miles – 1 May 1958

1st   C. Ubbiali (MV Agusta)
2nd   S.H. Miller (CZ)
3rd   H. Hallmeier (NSU)
4th   J. Autengruber (NSU)
5th   M. Schneider (NSU)
6th   R. Thalhammer (NSU)

Sammy made his debut on the CZ two-fifty at the Austrian Grand Prix, held at Salzburg on 1 May 1958, where he finished runner-up to Carlo Ubbiali (MV Agusta).

Next Sammy took in the Scottish Six Days Trial, after flying from Austria to England. But he did tell journalist Mick Wollett, before leaving, that: 'A pair of new engines were being prepared by CZ for the Lightweight TT.' These would follow: 'Normal CZ single-cylinder, double overhead camshaft lines, but would have twin plugs and coil ignition plus the six-speed gearboxes.'

As detailed in the preceding chapter, after the Scottish, and before the TT, Sammy completed a hat-trick of 250cc victories in the North West 200 on Terry Hill's NSU Sportmax machine.

TT Practice Begins

News of the arrival of the Ducati team bikes came in *The Motor Cycle* dated 5 June 1958: 'Organized confusion reigned in the Ducati camp where blue-overalled mechanics were readying the newly arrived mounts for the evening session. The Ducatis, all of which have desmodromic overhead valve gear [see separate boxed section within this chapter] are six in number and include the two original works models only differing in frame detail for Luigi Taveri and Romolo Ferri and two hack mounts for practice purposes.' It should also be noted that Fabio Taglioni, Ducati's design chief, had accompanied the team to the Island.

Sammy Miller's works 125cc machine for the 1958 Isle of Man TT was a desmodromic single-cylinder Ducati.

During the first practice session, on Wednesday evening, 28 May, Sammy had been fourth behind Luigi Taveri and the MV pairing of Tarquinio Provini and Carlo Ubbiali.

The Ducati machines were finished in royal blue, with a white prancing-horse emblem on the fuel tank.

Friday evening's practice on 30 May saw Sammy out on his works 247cc CZ. The machine now sported an additional gear ratio, making six in all.

Sammy's riding numbers for the 1958 TT were Ducati 28 and CZ 1.

Ducati 125 Desmo

During 1958, Sammy Miller was a member of the Ducati works team, riding the 125 Desmo single. This design had made its debut back in July 1956, when the prototype machine won its first-ever race, the Swedish Grand Prix at Hedemora, ridden by Gianni Degli Antoni. After their Scandinavian success, the Ducati squad travelled back to Italy. The Desmo's next outing was scheduled to be at Monza in early September, at the Italian Grand Prix. To prepare for this, Degli Antoni began track testing at Monza during early August. It was during one of these test sessions that, rounding the fearsome Lesmo curve, the 26-year-old Italian lost control and crashed heavily, receiving fatal injuries. This tragedy was a major blow to Ducati's racing ambitions, so much so that any serious attempt at the 125cc World Championship was not to be mounted until 1958.

The man behind the Ducati racing challenge was their chief designer Fabio Taglioni, who had joined the Bologna-based factory in the spring of 1954. Taglioni had spent his first year at his new employers designing and developing his first Ducati, the 98cc GS

The Ducati 125 Desmo single made its debut – a winning one too – at the Swedish GP in July 1956, with the Italian Gianni Degli Antoni at the controls.

(Gran Sport), also known as the Marianna. This was essentially a robust sohc sports/racing machine, brilliantly suited to the long-distance road events which were staged in Italy at the time, such as the *Giro d'Italia* (Tour of Italy) and the Milano-Taranto.

Following its successful arrival, Taglioni then turned his attention to not only designing new 125 and 175 ohc roadsters, but also a 125cc dohc version of the Gran Sport. This emerged in early 1956 and was known as the Grand Prix, and it was this which was to act as the spur to Taglioni's superb Desmo single.

Even at an early stage in the transformation of his bevel-driven single from single-overhead-cam to twin-cam design, Fabio Taglioni realised that this would probably not be enough to put Ducati on a par with the top 125 GP bikes, such as the MV Agusta single and the Gilera twin. So he produced his secret weapon: desmodromics.

The word 'desmodromic' was coined from the Greek words for 'controlled run'. The purpose of the design was to eliminate one of the chief problems of conventional spring-valve operation at high engine speeds, the phenomenon of valve float or 'bounce'. This was a particular weakness at the time, before the advent of four-valves-per-cylinder technology and the rev limiters found in modern engine management systems.

Valve bounce occurs when conventional valve springs are unable to respond quickly enough to close the valves onto their seats. In a desmodromic system, the troublesome springs are replaced with a mechanical closing system, much like that employed to open them, thus providing a positive action. This effectively eliminates the bounce, allowing the engine to rev higher.

Without a doubt, the 'desmo' was Taglioni's and Ducati's ace card, and was to prove central to the factory's efforts on first the race circuit and eventually in the showroom. But first he had to do something no

One of the 1958 Ducati Desmo models, seen at that year's Isle of Man TT. This tank-off view shows the engine and frame details off to advantage.

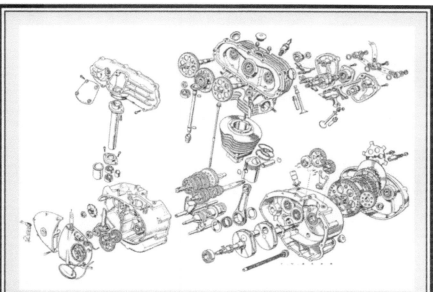

The 1958 triple camshaft Desmo single-cylinder engine. Features included twin plug ignition, five-speed gearbox, straight-cut bevel gears and titanium connecting rod.

one had managed to achieve in the two-wheel world since the first experiments had taken place with desmodromics many years before; make it work in practice!

The first Desmo prototype was simply a suitably modified dohc Grand Prix. Soon, however, purpose-built engines followed, and there were now *three* camshafts, not two, as on the valve-spring engine.

Much of the early testing was carried out on the bench. Then, when the basic principle had been proved to work, further extensive development followed over several months in the first half of 1956, on both bench and track. Power output was found to be around 17bhp at 12,500rpm, and – most significant of all – the Desmo valve gear passed all these tests with flying colours. Hundred-hour bench tests on full throttle caused no drop in the engine's performance, and no ill effects resulted from over-revving, even though track testers were at times letting the revs soar to over 15,000rpm – a truly fantastic figure at the time.

By the beginning of the 1958 season the 1956 Swedish GP victory was becoming a distant memory. But this did not mean that Taglioni had been idle. Far from it, in fact, because not only had he successfully created a new range of street bikes, but he had also carried out further work on the Desmo GP single *and* even found time to design a couple of twins – a 175cc valve model and a 125 Desmo as well.

Improvements to the Desmo single had not simply been reserved for the engine. They had also included a new double-cradle, tubular frame – in fact there were two types, one for the fast circuits, and one for twisting, slow courses. There was now also a choice of five or six-speed gear clusters (again depending upon circuit), while the full dustbin-type streamlining had been replaced with a new dolphin fairing to comply with FIM regulations introduced for the 1958 season. Because of this the brakes had needed modification, with repositioned air scoops on both front and rear wheels.

Race winner of the 1958
Ultra Lightweight (125cc)
TT, Italian MV Agusta star
Carlo Ubbiali.

The Lightweight Race

The first of the three races scheduled for the Clypse circuit on Wednesday 4
June was the Lightweight, which saw Sammy on his CZ. But it was not a
happy race for the Ulsterman. On lap five at Ballacoar, halfway point for the
10.79-mile (17.36km) circuit, Sammy locked the rear wheel and was
thrown, but he remounted to carry on with his fairing's screen shattered.
Sammy was later to comment that the CZ's: 'Brakes were weak and the
handling suspect.' Even so, he gamely battled on to come home sixth.
However, when one considers that a pair of privately-entered NSU
Sportmax machines ridden by Mike Hailwood and Bob Brown finished
third and fourth, one has to wonder whether Sammy would not have been
more successful on Terry Hill's similar model?

Lightweight (250cc) TT – 10 laps – 107 miles – 4 June 1958

1st	T. Provini (MV Agusta)
2nd	C. Ubbiali (MV Agusta)
3rd	S.M.B. Hailwood (NSU)
4th	R.N. Brown (NSU)
5th	D. Falk (Adler)
6th	S.H. Miller (CZ)

More success in the Ultra Lightweight

Even though Sammy's taller build better suited a 250 than a diminutive 125 machine, he enjoyed more success on the Ducati than he had a few hours earlier on the CZ. Ducati's team of four riders comprised Taveri, Ferri, Chadwick and Sammy. Team boss Fabio Taglioni's pre-arranged plan was that for seven laps Taveri was to go all out in an attempt: 'To ride the MVs into the ground,' (*The Motor Cycle*). After that it was to be every man for himself.

Besides the MV and Ducati machines, there was Mike Hailwood on a Paton, Fron Purslow on a valve-spring Ducati, Arthur Wheeler on an ex-works Mondial and, finally, a pair of works MZ machines. Powered by rotary-valve two-stroke engines, these latter bikes were ridden by Ernst Degner and Horst Fugner.

The first four laps saw a wheel-to-wheel battle develop between the two MVs and Taveri's Ducati. Then Provini was a shade too enthusiastic and crashed, and Taveri's engine began to smoke and he was eventually forced into retirement. This left Ubbiali in the lead, from Chadwick, Ferri and Sammy. By the finish Ferri and Chadwick had swapped places – Ferri put in a late burst, but in the end just could not catch the MV rider.

One of Sammy's teammates in the Ducati factory team was Dave Chadwick, seen here during the 1958 Ultra Lightweight (TT); others were Luigi Taveri and Romolo Ferri.

Sammy with his 125cc
Ducati, one of four riders
mounted on this
machinery in the 1958 TT.
Held over the 10.79-mile
(17.36km) Clypse circuit,
Miller took fourth position,
averaging 70.43mph
(113.32km/h).

Ultra Lightweight (125cc) TT – 10 laps – 107 miles – June 1958

1st	C. Ubbiali (MV Agusta)	
2nd	R. Ferri (Ducati)	
3rd	D.V. Chadwick (Ducati)	
4th	S.H. Miller (Ducati)	
5th	E. Degner (MZ)	
6th	H. Fugner (MZ)	

Following the TT, and before the Dutch TT at Assen, came the Leinster 200, where Sammy scored a victory on his own 350 Norton.

The Dutch TT

The 1958 Dutch TT at Assen marked a turning point in Sammy's riding career. He had been down to ride the CZ in the 250cc race, but when he arrived he found that the Czech machine had failed to arrive. In the 125cc race (which came after the 250cc event) he came home seventh, splitting the MZs of Degner (sixth) and Fugner (eighth).

Tarquinio Provini (MV Agusta), winner of the 1958 250cc TT.

125cc Dutch TT – 14 laps – 66.98 miles – 28 June 1958

1st	C. Ubbiali (MV Agusta)
2nd	L. Taveri (Ducati)
3rd	T. Provini (MV Agusta)
4th	A. Gandossi (Ducati)
5th	D.V. Chadwick (Ducati)
6th	E. Degner (MZ)
7th	S.H. Miller (Ducati)
8th	H. Fugner (MZ)

The 1958 125cc top three finishers. Left to right: winner Carlo Ubbiali (MV), runner-up Romolo Ferri (Ducati) and third Dave Chadwick (Ducati).

A determined-looking Sammy with the works CZ during the 1958 Lightweight TT.

The Dutch TT would be Sammy's last as a works Grand Prix rider – and his last race until 1960, when he took part in the Thruxton 500-mile endurance event for production machines on an Ariel Arrow.

So why did Sammy decide to walk away from racing? The truth is that he had become disillusioned – this process having begun while he was a member of the FB Mondial team the year before. In Sammy's eyes, racing was not a level playing field, and the performance of a particular machine was more crucial than the riding skill of the rider; however, in trials things were more equal and determination and riding ability – plus good machine preparation – were what counted. So Sammy decided to concentrate on the trials scene and to quit the glamorous Grand Prix scene.

When interviewed by John Craig for *Classic Legends* magazine during the late 1980s, Sammy commented: 'Looking back, maybe I should have kept on racing until the Japs came in, then I could have made some big money with them.' He went on to say: 'But then I might have been one of the dead heroes – and they're soon forgotten.'

Sammy was far from impressed with the CZ during the 1958 TT, later commenting: 'Brakes were weak and the handling suspect.' This is a practice week shot.

Chapter 4
Ariel

If one motorcycle more than any other is associated with Sammy Miller, it just has to be his legendary Ariel HT5 trials mount, GOV 132. Yes, Sammy rode – and won – on a great variety of machines on both dirt and tarmac, but it was that Ariel which is the best remembered today.

The Beginning of a Beautiful Partnership

And how Sammy and the Ariel began their relationship is a story in itself. At the time the Ulsterman was experiencing great difficulty locating the right size of sprocket for his James, prior to an entry he had made for the 1956 Scottish Six Days Trial. At the time it probably seemed inconvenient, but certainly not life-changing. However, as is often the case, it led by chance to something of far greater significance. In desperation Sammy telephoned Peter Howdle, then advertising manager for the James factory in Greet, Birmingham, to ask whether Peter could lay his hands on the required sprocket. By chance Sammy's road racing sponsor at the time, Belfast dealer Terry Hill, happened to hear of Sammy's problem. Taking matters into his own hands, Terry made a personal call to his friend Ernie Smith, Ariel's competition manager. The result of this conversation was an offer from Ernie of the loan to Sammy of a trials Ariel, for use in the Scottish and other competitive events that year.

The machine was a 497cc (81.8 x 98mm) HT5 ohv single, which had only recently been introduced, and its original design and development (by the factory) is fully described in a separate boxed section within this chapter. Sammy's own development and modifications are contained in the main text.

The 1956 Scottish Six Days

As *The Motor Cycle* began its report of the 1956 Scottish: 'A one-day sporting trial is usually short-term fun. The International Six Days Trial is almost invariably a grim race against stringent time schedules. But wherein lies the undoubted attraction of the Scottish Six Days Trial – an event which combines the observational hazards of a number of one-day sporting trials with the riding-to-time associated with the ISDT. Probably the best answer is provided by the organisers, the Edinburgh Club, who describe the event as "a sporting holiday in the Highlands" and ensure that everyone concerned is treated to a light-hearted rather than serious welcome.'

The 165 competitors were greeted at that year's Scottish – the 37th in the series – with sundrenched conditions in Edinburgh. And the following is how *The Motor Cycle* set the scene: 'Throughout the weekend preparations the weather remained as dry as it had been for the most part of the preceding two months. Though a few pessimists feared that a break in the fine conditions was imminent, most folk were optimistic about the weather for the days to come in the highlands. As starting time approached on Monday morning, smoke from Edinburgh's chimneys drifted lazily upward through the thin morning haze. Although the sun shone brightly from a clear blue sky there was an invigorating chill in the atmosphere. The route led competitors westward away from Edinburgh. After 28 miles [45km] had been covered they crossed the Firth of Forth by the swing bridge at

Although, as far as trials was concerned, Sammy's relationship as a works supported Ariel rider came at the Scottish Six Days in May 1956, he had already ridden an Ariel, albeit the HS Scrambler, as this previously unpublished photograph of him winning the Brian McClay Memorial Trophy at the Ards Club's event at Marino, Co. Down, on Saturday 28 January 1956

Sammy's debut on his Ariel HT trials mount, GOV 132, came in the 1956 Scottish Six Days. Finishing joint sixth with 38 marks, he was also awarded the Jimmy Beck Memorial Trophy for the non-Scottish rider who, in the opinion of the organisers, put in the best performance. The photograph here is from the 1957 Scottish Six Days.

Kincardine, then turned right to reach the first observed hill, Culross.' There followed some 50 miles (80.5km) of roadwork through scenery of increasing beauty, which brought competitors to the second observed section, Glen Ogle. By now rain had begun to fall. And as *The Motor Cycle* report said: 'Narrow, wet and slippery, the rocky hill was divided into six sub-sections, the difficulty and gradient of which increased as height was gained.'

The lunch control was at Tyndrum, some 20 miles (32km) beyond Glen Ogle. From Tyndrum riders followed the main road to Bridge of Orchy and then turned left on to the narrow, tortuous and broken Old Glencoe Road. The 15-mile (24km) run to Almafeadh lay through country of 'wild and desolate grandeur.' The rocky climb of Almafeadh was divided into eight sub-sections. Then, after nine miles (14.5km) of rough track, via Conduit and the village of Kinlochleven, riders were brought to Mamore. There followed a 16-mile run over the Old Mamore Road to Fort William, headquarters of the trial.

The Motor Cycle takes up the story: 'As riders handed in their machines at the end of the day's 148-mile [238km] ride it was rumoured that four men were unpenalised. They were S.H. Miller (497cc Ariel), S.R. Wicken, G.O.

McLaughlan (347cc AJSs) and A.J. Lampkin (499cc BSA).' Later officials tried to dock Sammy three marks; however, this was found to have been a 'clerical error', so Sammy *had* achieved a clean sheet for the first day.

The second day saw Sammy lose his first marks (four), and at the end of the third day Gordon Jackson led the trial on 12 marks lost, against Sammy's score of 23; from then on our man's score rose to 30 on day four and 38 on day five.

Then came the sixth and final day – with *The Motor Cycle* commenting: 'Fort William gave competitors an invigorating send-off on Saturday morning. As riders swing out of the closed control for the last time, bright sunshine was rapidly drying the roads after early morning rain and a stiff breeze whipped the waters of Loch Linnhe into a picturesque study of blue and white.'

Sammy did not lose any marks that day and finished joint sixth overall (with John Draper – 148cc BSA), both with 38 marks lost, compared to the winner Gordon Jackson with 16 marks conceded.

It had been a good start to Sammy's career as an Ariel rider. He was also awarded the Jimmy Beck Memorial Trophy, awarded to the non-Scottish rider who, in the organisers' opinion, puts up the best performance.

Scottish Six Days Trial – May 1956

1st	G.L. Jackson (347cc AJS)	16 marks lost
2nd	J.V. Brittain (346cc Enfield)	31
3rd	B.F. Bovey (201cc James)	33
	G.O. McLaughlan (347cc AJS)	33
5th	A.J. Lampkin (499cc BSA)	34
6th	S.H. Miller (497cc Ariel)	38
	G.J. Draper (148cc BSA)	38

Of course, at this time Sammy was also deeply involved in road racing, so it was very much a case of divided loyalties. And, as is related in Chapter 2, only a week after the Scottish Sammy was back in Ulster competing in the North West 200, in which he won the 250cc class on his Terry Hill NSU Sportmax.

Retirement in the ISDT

It was very much racing rather than trials that occupied Sammy's time during the summer of 1956. But, finally, from 17 to 22 September the ISDT was staged in Bavaria, based at Garmisch-Partenkirchen – and he rode as a member of the Irish Vase A team, together with D.F. Ryder and E.F.

Entered as a member of the Irish Vase A team in the 1956 International Six Days Trial in Germany, Sammy was forced to retire when in line for a gold medal on the fifth day, after his 499cc Royal Enfield (125) suffered a broken frame.

Richardson. His machine for the event was a 499cc Royal Enfield Bullet. However, he was forced out on the fifth day with a broken frame while in the running for a gold medal.

The Scott Trial Debacle

It was then back to the Ariel and the Scott Trial held on Saturday 3 November 1956. And as Allan Jefferies described for *The Motor Cycle*: 'The classic, crankcase-bashing blind over Swaledale, remotest, wildest and loneliest of the Yorkshire dales.' Jeff Clew accurately described the event thus: 'The Scott Trial, an annual event that is virtually a cross between a trial and a scramble.'

Although Sammy had read about the Scott, this was the first time he had competed – and was blissfully unaware of just how *tough* it really was. His itinerary shows just how ill-prepared he was. His plan saw him catching the midnight ferry from Belfast to Heysham in Lancashire, with three fellow Ulstermen, Billy Hutton, Dennis Campbell and Noel Bell. From Heysham the quartet planned to ride to Richmond, compete in the trial, then turn round and ride back to Heysham and return on the midnight boat to Belfast! However, this grand plan did not take into account just what the Scott Trial would do to man or machine…

Things began to go wrong when they reached Heysham and had to wait a considerable amount of time for the arrival of dawn, so they could ride their machines (which had no lights). And the quartet were not able to get any breakfast. There followed a ride across the Pennines to the trial. At the start, all four signed on and set off, and, as Sammy says: 'Somehow struggled our way round.' Noel Bell broke down out on the course and it was not until five in the evening that his machine was retrieved and put in working order again. After a nightmare ride in rain and fog they reached Heysham half an hour before the Belfast boat sailed. The final irony was not realising that they had to sign off at the end of the Scott, meaning they were all automatically excluded from the results!

The Suez Crisis

Hard on the heels of the Scott fiasco came another problem, the Suez fuel crisis, which caused the British government to introduce fuel rationing after petrol and oil supplies were threatened. In order to conserve existing stocks, motorcycle sporting activities were badly affected. This resulted in the majority of organising bodies having to abandon national events, and by Christmas 1956 things looked bleak indeed.

However, some more local events were allowed to continue, and so Sammy was able to return home to his parents over the Christmas period, which included being able to ride in the Ulster Centre Team Trial. Not only did Sammy win the event, but he also had the satisfaction of taking the Rusk Trophy (Walter Rusk being a famous Ulster road racer, and Norton and Velocette works star of the 1930s).

Headline Maker

The Motor Cycle dated 7 March 1957 carried the headline: 'win for Miller.' It continued: 'Brilliant Young All-rounder Successful in Hurst Cup Trial. Already well known as a successful road racer, scrambler and trials rider, Belfast's Sammy Miller underlined his versatility in winning last Saturday's national Hurst Cup Trial at Clanboye, Co. Down, Northern Ireland.' Organised by the Knock Club, the event was decided on a time-and-observation basis over six laps of a 17-section course. At that time Irish events were awarded marks differently from mainland British events. So with 866 marks awarded Sammy was the winner, against Gordon Blakeway (497cc Ariel) with 719 marks. The Best One-Make Team award went to Ariel (Sammy, Gordon Blakeway and Ron Langston), while Sammy was also a member of the victorious Club Tram (Queen's Island) – with Benny Crawford and C. Bell.

The following day, on Sunday 3 March 1957, Sammy was competing in the Cumberland County Club's 28th Alan Trophy Trial, the first national open event to be held that year. In spite of fuel shortages, entries – all solos – totalled 80. A notable feature of the trial was an experiment with a one-three-four system of marking (one for a dab, three for footing more than once, and four for a step). The winner was Arthur Ratcliffe (347cc Matchless), with Sammy finishing runner-up and winning the WT Tiffin Trophy. Again Sammy was a member of the Ariel team who won the One-Make Award.

Retaining the Irish Trials Championship Title

By winning the Patland Cup Trial on Saturday 6 April 1957 Sammy retained the title of Irish Trials champion. Organised by the Leinster club, the Patland was Eire's premier trial and he won by 81 marks (remember the different marking system for Irish events). The event was staged in Co. Wicklow over four laps of a 10-mile (16km) course, which included 25 observed sections. It is worth mentioning that Geoff Duke finished 13th riding a 497cc Ariel.

Once again Sammy was also part of the One-Make and Club winning teams.

Patland Cup – 6 April 1957

1st	S.H. Miller (497cc Ariel)	817 marks gained
2nd	M.C. Tracey (497cc Ariel)	736
3rd	B. Crawford (497cc Ariel)	707
4th	I.S. Crighton (499cc BSA)	683
5th	J.C. Dawson (348cc BSA)	666
6th	D.J. Campbell (497cc Ariel)	661

The 'Belfast Bombshell'

By now Sammy was beginning to attract serious press attention. For example, in the 18 April 1957 issue of *The Motor Cycle* Bob Currie penned a three-page profile, headed 'The Belfast Bombshell'. This was in response to the title already given by *The Motor Cycle* of 'Ireland's Leading All-rounder.' But, as Bob Currie pointed out: 'Yes, a hackneyed phrase, I know…yet, when a young man like Samuel Hamilton Miller comes along, a man who, in the relatively short space of three sporting seasons has scooped up the Irish trials, grass-track and sand-racing titles, made his mark in the scrambles field, achieved promotion to a factory trials team and exhibited his rear tyre to many prominent road-racing personalities, sure, and what else would you call him?'

An interesting extract from Bob Currie's feature back in April 1957 was the following: 'As one might expect from a man who built his own competition machine [the SHS], Miller is a rider who is also a competent mechanic; he really likes taking his coat off and getting to the root of the matter, adjusting and tuning, experimenting with his seat, handlebars and footrest positions until all is to his satisfaction. The policy pays dividends, of course, for unless the rider is thoroughly at home with his machine, he cannot hope to achieve the nicety of judgement necessary for success on the more ticklish parts of trials or scramble courses.' This, of course, was absolutely correct and helps explain why Sammy is just as committed and enthusiastic in everything he does, even today.

Bob Currie ended by commenting: 'An all-rounder we called him. That's just how he likes it. Were he to concentrate on, say, road racing alone, then Sammy Miller could no doubt become a world-beater; but he refers not to lay all his eggs in one nest. And, unlike the bird which does just that, Sammy Miller is no cuckoo.'

Preparing for the Scottish

Although he had signed to race works 125 and 250cc machines for the Italian FB Mondial team in the 1957 World Championship rounds, Sammy's next focus was the Scottish Six Days Trial, in early May.

The Scottish week began on the Saturday in truly magnificent weather; in fact it had been uncommonly good for some weeks north of the border. The

Sammy Miller's Ariel, GOV 132, seen here in its original guise during 1956.

scene at Gorgie Market, the trials assembly point, was bathed in brilliant, wall-to-wall sunshine. As *The Motor Cycle* said in its 9 May 1957 issue: 'the typical Scottish hill tracks were bone dry with the surface rocks and boulders loose and, for that reason, more likely than usual to offer little wheelgrip.'

But by the Saturday evening it was obvious in Edinburgh that hopes of continued dry weather were ill-founded. As one commentator described: 'A mixture of rain and sleet added a touch of real winter to the coldness of the wind.' Meanwhile, from the Highlands came reports of fresh layers of snow on the hilltops. And as old hands agreed, it would be wise to prepare for typical Scottish conditions – a mixture of everything from biting cold to summer heat, from heavy snow to brilliant sunshine. And probably a mixture of the lot in a single day!

The 1957 Scottish Six Days Trial

At 8am on Monday morning the first of the riders set off from Gorgie Market on their 141-mile (227km) run to Fort William, which included five observed hills. As they swept through the cobbled streets of Edinburgh's suburbs there was brilliant sunshine. Shortly after Menstrie, some 40 miles (64.4km) from the Scottish capital, the route deviated from first-class roads to introduce easy, ISDT-type terrain over narrow, winding tracks out in Stirlingshire and into Perthshire. The countryside changed to picturesque moorland with sheep and lambs in the hills, with streams tumbling from the heights. A newspaper of the day described the scene thus: 'In the brightness of the sun the colours – shades of green, yellow and brown – came to life as if they were in an oil painting. A few small clouds in the hard-blue sky cast shadows to enrich the scene almost beyond description. Stirling, historic gateway to the highlands, was presenting her county in its most alluring patterns, to encourage competitors on their journey northwards.'

From there the going began to become ever more difficult, and between Lochearnhead and Crianlarich came Glen Ogle, the first observed hill. Here, in the minds of the dyed-in-the-wool competitors, the Scottish Six Days really began.

Eventually, Fort William was reached and the locals were out in some force at Town Hall Brae to witness the sport on the last of the day's observed sections. At the end of that first day Sammy was not in the top 12, but on day two he was joint 11th on 13 marks lost. Then, on the next day, Wednesday, he once again dropped out of the leading bunch. On the Thursday he had climbed to 10th, having conceded a total of 30 points. On Friday he was joint eighth (37 points) and on the final day (Saturday) he was joint seventh having lost no further marks.

Sammy pictured in mid-November 1958 taking part in the Patland Cup Trial; organised by the Leinster club, the event was Eire's premier trial.

The winner was Johnny Brittain (346cc Enfield) with 22 marks lost. Although in Sammy's eyes, it wasn't his best Scottish performance by some margin, it was still a good result when one takes into account that he was still getting to grips with his machine. After a number of years on small capacity, lightweight two-strokes, the Ariel was just the reverse – a large displacement, relatively heavyweight four-stroke.

Sammy now began his road racing season, at first on Terry Hill's NSU Sportmax in the North West 200 a week after the Scottish, followed by the TT and Grand Prix events on factory FB Mondials.

Moving to Birmingham

Essentially, Sammy's racing season came to an end after the Italian Grand Prix at Monza in early September 1957. This was also to coincide with FB Mondial, together with Gilera and Moto Guzzi, announcing its retirement from big-time racing. And this was to influence Sammy's plans in a far bigger way than he could ever have dreamed of at the time.

As we know, he had already become a works-supported rider for the Ariel factory in Selly Oak, Birmingham. But he now decided to take up the offer to join the competition department of Ariel Motors.

Ernie Smith had been impressed, not only by Sammy's obvious riding potential, but also by his mechanical ability, and realised that the Irishman would make a very positive acquisition if he could only persuade Sammy to move to Birmingham. As Jeff Clew recalled: 'The offer came at just the right time, for Sammy was beginning to get just a little disenchanted with road racing and was looking for somewhere he could deploy himself to a greater advantage and more satisfaction.'

And so, one day in the autumn of 1957, and with mixed feelings, Sammy left his Belfast home and headed for the docks, with all his worldly goods strapped to GOV 132. On one hand he looked forward to a fresh challenge – which involved making a living in the motorcycle industry, rather than simply riding them or working on them. Yet, on the other hand, he realised that his mechanical skills were those he had picked up himself; it was therefore very much a case of pitting his enthusiasm and skills acquired against those of a factory organisation. Would he make the grade? Only time would tell, but he was quietly confident in his own ability to pull it off. He was determined that things would work out and he would do what was necessary, including attending evening classes, to improve his career.

Selly Oak

Birmingham was several times larger than Belfast and Sammy got something of a shock, thinking that he had arrived in Birmingham when, actually, he was approaching the outskirts of Wolverhampton! Eventually he reached his destination at the Ariel works in Selly Oak, best described at that time as being a major industrial area of the city of Birmingham.

As for the factory itself, this occupied both sides of the road, with the competition shop and the assembly shop on one side, and the remainder of the operation on the other side.

The competition shop itself was a single-storey structure comprising one large room kitted out with benches and a quartet of trestles. Sammy was provided with his own work bench and trestle, thus allowing him space enough to work on his own motorcycle and also assist in the preparation of the HS scrambles machine. Besides these duties he also undertook the occasional road test.

The Weight Saving Begins

Right from the beginning of his time at Ariel, Sammy was to conduct an ongoing weight-saving exercise. At first, not knowing how Ernie Smith would react, Sammy says he played it 'cool'. As Jeff Clew revealed in his 1976 book: 'There was an occasion when he carefully parked the machine with the exhaust pipe facing the wall, so that Ernie Smith could not see that it was now upswept! Nothing was said and eventually Sammy got down to the weight reduction exercise in earnest.'

To illustrate what Sammy's life was like during those early days at Ariel it is worth saying that when work was finished for the day, he would return to Ernie Smith's home, as the latter had been generous enough to offer him accommodation. At that time his life was certainly full – working at Ariel, trials riding or racing at weekends and spending three nights a week at evening classes, studying for his City and Guilds in engineering. He had also struck up a friendship with Johnny Harris and Roy Peplow (both well-known riders in their own right). Eventually Sammy moved into lodgings in Moseley, not far from Selly Oak. His landlady was a certain Mrs Embleton – known more usually as simply 'Mrs E'.

The Southern Trial

Sammy's picture and a headline entitled: 'Sammy Miller (Ariel) wins the Southern' adorned the 30 October 1957 issues of *Motor Cycle News*, which went on to say: 'When provisional results were made available on Sunday evening it emerged that the young Belfast rider, Sammy Miller, had won the previous day's Southern Trial.' The Ariel team – consisting of Sammy plus Gordon Blakeway and Ron Langston (all on five-hundreds) also took the manufacturers' award, while Frank Wilkins won the sidecar class. The 40-mile (64.4km) course began from the Seven Thorns Inn, Bramshott, near Hindhead, Surrey and was organised by the Haslemere Club.

Southern Trial – 26 October 1957

1st	S.H. Miller (497cc Ariel)	37 marks lost
2nd	J.R. Giles (498cc Triumph)	41
3rd	E. Adcock (197cc DOT)	48
4th	G.S. Blakeway (497cc Ariel)	49
	R.J. Langston (497cc Ariel)	49
6th	B.W. Martin (348cc BSA)	51

Sammy in action winning the Ards Motorcycle Club Turner Memorial Trial near Belfast on 8 November 1957. It was a round of the Irish Trials Championship.

The following weekend Sammy took in the Scott Trial. To show the progress he had made, he came home with a combined loss (the Scott having points deducted for both observation and speed) of 125, compared to the winner Artie Ratcliffe (199cc Triumph) with a score of 104.

Boxing Day, 1957. Sammy, centre, prior to the start of the Walter Rusk Trophy, which he won. Walter Rusk was a famous Ulster road racing star in pre-war days, riding works AJS, Norton and Velocette machines during the 1930s. Sammy won the trophy 17 times in succession, but eventually he decided that travelling over to Ireland each year from England was too much.

The Turner Memorial Trophy

Sammy returned to his native soil the following weekend to retain the Turner Memorial Trophy in the Ards MCC's trial on Saturday 8 November 1957. This was a round of the Irish Trials Championship, and the first such event he had competed in that season (he had won all of them the previous year!).

Back in England two weeks later, he took part in the Birmingham MCC's 23rd British Experts Trial, finishing in eighth position, with a loss of 101 marks compared to the winner, Gordon Jackson (347cc AJS), with 78.

Then, on Saturday 14 December 1957, Sammy finished runner-up to Peter Stirland (346cc Enfield) in the national Hoad Trophies Trial in Sussex, with 33 marks lost to Stirland's 26. The following day in the Southern Experts the same rider won, while Sammy was sixth.

He then returned home to Belfast, where on Boxing Day he retained the Walter Rusk Trophy at the Ards Club's event at its traditional home at the Lead Mines, Conig – over much of the course which was used in the Hurst Cup Trial!

Boxing Day, 1957. Sammy, centre, prior to the start of the Walter Rusk Trophy, which he won. Walter Rusk was a famous Ulster road racing star in pre-war days, riding works AJS, Norton and Velocette machines during the 1930s. Sammy won the trophy 17 times in succession, but eventually he decided that travelling over to Ireland each year from England was too much.

1958 – The Year of Decision

There is no doubt that for Sammy 1958 was a year of decision. He began it still a factory-level road racer and ended it having chosen trials over the glamour of racing. Now that FB Mondial had quit, other marques showed their interest, namely Ducati (125cc) and CZ (250cc).

The year got underway with the Vic Brittain Trophy Trial held near Bridgnorth, Shropshire, on Sunday 5 January. The winner was Brian Martin (348cc BSA), with a loss of 17 marks. Close behind came John Draper (348cc BSA) with 19, while Sammy lost 20, the same as the previous year's winner Johnny Brittain (346cc Enfield). Sammy also won the 351 to 500cc award.

By now the name Sammy Miller was becoming as established as a trials rider as it had already become in road racing, and to be honest perhaps more so. This meant that as a rising trials star he was beginning to take in more trials events – and more nationals too. In truth, attempting to list every one in the way I have done with the road racing stars in this series would need a multi-volume approach. Thus what you have here is a comprehensive record of the major achievements and important milestones, together with the technical advances Sammy introduced into the sport of trials riding, rather than simply a complete event-by-event approach. If anyone needs convincing that this is the right approach to *Sammy Miller: Motorcyle Legend,* the mere mention of the fact that he went on to record over 1,400 trials *victories* alone should suffice.

Racing v Trials

In mid-February came news that Sammy had been offered a works ride for the Ducati team, and as *Motor Cycle News* commented, he: 'Will shortly have to curtail his activities as a member of the Ariel trials team in order to start training for his first race on a works Ducati. This will be at Imola at Easter.'

A Double Trials Success

Sammy again made news at the very beginning of March 1958, by carrying off the coveted Hurst and Alan trophies on Saturday 1st and Sunday 2nd. As *Motor Cycle News* reported: 'Irish eyes have good cause to be smiling this week…with Sammy Miller working a double wonder on his 497cc Ariel.' It continued: 'The MCUI event in the Emerald Isle on Saturday put Sammy right in the forefront, playing as he was the principal role before his fellow countrymen. On Sunday, in Cumberland County, he proved himself no less a popular winner, sweeping all opposition aside in the 29th Alan Trophy National Trial.'

Ariel Arrow

Besides his legendary exploits aboard his HT5 five-hundred ohv trials mount, GOV 132, Sammy Miller was also deeply involved in the Arrow two-fifty twin-cylinder two-stroke; not only riding examples in various events, including climbing Ben Nevis and racing in the Thruxton 500-mile endurance race, but also in its development.

The Arrow (and its more sporting sister, the Golden Arrow) were derived from the earlier Leader (which itself had entered production in late 1958).

Essentially, the Arrow/Golden Arrow were born of a need to reach sales targets that the fully-enclosed Leader had trouble meeting. When the first of the Arrow series was launched in a blaze of publicity at the very end of 1959 it was immediately evident that the newcomer was very much an 'undressed' Leader.

There is no doubt that by introducing the Arrow, Ariel gave itself something of a lift. One has to take into account that with the Leader not reaching its sales targets *and* the entire four-stroke range having been discontinued, the marque's entire fortunes rested on the success of the two-fifty twin-cylinder two-stroke duo of Leader/Arrow.

By utilizing the engine unit, transmission, frame and trailing-link front fork, the Arrow's development and production costs had been kept to a bare minimum. Moreover, experience had shown that these components were generally reliable.

In its general appearance, the Arrow gave the impression, at least, of being different from its older brother. The engine-gear unit was exposed and the exhaust pipes as well as the silencers were chromium plated. At the rear, a conventional valanced mudguard, supported cantilever style, had been grafted onto the rear of the frame beam. The upper shell pressing, which occupied the position of a fuel

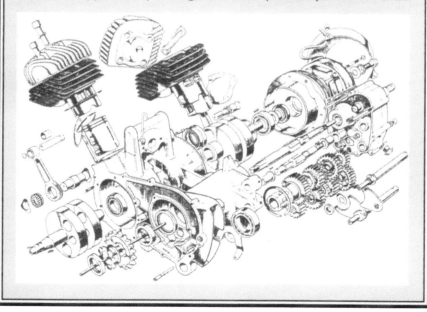

The earliest version of Ariel's 247cc (54x54mm) parallel twin two-stroke power unit.

The Arrow Super Sports – affectionately known as the 'Golden Arrow' – was launched in January 1961; thus making three versions of the basic design: Leader, Arrow and Arrow SS.

tank on a more orthodox motorcycle, extended forwards of the steering head to form brackets which supported the 6in (153mm) diameter Lucas headlamp.

The 249cc (54 x 54mm) parallel twin two-stroke engine, with slightly inclined cylinders, together with its integral four-speed gearbox, was taken directly from the Leader. This meant a one-piece die-cast aluminium crankcase, also comprising the inner half of the primary chaincase and the gearbox shell. Supported on a trio of ball race bearings, the two-piece crankshaft had a key and taper coupling in the middle. On the offside (right) end of the shaft was a Lucas 50-watt alternator which supplied lighting and ignition current.

As with the Leader, there were light-alloy cylinder heads, with separate cast-iron cylinder barrels. Both the Leader and the Arrow/Golden Arrow used a single Amal Monobloc carburettor.

One of the Leader's strongest features was due to the torsional rigidity of its box frame, formed by welding together along the machine's centre line two 20-gauge steel pressings. The frame was unaltered for the Arrow, and, as before, the beam embraced the steering head at the front and the upper mountings for the rear shock absorbers.

As with the Leader, within the beam was located a rectangular 2.5 gallon (11.4l) fuel tank.

The suspension, as mentioned earlier, also followed the Leader. In other words, at the front was the by now well-known trailing-link front fork, which provided almost constant wheelbase irrespective of wheel deflation. Pivoted on nylon bushes, the trailing links incorporated downward-projecting lugs, which were attached to the lower ends of the spring, and damper Armstrong-manufactured shock absorbers concealed within the fork leg pressings. Two-way damping was provided. The damper rods projected upwards through the fork yoke to provide anchorage at the top.

The Arrow retained the 16in diameter wheel rims and the 3.25 section tyres from the Leader, but the full-width 6in x 1in (152mm x 28.5mm) brake hubs were now of cast iron rather than aluminium with an iron liner. This was done mainly on cost lines, but it also solved a problem as a few of the aluminium hubs had suffered cracking in service.

There is no doubt that the arrival of the Arrow helped Ariel's sales significantly; for example, in one month alone in 1960, a total of 1,600 Leader and Arrow models were produced.

When Ariel announced its 1961 range in October 1960 there were three main changes for both the Arrow and Leader. These were: high-compression cylinder heads, repositioning of the anchorage for the floating front brake plate and an increase in fuel tank capacity from 2.5 to 3 gallons (11.4 to 13.6l).

The next development was the launch, in January 1961, of the Arrow Super Sports (more widely known as the 'Golden Arrow').

Unlike many so-called 'sports' models of the period, the newcomer brought real improvement, not only to the looks, but also to the performance. The compression ratio had been raised from 8.25 to 10:1; there was a larger Monobloc carb and a larger main jet, while the factory had given attention to the inlet passages in the crankcase casting. However, due to the design of the crankcase, fitting twin carburettors was ruled out, at least as far as series production was concerned. Even so, power output was now up to a claimed 20.2bhp at 6,650rpm, while maximum speed was 81mph (130km/h).

Thereafter, Ariel introduced several technical improvements to the Leader/Arrow/Golden Arrow range. A notable one concerned the brakes. Prior to this, for some time, a water-excluding flange device had been pioneered by Sammy Miller, whose HT5 trials mount featured Leader-type wheel hubs. At first the factory only incorporated this measure on the front wheel, but eventually Ariel incorporated this feature into the rear hub too.

In fact, as the main text reveals, Sammy Miller featured quite strongly in the Arrow's development story, but as was common practice in the British motorcycle industry, received little or no credit at the time.

The final version of Ariel's two-stroke was the 200 Arrow (199.4cc by reducing the bore size to 48.5mm), which was launched in May 1964.

Sammy Miller testing one of the Arrow Super Sports models at Silverstone in 1961.

Hurst Cup Trial – 1 March 1958

1st	S.H. Miller (497cc Ariel)	873 marks gained
2nd	B. Crawford (497cc Ariel)	828
3rd	J. Brittain (346cc Enfield)	769
4th	B.W. Martin (348cc BSA)	758
5th	G.L. Jackson (347cc AJS)	753
6th	G.J. Draper (348cc BSA)	750

Alan Trophy Trial – 2 March 1958

1st	S.H. Miller (497cc Ariel)	36 marks lost
2nd	J.V. Smith (499cc BSA)	43
3rd	A.J. Lampkin (499cc BSA)	46
4th	J.B. Houghton (197cc James)	47
5th	R.J. Langston (497cc Ariel)	48
6th	G.S. Blakeway (497cc Ariel)	52

Sammy pictured with Ariel HT5 GOV 130 instead of the usual GOV 132, in early 1958. This machine is very similar to the one that Ariel sold to its customers.

In Belgium

Sammy then travelled to Belgium for the 11th International Lamborelle Trial – held near the site of the Battle of Waterloo, to the south of Brussels. This was won by Gordon Jackson (347cc AJS) with a loss of 14 marks. Sammy tied for third place with Jeff Smith (499cc BSA), both riders losing 20 marks. The previous day, Sammy had missed victory in the national Cotswold Cup Trial, which had been postponed from the previous September, by one point also from Gordon Jackson.

In the very same week *Motor Cycle News*, dated 12 March 1958, carried a feature on Sammy in its popular 'Sporting Profile' series.

During much of April and May, Sammy was involved in the road racing side of things, that was, of course, with the exception of the major trials event of the year, the Scottish Six Days.

Runner-up in Scotland

And so to the 39th Scottish, with 205 riders weighing their machines in. As for Sammy, he had just returned from the Austrian Grand Prix, where he had made his debut for the CZ factory in the 250cc event, finishing second to Carlo Ubbiali (MV Agusta).

Although Gordon Jackson (347cc AJS) scored what *MCN* described as an 'outstanding' win, with the loss of only six marks, Sammy and his Ariel were always close. Sammy lost his chance of victory on the notorious Loch Eild Path on Friday when he brought his penalty points up to 13, but it had been a thrilling tussle throughout the week, with, as *Motor Cycle News* commented: 'Two totally different styles of riding – Jackson appearing always confident and steady, while Miller had numerous very awkward situations to deal with.' Another factor was the weather, which during the first four days was truly atrocious, particularly on the Wednesday when conditions were described by *MCN's* Bob Snelling as: 'By far the worst since the war.'

Scottish Six Days Trial – May 1958

1st	G.L. Jackson (347cc AJS)	6 marks lost
2nd	S.H. Miller (497cc Ariel)	13
3rd	A. Ratcliffe (199cc Triumph)	24
4th	G.S. Blakeway (497cc Ariel)	26
5th	J.V. Brittain (346cc Enfield)	28
6th	R.S. Peplow (199cc Triumph)	30

The 39th Scottish Six Days Trial took place in May 1958. After travelling back from Austria, where he had debuted on a CZ racer in the Salzburg Grand Prix, Sammy put in a superb performance to finish runner-up to Gordon Jackson (347cc AJS) on his Ariel.

Sammy's Manx

A record number of 149 riders competed in the increasingly popular Manx Two Day Trial in early September 1958. Sammy emerged victorious with a loss of 19 marks, and he was followed by J. Minnis (197cc Greeves) and D.G. Langston (347cc Ariel) with 30 and 34 marks respectively.

Starting from the TT grandstand in Glencrutchery Road and finishing in Peel, the trial took riders over moorland tracks and an assortment of mud, rocks and water splashes in the south of the Isle of Man, clear of Snaefell racing activities (the Manx Grand Prix was being staged at the same time).

The Manx Two Days also marked the beginning of the 1958–59 British trials season.

The ISDT

In mid-August the ACU confirmed that it had received entries from several British manufacturers for the forthcoming ISDT, including four from the Ariel concern, these being Gordon Blakeway, Ron Langston, Tim Gibbs (reserve) and Sammy Miller – all on 497cc singles. No British manufacturers or the ACU had been involved in the previous year's events, which had been held behind the Iron Curtain in Czechoslovakia.

The event was the 33rd in the series and based at Garmisch-Partenkirchen, in the shadow of the Bavarian Alps.

Some 213 of the original 257 competitors came under starter's orders. The non-arrival of the 19-strong Russian and 13-strong Romanian contingents accounted for the bulk of the non-starters. There was also a last-minute addition to these when Sammy was struck down with a sudden and severe bout of food poisoning; his trial was thus over before it had even begun.

A Clean Sheet

On Sunday 19 October, Sammy made headlines by not conceding a single mark. This came when he won the 28th Alec Ross Trophy and Midland Centre Trial, which started from Studley, Warwickshire, and was organised by the Pyramid MCC with help from the Redditch Club on behalf of the Midland Centre of the ACU.

The 50-mile (80.5km) course was run as a figure of eight, with odd numbers taking the Worcestershire loop first and even numbers the Warwickshire loop.

Alec Ross Trophy and Midland Centre Trial – 19 October 1958

1st	S.H. Miller (497cc Ariel)	0 marks lost
2nd	R.R. Cooper (347cc Ariel)	4
3rd	W. Fox (497cc Ariel)	11
	J.L. Harris (346cc Enfield)	11
5th	J. Grazier (497cc Ariel)	14
6th	N.J. Crump (497cc Ariel)	17

Southern Win for Sammy

A week later Sammy was the clear-cut winner of the National Southern Trial held on Saturday 25 October 1958. The event began at 10.30am from the Brands Hatch pavilion, Farningham, Kent, and although it was considered there was ample time to cover the 35-mile (56km) course in daylight, many of the later numbers (which included Sammy) arrived at the special test at dusk. However, as *Motor Cycle News* commented: 'Even under these conditions the winner proceeded to make the fastest time.'

Southern Trial – 25 October 1958

1st	S.H. Miller (497cc Ariel)	32 marks lost
2nd	B.W. Martin (348cc BSA)	42
3rd	J.R. Giles (199cc Triumph)	45
4th	J. Simpson (197cc Greeves)	48
5th	R. Peplow (199cc Triumph)	51
6th	G.L. Jackson (497cc Matchless)	52

For the rest of 1958 and into 1959 Sammy put in a number of excellent performances, but it is worth noting that not only was the Triumph Tiger Cub becoming a threat (notably in the hands of Roy Peplow), but in December, at the British Experts Trial, Brian Martin debuted a specially prepared two-fifty BSA C15 Star, with the registration number BSA 250. The BSA competition department had been working behind the scenes to create a competition version of the new unit construction road bike which had been launched a short while earlier. As one commentator said: 'The day of the lightweight trials bike was coming.' But Sammy, with his weight-saving development of GOV 132, would postpone the inevitable for some years yet.

Sammy Masters the Scott

Perhaps more than any other event of 1958, it was the national trade-supported 44th annual Scott Trial which highlighted Sammy's progress.

Sammy negotiating rocks
and other debris on his
legendary Ariel GOV 132.

Remember, it had only been two years previously that he had not even been credited as a finisher in the event!

The Scott was generally agreed to be the toughest of all the major one-day trials events. As many would agree, simply to finish the Scott was an achievement. But Sammy's performance in November 1958 was far, far more than this.

This is how the 12 November 1958 issue of *Motor Cycle News* began its report: 'True to its tradition, Saturday's Scott Trial was much more than an important Yorkshire Trial. It was a super moto-cross, and one of the toughest solos only events of its kind in the world. To win called for an outstanding combination of Sammy Miller's racing and trials skill. The 48 survivors of Saturday's 166-strong starting paddock can thus thank the Darlington and DMC for one of the most exhausting day's sport they will experience this season.'

For the 1958 Scott, for the first time the Yorkshire Centre ACU organisers introduced a penalty of one mark per minute instead of for every two minutes beyond the standard time set by the fastest rider. More than ever this eliminated any possibility of studying sections and the accent was on speed. Speed over the wild and everlasting hills of the North Riding, where nature blessed the rocks, mud and streams with a cold but sunny day.

Roadwork was non-existent. After the start, the only tarmac riders saw was when crossing the road from one hazard to another with police on point duty.

Scott Trial – 8 November 1958

1st	S.H. Miller (497cc Ariel)	110 marks lost
2nd	G.L. Jackson (347cc Ariel)	126
3rd	R.J. Langston (497cc Ariel)	139
4th	B.G. Stonebridge (249cc Greeves)	150
	A.J. Lampkin (499cc BSA)	
6th	J.V. Smith (499cc BSA)	155

Words of Wisdom

In the 27 November 1958 issue of *Motor Cycling* Sammy penned a feature entitled 'Trials Riding with the Ariel HT5.' In this he not only dished out a series of helpful hints and tips regarding the preparation of the HT5 (and its smaller capacity sister, the HT3), but also revealed something about his own techniques, of both machine preparation and riding.

Here are a few extracts from this article:

'Naturally, each of us has his own riding technique. I have heard people say that my stance is so unusual that S.H. Miller (497 Ariel) can be identified before either face or number is clearly visible.' Sammy continued: 'OK, I admit it – I do stand up and lean forward, and there's good reason. In that position, I have more control of the front wheel and can steer much better. This is most useful among rocks, where my drill is to go slowly, plonking through and following a previously selected path rather than rushing the section. Submerged hazards I hate most of all – who doesn't? – and among these, again, a suddenly wayward front wheel can be more readily controlled from the forward-leaning, upright stance. Consequently, I regard riding position as particularly important. My saddle is mounted as low as possible; even the standard HT3 and HT5 seat can usefully be lowered for the short rider. The object is to enable the pilot to foot easily and continuously if necessary. I believe that hardly any sections are so hard that rigorous footwork can't get the competitor through and, accordingly, I arrange my saddle so that both feet can be well on the ground when the occasion arises. After all, a three-mark debit for footing is better than being penalised five for a stop.'

Sammy also went on to reveal: 'A personal fad is control lever angle. I don't really know why, but I like my clutch lever horizontal and the front brake lever a shade down; silly, but I do! If convenient, levers are better welded to the bars than clamped, then they can't swing round out of reach.'

He ended up: 'Two pet points of mine are: first, arrive with half an hour to spare at the start, for a last-minute rush is most unsettling; and, secondly, make a quick survey of even the simplest sections.'

Winning the Hoad

Runner-up the previous year, Sammy made no mistake when winning the solo class of the national Hoad Trophies Trial held in Hampshire in mid-December 1958. As *Motor Cycle News* said in its front page story: 'He rode brilliantly throughout the day and his climb of Warren Hill will long be remembered by all those who had the good fortune to see it.'

Heavy and cold rain persisted throughout the morning, but soon after midday the clouds broke and competitors were able to enjoy a 'severe but well organised event in much better conditions' (*MCN*).

Hoad Trophies Trial

1st	S.H. Miller (497cc Ariel)	34 marks lost
2nd	P.N. Brittain (346cc Enfield)	44*
3rd	P. Stirland (346cc Enfield)	44*
4th	R. Peplow (199cc Triumph)	45
5th	J.V. Brittain (499cc Enfield)	47

*by special test

'Miller's Frosty Colmore'

The *Motor Cycle News* front page said it all. With mist covering much of the Cotswolds and frost decorating the countryside with nature's icy fibres, the national Colmore Trial run in early February 1959 was certainly a wintry affair. Sammy won the event by three points from Johnny Giles (199cc Triumph).

And the Colmore success was just to be the start of things for Sammy in 1959.

Next came another national success a couple of weeks later when he won the Victory Trial as *MCN* said: 'Convincingly upholding his decision to abandon road racing to concentrate on trials, Belfast "banger" expert Sammy Miller (497 Ariel) displaced last year's Victory Trial solo winner Gordon Jackson (347 AJS) by two marks on Saturday.' Just as significant was a modification to his Ariel HT5. As the 25 February 1959 issue of *Motor Cycle News* reported: 'Sammy Miller has an Ariel Leader hub and brake fitted to his trials machine. It is lighter than the normal rear brake and is cable operated. Riveted to the six-inch hub can be seen a "water excluder". Having used this modification for over a month, Sammy is well pleased with its performance.'

Victory Trial – 21 February 1959

1st	S.H. Miller (497cc Ariel)	14 marks lost
2nd	G.L. Jackson (347cc AJS)	16
3rd	J.V. Smith (249cc BSA)	18
4th	L.A. Ratcliffe (199cc Triumph)	19
5th	J.G. Draper (249cc BSA)	21
6th	P.N. Brittain (346cc Enfield)	23

Third Year Running

In winning the Ulster-based Hurst Cup Trial for the third year running, Sammy set the organisers, the Knock Motor Cycle and Car Club, a dilemma. The rules said he had now won the award outright, and as one commentator put it: 'If so, how can there be a Hurst Cup Trial with no Hurst Cup?' The 1959 event was the 25th in the series – it was also proclaimed the toughest – as evidenced by the fact that of the 72 starters only 27 finished!

Hurst Cup Trial – 28 February 1959

1st	S.H. Miller (497cc Ariel)	595 marks gained
2nd	B. Crawford (497cc Ariel)	529
3rd	G.L. Jackson (347cc AJS)	508
4th	J.V. Smith (249cc BSA)	474
5th	J. Brittain (346cc Enfield)	445
6th	B.W. Martin (249cc BSA)	395

The Alan Trophy Trial Again for Sammy

The following day, having crossed the Irish Sea, Sammy and many other stars took part in the Cumberland county club's 13th Alan Trophy Trial on Sunday 1 March. As in Ulster, conditions caused the heaviest batch of retirements yet seen. But these conditions did not seem to affect Sammy, as he repeated his previous year's success in the event. Riding 'confidently' (*MCN*) throughout, he dropped only 19 marks in 50-odd sections to finish with a 22-mark advantage over the runner-up Roy Peplow (199cc Triumph).

Alan Trophy Trial – 1 March 1959

1st	S.H. Miller (497cc Ariel)	19 marks lost
2nd	R.S. Peplow (199cc Triumph)	41
3rd	J.R. Sayer (199cc Triumph)	43
4th	P. Brittain (346cc Enfield)	45
5th	J. Brittain (346cc Enfield)	47
	A.J. Lampkin (249cc BSA)	47

As for the Ariel works team for 1959, Bennie Crawford had been temporarily drafted into the squad after Gordon Blakeway had broken a leg while competing in the British Experts event at the end of the previous year. Meanwhile, Frank Wilkins and his future wife Kay remained the factory's number-one sidecar crew.

During March, Sammy, together with several other riders, took part in Belgium's international Lamborelle Trial on Sunday 15th. The event, organised by the *Union Motoriste de Bruxelles* had attracted 153 competitors from France, Germany, Holland and Switzerland, as well as from Great Britain and the host country.

Most important of the fully-international one-day trials in the Continental sporting calendar, the 12th Lamborelle was to prove a great British success, with the Best Performance and Best 250cc awards going to Johnny Giles (199cc Triumph), while Sammy and his Ariel were named Runner-up and Best 500cc.

The starting point was at Ohain (between Brussels and Louvain) and the trial began in fine weather, but later the rain made the going much tougher.

Lamborelle Trial – 15 March 1959

1st	J. Giles (199cc Triumph)	30 marks lost
2nd	S.H. Miller (497cc Ariel)	34
3rd	R. Sayer (199cc Triumph)	35
4th	J. Draper (249cc BSA)	42
5th	G.L. Jackson (347cc AJS)	43
6th	R.J. Langston (347cc Ariel)	44

The best placed continental rider was A. Piron (Belgium, 199cc Triumph) with a loss of 51 marks.

March ended with Sammy stamping his authority on the national Bemrose Trial in Derbyshire. He won with 11 marks conceded compared to the runner-up, Gordon Jackson (347cc AJS) with 19. This event also marked a successful return for Gordon Blakeway to the Ariel team, who celebrated by winning the Best-One-Make award.

Yet more successes came in April, including the Travers Trophy Trial and the Cleveland Trial. In winning these he simply consolidated his lead in the ACU Trials Star table.

Golden Jubilee Scotland

In 1959 the Edinburgh and DMC's international Scottish Six Days Trial celebrated its golden jubilee, and this began from Scotland's capital city at 8am on Monday 4 May.

At the end of that first day Sammy led, but only after his teammate Gordon Blakeway had picked the wrong path in front of hundreds of spectators in Fort William on the final section at Town Hall Brae; Gordon up to then had the only clean sheet of the trial! So, after day one, the scores stood at: Sammy one mark lost, Roy Sayer (199cc Triumph) three and then Roy Peplow, Alan Lampkin and Gordon Jackson all on four.

However, it was not to be Sammy's week, as after leading on Monday and again on Wednesday he lost eight of his 22 marks on the Loch Eild Path's gigantic hill on the Friday. In the end he finished third, but then he had to dash off to Ireland without receiving the Nelson Challenge Trophy from the Lord Provost of Edinburgh.

Scottish Six Days Trial – May 1959

1st	R.S. Peplow (199cc Triumph)	18 marks lost
2nd	G.L. Jackson (347cc Ariel)	20
3rd	S.H. Miller (497cc Ariel)	22
4th	J.R. Sayer (199cc Triumph)	27
5th	W.H. Martin (249cc James)	33
6th	W. Wilkinson (249cc Greeves)	57

Sammy is shown here at Tyndrum during the 1959 Scottish Six Days. But it was not to be Sammy's week, as after leading on Monday and again on Wednesday, he finished third on 22 marks compared to the winner Roy Peplow's 18 and runner-up Gordon Jackson's 20.

Even though Sammy had not won the Scottish, he was fast becoming *the* man to beat in the trials world, and this progress simply gathered pace as 1959 unfolded. But, unfortunately, there was no possibility of taking part in the ISDT, as because the Czechoslovakian team had won the Trophy team award in 1958, the 1959 event was to be staged behind the Iron Curtain. Although entries could be arranged on a private basis, the ACU had banned direct factory representation.

The Mobil Oil Advertisement

During December 1959 the Mobil oil company ran an advertisement heralding Sammy's run of trials successes throughout that year. He had won the Victory Cup Trial, the Hurst Cup Trial (for the third year in a row), the Bemrose Trophy Trial, the British Experts Trial, the Manx Two-day Trial and the Travers Trophy Trial. Besides these he had also taken the Class Award in the St David's Trial, the Cotswold Cup Trial, the Kickham Trial, the Traders Cup Trial, the Scottish Six Days Trial, the Red Rose Trial, the Allan Jefferies Trial, the West of England Trial and the Scott Trial. As Jeff Clew pointed out in 1976: 'No other trials rider could boast such a string of successes that year.' This was, of course, absolutely true and heralded Sammy's years of unparalleled success, which he achieved riding his Ariel HT5 GOV 132.

All Change at Ariel

In August 1959 Ariel motors quietly discontinued its entire four-stroke range of motorcycles, which not only included the Square Four, the Huntmaster twin and its range of road-going singles, but also the HT5 and HT3 trials models. From then on the company concentrated exclusively on the twin-cylinder, two-stroke Leader and Arrow series. There is little doubt that this decision was made by the BSA Group management, rather than being an in-house one. Not only did this sever an historic link with the type of engine, which could be traced back to the origins of the marque itself, but, more significantly to the Sammy Miller story, it also meant the demise of Ariel's works trials effort and the closure of the competition shop. Sammy was retained on the company's payroll, however, and was able to purchase GOV 132 for the nominal price of £1. This meant that, in practice, Sammy had now reverted to a privateer. His reserve bike, registration 786 GON, which had largely been built from spare parts, was also now his own property.

Politics

As Jeff Clew said: 'Politics were coming into play and it was obvious that full [works] support was now going to be given to the two-fifty BSA [C15] lightweight, competition versions of which had been announced on a production basis, during September. Ariel Motors was no longer quite as autonomous as it had been after the acquisition by the BSA Group.'

Instead of his employment in the competition shop, which as we know was now closed, Sammy began work instead in the development department, where he fabricated various special components. This also brought him, for the first time, into direct, almost daily contact with Ariel's design staff, and provided an insight into the working of a large motorcycle factory. Going into all that happened, both at Ariel's Selly Oak works and later when the company transferred to the giant BSA facilities in Small Heath would take a chapter in itself. Suffice to say, Sammy's own ideas and development were often either shunned or reintroduced later as part of

Mid-1959 saw the demise of Ariel's factory trials team. Although Sammy was retained on the payroll and able to purchase GOV 132 for the nominal price of £1, he was now, effectively, a privateer.

someone else's alleged activities. As Jeff Clew pointed out back in 1976: 'Sammy has a whole fund of stories, many of which would seem to suggest that the management itself was highly successful in engineering the eventual downfall of the company, and then the BSA Group to which it belonged.' Jeff continued: 'Ideas and suggestions were ruled out of hand unless they happened to conform to established practice. If a particularly good idea came along, it was frequently rejected, then resurrected some while later, when the person who had re-invented it could take full personal credit.'

One example of the above was the saga of the Leader/Arrow brakes when they were modified to improve wet weather performance. Water excluders which had been developed and proved by Sammy on his trials bike were subsequently fitted to the production bikes, but without any form of credit to the person who had actually done the original work – a surefire way to stifle original thinking and initiative on the part of one's workforce!

Then there was the case of a special one-off tubular duplex-framed Arrow. Sammy had come up with the concept and fitted it with BSA forks, smaller wheels equipped with knobbly tyres and an Arrow engine with upswept exhaust system and chrome-plated mudguards. The completed motorcycle was the centre of attention wherever it went. In many ways it was a forerunner of the Street Scrambler or Trail bike, which was to become so popular from the late 1960s onwards, particularly in North America.

Sammy's move from works rider to privateer did give him the advantage of being able to do far more development work on his machine. One of the first moves was to fit the smaller, lighter brake hubs from a Leader/Arrow, as shown here, and a tucked in, hi-level exhaust system.

However, instead of embracing this enterprising project, while Sammy was away riding in the Scottish Six Days Trial, the machine was quietly confiscated and sawn up! Sammy only found out when he returned from north of the border. So why did this happen? Jeff Clew's view was quite simple. He said 'It had become too much of an embarrassment, for although the machine was constructed quite legitimately, the design concept had not originated through "official" channels.' This sort of carry-on could only be described as commercial suicide.

ISDT

Often dubbed as 'The Olympics of Motorcycling', with gold, silver and bronze medals for individual riders' efforts, the ISDT (International Six Days Trial) brought together more nations than any other competitive event in the two-wheel sporting calendar.

But how did it all begin?

In December 1897 the Automobile Club of Great Britain and Ireland was founded to look after the interests of the early motorist. No distinction was made at that time between four-, three- and two-wheel vehicles! In the 'Emancipation Run' to Brighton in 1897 the only British-made vehicle to complete the course was a tricycle. Sport has always been a major interest of motorists, and in 1900 the ACGBI promoted the 'Great 1,000 Miles Trial.' Among the entrants were two quadricycles, two motor tricycles and one tricycle with a trailer. A couple of Werner two-wheelers were also entered, but did not start. By 1903 the development of the motorcycle was such that 93 members of the motorcycling branch of the parent body set up the Auto Cycle Union. In the very first year of its existence the ACU organised a 100-mile (1,600km) trial which became an annual event as the ACU Six Day's Reliability Trial. The object of the event was to satisfy the sporting urge to demonstrate the advantages of one machine over another. In 1913 it was decided to incorporate into the event, under FIM rules, the first International Touring Trial.

This 1913 event is generally regarded as the first ISDT. And even though the international element was only a class in the ACU's 1913 trial, it did set the pattern for the future. Its purpose was to provide a prolonged test and demonstration of the reliability and efficiency of the motorcycle.

The 1914 event, which would have been the first full International, was cancelled due to the outbreak of World War One that summer. And so the ISDT did not resume until 1920.

Thereafter, it rapidly established itself as the most important test for the world's manufacturers of standard production motorcycles. Its tradition as a punishing ordeal for both men and machines continues today with the International Six Days Enduro

(ISDE), which replaced the ISDT from 1981. However, the days of standard production *road-going* motorcycles have long gone; today they are very much specialised motocross-based machines.

For the ISDT, manufacturers were invited to enter three-man teams for the Gold Medal. This was to become known as the Trophy, and national Trophy teams took part. There was also a Vase awarded to the most outstanding individual rider. It was the lure of the Vase that drew some notable competitors who, even without sponsorship, were prepared to pit themselves against the best in a marathon of cross-country riding through mountains, forests and sometimes even peat bogs. But, inevitably, it was the manufacturers' greater resources and their ability to put first division riders under contract that ensured the honour of the Gold Medal was theirs.

National pride, as well as commercial benefits, motivated the teams to achieve unprecedented feats of heroism and engineering excellence. Inevitably there were some fatalities and serious incidents. On some occasions during the early days of the event riders set out over rugged terrain, never to be seen again. However, despite the arduous nature of the ISDT there were many instances of teams working together, humour and high spirits on and off the course.

During the 1930s the ISDT was dominated by the Italians, and then, from 1932 onwards, it became a straight battle between Great Britain and Germany.

The 1939 event, later to become known as 'The Salzburg Incident', was run on the very eve of war. In fact, many competitors were forced to flee west during the week and the results were annulled, post-war, by the FIM.

Although Czechoslovakia won the first post-war ISDT Trophy in 1947, Britain won the next four (1948–51 inclusive). The Czechs then regained it in 1952, and the British took the premier honours in 1953 and 1954. This, however, was to prove the start of the British decline. Having dominated for so many years the large capacity four-strokes (such as the Ariel 500) were outclassed by the end of the decade and were replaced by smaller capacity two-strokes.

Although Austria won the Trophy contest in 1960, either side the Czechs, West Germany and East Germany held sway until the Italians won for three years (1979, 1980 and 1981). As we know, by the final year the event had become the ISDE. The switch from 'Trial' to 'Enduro' heralded a change (effectively begun before the end of the 1960s) from a trial of reliability of standard production machinery to specialised enduro bikes, which often had more in common with motocross bikes. Press coverage, certainly in Britain, also suffered. The new Six Days no longer appeals to the vast majority of normal motorcyclists who ride on the road, whereas before, because many of the bikes were what they themselves owned, interest was always considerable.

Sammy Crowns His Year

At Llandrindod Wells in mid-Wales, on Saturday 28 November 1959, Sammy crowned his year by making a best solo performance in the 25th British Experts Trial. It was also his first 'Experts' win.

The 60-mile (96.5km) route embraced 14 main observed sections, and it would be true to say that anybody who was anybody in the British trials scene took part, thus fully justifying the event's title.

Sammy put in a magnificent performance to finish five marks clear of the runner-up Johnny Giles (199cc Triumph).

British Experts Trial – 28 November 1959

1st	S.H. Miller (497cc Ariel)	39 marks lost
2nd	J.R. Giles (199cc Triumph)	44
3rd	E. Adcock (246cc DOT)	48
4th	G.J. Draper (249cc BSA)	49
5th	J.R. Sayer (199cc Triumph)	50
6th	J.V. Brittain (346cc Enfield)	52
	G.O. McLaughlan (347cc AJS)	52
	R.S. Peplow (199cc Triumph)	52

To round off 1959, Sammy's performances seemed if anything to benefit from being a privateer rather than a works rider. Certainly, when studying the press reports of the day one cannot be anything other than mightily impressed with the level of success being achieved as the 1950s came to a close and the 1960s began.

The year was to end on a high note when Sammy not only won the silver jubilee British Experts Trial, but also, a day later, was equally successful in the Knut Trial, which then qualified him for entry into the next British Experts event. Then, to bring the year to a close, he was awarded the 1959 ACU Trials Star title – the highest compliment that could be achieved in the trials world at that time. In fact, looking back 1959 had been a truly remarkable year and, in fact, the Mitcham Vase Trial had been the only national-status event in which Sammy had finished without winning either the premier award or a class cup.

The Most Successful Rider

In the 28 January 1960 issue of *The Motor Cycle* Jeff Smith penned a three-page feature with the headline: 'What Makes Sammy Tick?' A sub-heading was entitled: 'A Critical Appraisal of Sammy Miller, Most Successful Trials Rider of Today.'

This is how Jeff began his article: 'Leaning well forward over the handlebars, his long lean body swinging from side to side in that way many decry as untidy, his normally friendly face contorted in a frown which reflects the concentration and determination of his efforts: that could be Sammy Miller tacking almost any observed section. His mount is a five-hundred – an Ariel – and that at a time when more and more riders are turning to little 'uns in the belief that the five-hundred has had its day; too powerful, they say, and too heavy – and too expensive! How does it happen then, that Miller, reigning British expert, holder of the ACU Trials Star, can run contrary to majority opinion? How is it that he can demonstrate his point not only decisively but repeatedly? It can't all be the result of intervention by the Irish "wee folk"; much of the true answer can be found by studying the tall, quiet Ulsterman and by trying to understand his personal approach to the game.'

The Machine
Even when he was a member of the Ariel factory team, Sammy was looking at the improvement of his machine. Becoming a privateer actually made his task easier, in that he no longer had to 'toe the factory line', so to speak.

Sammy's now ex-works Ariel perhaps conjured up, to the uninitiated, a vision of a model worlds apart from anything a layman could hope to own. Most factory machines were very similar to their production trials brothers. In truth, becoming a privateer was the signal that allowed Sammy's bike to become ever-more different, because now he was able to do what he liked in the way of development and did not have to have one eye on the fact that he was a factory entry.

Lightness was his principle aim. By the beginning of 1960 the bike weighed stood in the region of 270lb (122.5kg). That was, of course, well below the weight of most trials five-hundreds and, indeed, could beat some of the existing two-fifties. Many, many hours of careful thought and patient work had been lavished by Sammy on machine preparation. But he was, said Jeff Smith, 'rightly reticent' about the finer and less obvious points; however, some of Sammy's modifications were all-too evident to the keen eye. And some, too, were entirely of an individualistic nature and some, said Jeff, 'defy convention'. Of course, this latter trait was to become very much a Miller stamp, not only with his Ariel, but also with later efforts for factories including Bultaco and Honda.

Light Alloy Wheel Rims

Sammy now used Italian light alloy wheel rims, to add to the Ariel Leader-type hubs, while the rear chain sprocket was so liberally drilled that one observer commented: 'I don't know how it hangs together.'

The use of light alloy did not end there. It was also to be found in the engine forward mounting plates, the fuel tank, the mudguard stays (which were of a very light gauge) and the chain guard. There was even the use of alloy for both the front and rear number plates. The gearbox mounting plates had also been drilled for lightness, while further fractions were saved by using welded-on pivot blocks for the control levers. Then there was the oil tank, which was not only smaller than the stock HT5 component, but also wrapped partly round the seat tube.

As far as the engine and transmission were concerned, these too had received the Miller treatment. One only had to inspect the much-lightened clutch to realise the level of his attention to detail.

Jeff Smith thought: 'Much of the preparation is a legacy of Miller's road racing experience. Like that other brilliant Ulsterman Bill Nicholson, Sammy is more than just an engineer. He is a very fine engineer. Someone once asked Nicholson the recipe for success in trials and he replied: "never be satisfied with yourself; always keep practising." That could equally well be Sammy's maxim, for he practices hard and regularly and never seems entirely satisfied with his prowess. Some of his antics during these training sessions would confound the profoundest pundits – and they certainly contradict all the known laws of gravity.'

Continuing in the Winning Groove

Moving into the 1960s seemed to add an additional stride into Sammy's performances. He simply kept improving!

Typical were his victories in a two-country weekend at the very end of March 1960, when he won the Hurst in Northern Ireland on Saturday, Ulster's major trial (for the fourth time in succession), and then across the water in Cumberland, where he put up the best performance in the National Open Alan Trophy on Sunday for the third year (which he then got to keep).

Dealing with the Hurst first, in its entire history only one other rider had won four times. This was fellow Ulsterman Bill Nicholson, but his victories were not successive.

At the second trial, for close on 40 years the Alan Trophy (which in 1960 was valued at 200 guineas) had eluded the grasp of generations of top riders who had aimed to make it their own property – but with his third successive victory this was exactly what Sammy achieved. The Alan Trophy had been presented shortly after World War One by Captain Alan Roberts, whose nephew was among the landowners who gave permission for their property to be used in the 1960 event, the 31st in the series.

Alan Trophy Trial – 29 February 1960

1st	S.H. Miller (497cc Ariel)	25 marks lost
2nd	J.V. Smith (249cc BSA)	36
3rd	W. Wilkinson (246cc Greeves)	40
4th	G.S. Blakeway (199cc Triumph)	41
5th	L.A. Ratcliffe (199cc Triumph)	44
	D. Younghusband (246cc DOT)	44

Ben Nevis

During early 1960 Sammy, together with Jeff Smith, attempted to climb Britain's highest mountain, Ben Nevis.

Sammy's machinery was a much-modified two-fifty Ariel Arrow (registration 695 AOH), which he had nicknamed 'Crocodile'. A larger rear wheel sprocket provided a bottom gear ratio of around 31:1 and a top of some 9:1. The front wheel was increased to 20in in diameter to provide

During early 1960 Sammy,
together with Jeff Smith,
attempted to climb
Britain's highest mountain,
Ben Nevis. Jeff rode a
BSA C15T (trials), Sammy
a modified Ariel Arrow.

more ground clearance; the rear wheel was 18in in diameter (standard fitment being 16in front and rear). A trials-type rear tyre was fitted to improve grip. Although no changes had been made to the power unit, the exhaust system was now siamesed, with the single silencer upswept.

Jeff's mount was his C15 BSA trials bike fitted with a knobbly scrambles tyre. The third member of the team was Ian MacDonald, the Scottish photographer for *The Motor Cycle*, who undertook the climb on foot.

Table talk the night before the attempt 'ranged far and wide', said Jeff. 'We reflected on the massacre of the MacDonald clansmen in 1692 by the Campbells in that beautiful yet gloomy vale of Glencoe through which we had passed on the way up; on the fickleness of highland weather; and on the possibility of meeting some raging haggis or hairy yeti above the snowline. Finally, before going to bed we pored over a map of the mountain in the comfortable lounge of the Highland Hotel.' Leaving the hotel the following morning they headed straight to the shore of Loch Linnhe (a sea loch) to zero the altimeter – the latter having been purchased from an ex-WD (War Department) stockist for £2. Next it was road work to Achintee at the mountain's foot. After that the hard work began. As Jeff Smith recalled:

As this picture shows, scaling Ben Nevis was no easy task!

Eventually, Jeff and Sammy encountered the snowline, making the going even more hazardous.

'Glen Nevis seemed about to burst with the coming of spring. In spite of the northern latitude, trees and hedgerows already held promise of the full months to come. But when we climbed through the last gate and reached the mountain a light rain began and the great berg looked uncompromising and hard. The stunted hawthorn bushes, the dead ferns, the heather burnt red by an arid summer sun, showed no signs of life and added to the gaunt and unyielding aspect up front.'

At first the path was rugged but not too difficult, and the two riders set off confidently; however, as the altitude rose so did the difficult nature of their task become ever more apparent.

The terrain changed Gorgie almost every minute. When the pair reached 2,000ft (610 meters) the first snow was encountered. At 2,800ft (869m) they encountered 'A vast stretch of snow which looked impassable.' But somehow the pair managed to reach 3,650ft (1,112.5m) before having to leave their machines and 'trudge upwards over another 400ft [122 m] into a world of dazzling whiteness. We'd made it to the top! We shouted and screamed and knew how Hilary felt on Everest.'

But, unfortunately, as they were soon to discover, a shock was in store. This is how Jeff Smith described what transpired in March 1960: 'Suddenly, as though it were a veil being lifted by a malicious hand, the cloud was gently but quickly folded back. Below it we espied a valley in which the wind had carved fantastic shapes in the snow. And there, on the other side, towering above a magnificent, fantastic and hopeless sweep *was the true summit*. Olympians one minute, we were dwarfs the next.'

Then it was time for the homeward journey. Dusk was falling by the time they reached the hotel. The pair had travelled what Jeff described as: 'A mere 14 miles (22.5km) and taken 7½ hours doing it. Dark fingers crept across the vastness of the highland sky. And thus ended one of the most memorable days of my life.'

In reality no written description can adequately describe just how *difficult* this trip really was. At times it was definitely very dangerous, at times it was back breaking work when they had to manhandle their machines, and as they got further up the mountain it was bitterly cold.

Ken Whistance

During Sammy Miller's time at the Ariel factory in Selly Oak, Birmingham, (and later when the marque was moved to BSA's Small Heath works), the man in charge of the company was Ken Whistance.

Born in the West Midlands (known to the locals as the Black Country), K.J. (Kenneth John) Whistance was the son of a local motorcycle dealer and served his apprenticeship in his father's dealership.

Ken Whistance (in striped suit), Ariel's factory manager, with Sammy and Ernie Smith (who as Ariel's competition boss had signed up the Ulsterman in 1956), after Sammy had won the 1964 ACU Trials Star.

Ken Whistance got his driving licence the day he reached 14 years of age (which was possible in those far-off days), and, as a member of the West Bromwich Motor Cycle Club, he entered the world of trials, and the branch of motorcycle sport at which he was something of a star turn – motoball (essentially a form of football with the players mounted on motorcycles).

Ken was also a road racer of some note and in 1933 he was signed up by the Birmingham factory of New Imperial, to ride for the works team in the Junior TT. But it was to prove a disastrous year for New Imperial, with a whole trio of riders being forced to retire. In fact, Ken Whistance's machine was the last to make its exit – with big-end problems on the third lap.

After serving his apprenticeship Ken had moved into the industry proper. In those days, during the inter-war period of the 1930s, Birmingham was the centre of the motorcycle trade, with countless factories, large and small, scattered all over the area. One of his first major tasks came with the development of the wartime Wellbike – a small motorcycle that could be folded up for easy transport by troops in the field. After the war, this was developed into the civilian Corgi, built and distributed by Brockhouse Engineering of Southport, Lancashire. Then came a spell with BSA at the company's Small Heath works in Birmingham. Finally, in 1953, he moved to nearby Selly Oak and Ariel.

As a Director and General Manager, Ken Whistance fought to keep Ariel independent of BSA (which had purchased the company from Jack Sangster in 1944).

Together with Ariel's Chief Designer Val Page, Ken Whistance was largely instrumental in the birth of the new two-stroke range, which began in 1958 with the launch of the revolutionary Leader.

But, ultimately, Ariel suffered a drop in sales like virtually everyone else in the British motorcycle industry, and even though Ken Whistance and other management and workers at Selly Oak battled valiantly to keep Ariel a separate operation, it ended when the BSA directors axed their works – resulting in Ariel being moved lock, stock and barrel in mid-1962 into a small corner of the BSA complex in Small Heath.

However, Ken Whistance was retained as Ariel's General Manager, but after 1962 he and the rest of Ariel were increasingly sidelined in BSA's plans. He finally quit the company, and thus the BSA group, in September 1965, to become managing director of another engineering company in the Midlands, Concentric Group. His parting words were: 'It has been a most difficult decision for me to make but I feel I shall find greater scope outside the industry.'

Back to Trials Action

Then it was back to winning ways in the trials world, but not so in the 1960 running of the Scottish Six Days. Even though Sammy won the 500cc cup he had, by his standards, a bad trial, dropping from 0 marks and joint leader at the end of the first day, to seventh at the end of the final day and a loss of 34 marks.

Scottish Six Days – May 1960

1st	G.L. Jackson (347cc AJS)	16 marks lost
2nd	G.J. Draper (249cc BSA)	20
3rd	J.V. Smith (249cc BSA)	22
4th	A.J. Lampkin (249cc BSA)	26
5th	J.V. Brittain (346cc Enfield)	30
6th	G.O. McLaughlan (347cc AJS)	32
7th	S.H. Miller (497cc Ariel)	36
8th	B.W. Martin (249cc BSA)	37

Welsh Two Day Trial

Truly brilliant weather greeted riders for the Welsh Two Day Trial in late May. This event was based as nearly as possible on the ISDT, and there were a dozen riders who had been entered by the ACU in order that their capabilities could be more fully assessed.

Sammy with the Ariel Arrow he rode in the Welsh Two Day Trial held over 26–27 May 1960.

The list comprised:

Andre Baldet (246cc Greeves)

Ian Hillier (246cc Greeves)

Mick Dismore (249cc James)

Roger Kersey (246cc Greeves)

Mick Waller (347cc AJS)

Tony Davis (347cc AJS)

John Thomas (347cc AJS)

Roy King (499cc BSA)

Colin Moran (498cc AJS)

John Piggott (592cc Matchless)

Eric Chilton (649cc Triumph)

Sammy Miller with the Ariel Arrow he had used on the Ben Nevis expedition. This time, however, the machine gave trouble, retiring before the first day was out with gearbox problems.

Back to Racing

Then, on Saturday 25 June 1960, Sammy made a return to racing, when he and former World Champion Cecil Sandford shared an Arrow in the Thruxton 500-Mile race for production machines. As *The Motor Cycle* reported: 'Oddly enough – and yet, perhaps, not so unexpectedly – it was the 250cc class that provided the closest tussling. After six hours of racing

The Arrow was the same bike as he had used in his Ben Nevis adventure. But this time it gave trouble, retiring on the first day with gearbox gremlins.

On Saturday 25 June 1960 Sammy made a return to racing. Sharing an Ariel Arrow (11) with co-rider Cecil Sandford, the pair finished runners-up in the 250cc class of that year's Thruxton 500-mile race for production machines.

Syd Lawton's Crusader Sports Royal Enfield (Ray Prowting and Mike Munday) and Arthur Taylor's Ariel Arrow (Cecil Sandford and Sammy Miller) were on the same lap and breathing down each other's necks. It could have been anybody's victory until oil on the Arrow's contact breaker cut the speed and the Crusader romped away to finish a lap ahead.' Actually, the Arrow's problem had begun much earlier when Sammy had stepped off in the early stages and damaged the contact breaker cover. The cover was discarded, but the pit crew had overlooked the fact that the topmost of the holes for the three securing screws was actually drilled right through the primary case. It was from this small orifice that oil may well have come out and probably with it the class race victory. Nonetheless, it was still an outstanding performance – and from two riders who had been out of the tarmac sport for some considerable time.

Thruxton 500-Mile Race – 250cc class – 25 June 1960

1st	R. Prowting/M. Munday (247cc Royal Enfield)	197 laps
2nd	C.C. Sandford/S.H. Miller (247cc Ariel)	196
3rd	R. Good/B. Fortesque (247cc Ariel)	193
4th	R. Dowty/B. Potter (247cc Royal Enfield)	192
5th	R. Difazio/A. Mustard (249cc BSA)	189
6th	A. Morris/G. Dunn (249cc BSA)	188

The Ernie Earles Four

Sammy's involvement with the Arrow even took in the very interesting Ernie Earles-built 496cc four-cylinder sidecar racing outfit. This utilised a pair of Arrow engines mounted side-by-side. Although very fast when it kept going, the power unit was extremely temperamental. Raced by the highly experienced Birmingham-based Bill Boddice, the Earles Arrow machine first appeared in 1960 and was campaigned, with limited success, until the end of 1962. As with the Arrow-engined 250cc solo racers, notably the Hermann Meier-tuned machine which finished seventh in the 1960 Isle of Man TT, had the factory given its full backing there is little doubt that the Arrow could have been much more successful in racing than it actually was. In fact, in the author's opinion, it could have been a much bigger threat to the Continental and Japanese machines than the various Greeves, Cotton and DMWs which appeared from late 1962 onwards.

The Ernie Earles four-cylinder Arrow engine – fast but temperamental.

Bill Boddice with Sammy in the chair of the former's Ernie Earles Ariel Arrow four-cylinder racing sidecar outfit, August 1960. The car in the background is a Ford Zephyr.

The 1960 ISDT, the 35th, was staged in Austria. Sammy had been selected to represent Britain in the Silver Vase contest, riding a 246cc Greeves. Here he works on the machine prior to the start; looking on in the white coat is Malcolm Edgar of Castrol. After a cylinder head retaining sleeve-nut sheared, Sammy was eventually forced to retire after some 60 miles (96.5km).

ISDT Selection

The 1960 ISDT was the 35th and held in Austria, with its headquarters in the tiny mountain resort of Bad Aussee, over 5,000ft (1,524m) above sea level and some 45 miles (72.4km) east of Salzburg. Sammy had been selected to represent Britain in the Silver Vase competition, riding a 246cc Greeves. His teammates were Fred Billot (347cc AJS), Bryan Sharp (246cc Greeves) and Mick Waller (347cc AJS).

The event took place in mid-September with 248 entries from no fewer than 17 countries. But it was not to be a happy memory for Sammy, as *The Motor Cycle* of 22 September 1960 vividly reported: 'The route headed west from Bad Aussee along the shores of the beautiful Hallstatter See. It was not far from there that the British Silver Vase team had an almighty setback. Sammy Miller's two-fifty Greeves began to lose power. A cylinder head retaining sleeve-nut had sheared and was allowing the joint to leak. By superhuman riding he reached the next check at Gosau on time – but he was forced to retire on the lower slopes of the Grossglockner, some 60 miles [96.5km] from the start.'

So, yet again, the ISDT had proved a jinx event for Sammy.

Even Lighter

The Motor Cycle dated 20 October 1960 called it the 'Featherweight Five-hundred'. It went on to say: 'To carve anything more from what must already have been Britain's lightest five-hundred might seem impossible. Yet Sammy Miller has done it; that Arrow-grey Ariel he rode in last Sunday's Alec Ross Trial was lighter by 20lb [9.1kg] than its predecessor. So what does that make it now? Sammy isn't saying – but a guess of around 250lb [113.4kg] would not be far out.'

Still registered GOV 132, the machine now sported a frame of Sammy's own design and construction, manufactured in Reynolds S31 tubing – a diamond pattern with single top, front-down and seat tubes.

From below the seat nose twin tubes diverged to run rearward to the rear suspension unit upper mounts. Additional tubes acted as struts between the base of the seat tube and the damper upper mountings. And that was it: engine, gearbox and dural mounting plates completed the structure. Sammy had retained the swinging-arm as before, with its nearside (left) arm serving as a rear chain oiler.

There was no separate oil tank; instead the seat tube (2¼in x 16 gauge) served as an oil container, with a capacity of 2.75 pints. A fabricated box at the top of the tube contained the filter.

Duralumin bolts were employed wherever practicable; steel bolts were drilled longitudinally and their ends plugged to prevent the ingress of mud – even the kickstart lever was so treated.

Sammy had also used glass-fibre to play an important role in the weight-saving exercise, and so the complete primary chaincase was of this material – the weight being half that of the original aluminium component.

An upholstered seat with glass-fibre underpan saved yet more – even the competition plate, registration plates and magneto cover were now of plastic.

An aluminium crankcase shield replaced the former steel component, while a rubber pad was placed between the shield and crankcase.

A German-made Magura twistgrip was entirely of alloy, while Sammy had spent considerable time drilling even more items, for example both wheel spindle ends, to accept a tommy-bar, while a single tank bolt was slotted for a coin, which saved the weight of a box spanner in the tool kit.

Using the original malleable-iron Ariel front-fork top yoke as a pattern, Sammy had cast a new one in light-alloy, saving yet more weight.

As before, the wheels featured alloy rims on Ariel Leader hubs, with water-excluding flanges riveted to the shoe plates.

Extreme narrowness had been another priority, so a modified inlet tract and mounting flange had repositioned the carburettor more nearly parallel with the frame tubes. Similarly, the exhaust header pipe was even more tucked in than before, joining up to Sammy's specially created miniature silencer. All in all it was a brilliantly conceived job and one that its builder could be genuinely proud of.

The wins kept on coming, an exception being the British Experts in mid-December; however, with yet another excellent year's performances Sammy retained his ACU Trials Star for another 12 months. Another aspect of 1960 had been the emergence of television trials, notably via the BBC.

1961

Another win came in the Colmore Cup Trial, for the third successive time, then it was on to Sammy's favourite weekend double, the Hurst Trial on the Saturday and the Alan Trophy Trial the following day. He even had time to take part, at around the same time, in a Midland Centre scramble, where he finished runner-up on a BSA C15S; at the same meeting he was third in the team race – the first 250cc home.

Also early in 1961 Sammy was linked with the Bultaco firm for the very first time. Anneley's of Blackburn had just been appointed the British Concessionaires for the Spanish make and Norman Culley of Bury, a very active North Western Centre member, had been appointed their scrambles and trials manager. *The Motor Cycle* of 9 February 1961 said: 'Team members have not yet been decided, although Sammy Miller is very interested. He recently tried a scrambler and was impressed with the engine [at that time a 196cc unit], although he suggested that frame modifications were necessary.'

Norman Culley also told *The Motor Cycle*: 'We are also trying to get him interested in the road racer.' But on this front Dan Shorey had already been signed, shortly to be followed by Sammy's fellow Ulsterman and schoolboy friend Tommy Robb. The racing side of the British Bultaco operation was being run by Ken Martin, a road racer himself.

Runner-up in the Scottish

Then, in early May, came the annual Scottish Six Days. Yet again Sammy was to be denied victory in this event, but he did the next best thing by finishing runner-up to AJS-mounted Gordon Jackson. And with only a single mark deducted, no one could have begrudged Jackson his success.

The Motor Cycle dated 11 May 1961 began its report: 'Incredible. Fantastic. Stupendous. You can milk filmdom dry but you won't find a superlative that will fit Gordon Jackson's performance in winning last week's Scottish Six Days Trial.' And in this event Gordon Jackson was certainly often the man to beat during the late 1950s and early 1960s.

Scottish Six Days Trial – May 1961

1st	G.L. Jackson (347cc AJS)	1 marks lost
2nd	S.H. Miller (497cc Ariel)	5
3rd	R.S. Peplow (199cc Triumph)	17
	R. Sayer (199cc Triumph)	17
5th	P.N. Brittain (346cc Enfield)	22
6th	J.A. Sandiford (249cc BSA)	23

More Long-distance Racing

During May, Bemsee ran their 1,000 kilometre race for production machines at Silverstone. Among the 250cc entries it looked like being a big day for Cecil Sandford and Sammy, out once again on Arthur Taylor's Ariel Arrow. *The Motor Cycle* takes up the story: 'Running like a sewing machine, way in front of the other quarter-litres, the Arrow seemed unstoppable. But only 11 laps from the finish Cecil cruised to an inexplicable halt at Becketts – and started to push home.'

Then came the 500-miler at Thruxton at the beginning of July. But again, after leading, the pair struck trouble, when after completing 65 laps the Ariel's engine seized.

New Trials Season

The national British trials season got underway in mid-September 1961, but Sammy, even though he had only lost five marks and won the 500cc class in the Mitchell, was described by *Motor Cycle News* as 'off form', as by now the public and press alike expected a victory every time he ventured out.

During May 1961 Bemsee ran a 1,000 kilometre race for production machines at Silverstone. Here Sammy is shown at speed aboard Arthur Taylor's Ariel Arrow. When seemingly set for victory the machine struck trouble; the same thing happened a few weeks later in the Thruxton 500-miler.

Only a week later, however, Sammy was back on top, with victory in the Southern Trial organised by the Kent & Sussex Motor Cycle club.

Then he was off to compete in the ISDT as a member of the British Vase B team on his 500cc Ariel. In 1961 the ISDT was staged once more in Wales, with Llandrindod Wells as its base. Although Britain's Trophy and Vase A did not do very well, the Vase B team came home third in the Vase contest, a fine result. And of the 16 gold medals won by British riders, Sammy's was the second-best-placed competitor. So, at last, he had something to cheer himself with regarding the ISDT.

The Belgian Lamborelle Trial

By the end of 1961, Sammy had won the Belgian Lamborelle Trial once more, the rugged Ilkley Grand National (with fastest time of the day), the John Douglas Trial, the Wye Valley, the Bemrose, the Red Rose, the Beggars Roost, the Welsh Two Day, the Manx Two Day, the Irish Experts and several others. And he would probably have won the Scott Trial too, but he had taken some four minutes longer to complete the moorland course. Actually, the winner Arthur Lampkin (249cc BSA) tied on marks lost on observation, but the BSA rider took the honours of being best on observation for going the furthest cleanest.

Sammy also came runner-up (to Gordon Jackson) in the 1961 British Experts two weeks after the Scott in late November.

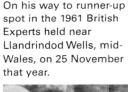

On his way to runner-up spot in the 1961 British Experts held near Llandrindod Wells, mid-Wales, on 25 November that year.

The 24th Southern Experts Trial

Then in mid-December Sammy won the 24th annual Southern Experts Trial. It was a special test which finally gave Sammy a repeat of his 1960 victory, after tying with Gordon Jackson on observation with a debit of six. Set out in an area of Wotton-under-Edge and Dursley, the 30-mile (48km) course contained 50 sub-sections for solos and eight less for sidecar competitors.

Southern Experts Trial – 17 December 1961

1st	S.H. Miller (497cc Ariel)	6 marks lost*
2nd	G.L. Jackson (347cc AJS)	6*
3rd	D.G. Langston (249cc BSA)	8
4th	S. Ellis (199cc Triumph)	13
5th	J. Giles (199cc Triumph)	21
6th	J.V. Smith (249cc BSA)	22

* decided by special test

Receiving the ACU Trials Star for another year in 1961.

1962 Starts Badly

Practice was a byword for Sammy; however, as he found out it could also be dangerous. Home for the annual Christmas holiday, he was out on Friday 29 December after winning the Boxing Day Walter Rusk Memorial Trial for the ninth time in succession, when, in his own words, 'my back went click – and I was out.' This resulted in him being confined to bed with a slipped disc, and on the following Monday he telephoned journalist Charlie Rous at *Motor Cycle News* to say that the dislodged vertebrae had been reset, but that it would keep him out 'for a few weeks.' Sure enough, Sammy was a non-starter in the Vic Brittain Trial the following weekend.

Back in Action

However, rivals who thought they had seen the last of Sammy for some time suffered a rude shock when he not only reappeared with his Ariel, but also beat a star-studded field in the annual Neath club's national St David's Trial on Saturday 13 January 1962! *Motor Cycle News* simply said: 'The Irish Wizard Again!'

So just how had Sammy got back in the saddle so quickly? For a start determination was one of his strongest traits. For most people a slipped disc really would have meant weeks rather than days; however, anxious not to miss too many trials right in the middle of the season, he disdained the conservative methods of conventional medical advice and sought the aid of a non-professional man, a football trainer with a talent for slipping bones into place quickly. With a few words of sympathy, some pressure skilfully applied, a click – and the offending disc was back in place. Some strapping to ensure that the errant joint remained in place meant that Sammy was back in business.

St David's Trial – 13 January 1962

1st	S.H. Miller (497cc Ariel)	23 marks lost
2nd	B.W. Martin (249cc BSA)	29
3rd	J.A. Sandiford (249cc BSA)	30
4th	P.T. Stirland (249cc BSA)	31
5th	D. Langston (249cc BSA)	32
6th	J.V. Brittain (247cc Enfield)	34

At the beginning of February 1962 it was announced that the Thames Ditton sporting dealers, Comerfords, whose flag in road racing was carried by John Hartle, would be extending their interest into the trials sphere, via none other than Sammy Miller, in all national events.

The Double Act Again

Towards the end of February, Sammy was once again not content with winning the Irish Hurst Cup for the sixth year in succession, and he made the overnight dash across land and sea from the Emerald Isle to Cumberland for the following day's national Alan Trophy Trial – and emerged victorious for the fifth year running. As *Motor Cycle News* commented: 'What a record!'

But this was only the start, as a week later he scored an even more impressive double when he first travelled down to the Cotswolds to annex the Cotswold Cup, then hopped over the channel to Belgium to carry off the top award in the 10th international Experts Trial at Braine-le-Chateau, Belgium.

Then in mid-March Sammy ventured across the English Channel once more and won the Lamborelle Trial for the fourth time in succession. Yet he nearly did not compete in this Belgian classic. After motoring down from Birmingham with Peter Fletcher, they missed the 4pm ferry at Dover by 10 minutes and then had to rush all the way to Brussels, reaching their hotel at 3.45am. After only a few hours' sleep, Sammy set about tackling the 32 sections on the two-lap circuit of 37 miles (59.5km) each. He did this, losing only 15 marks in the process, less than half the number lost by Johnny Giles, the runner-up.

Lamborelle Trial – 19 March 1962

1st	S.H. Miller (497cc Ariel)	15 marks lost
2nd	J. Giles (199cc Triumph)	33
3rd	R. Vanderbecken (Belgium, 199cc Triumph)	34
4th	W. Wilkinson (246cc Greeves)	36
5th	D. Clegg (246cc Greeves)	39
6th	R. Peplow (199cc Triumph)	41

Lightening the Ariel Still Further

In preparing his Ariel for the Scottish Six Days the following month, Sammy carried out yet more weight-saving measures. The latest ones included Hylite titanium alloy of 80-ton tensile strength instead of steel for the front wheel spindle; titanium also being used for the rear-fork pivot pin and rear spindle. The rear sprocket was now of light-alloy, not steel, and a cast light-alloy brake pedal had been made, using the steel original as a pattern. Sammy's drill had also been hard at work on the gearbox, perforating the gear pinions and hollowing-out the kick-starter and gear pedal shafts.

The Ariel Factory

Ariel was one of the mainstay British motorcycle marques from its foundation in 1902 until its ultimate demise in 1965. During this time it produced many famous models, from small-capacity commuter bikes right through to 1000cc four-cylinder range-toppers – what would now be referred to as superbikes.

Much of the early history of Ariel was overseen by the Sangster family, Charles and later his son, Jack, who were key figures in the birth and growth of the British motorcycle industry. Some of the

A May 1955 advertisement for the Ariel range, headed by the 1000cc Square Four.

Illustration of the Ariel factory.

nation's greatest designers worked for Ariel over the years – men like Val Page, Bert Hopwood and Edward Turner.

Val Page was with Ariel, off and on, from the mid-1920s until the late 1950s. His first contribution was a series of single-cylinder models with overhead-valve or side-valve engines, the basics of which would endure until the end of the 1950s when a brand-new series of 250cc two-stroke twins – the Leader and, later, the Arrow – came from the pen of the same man.

Edward Turner's most enduring contribution to Ariel was the immortal Square Four, most famous in its 1000cc guise (but also built originally as a 500, followed quickly by a 600 – both with ohc, whereas the 1000 made do with ohv); however, Turner also helped revitalise the Ariel brand in the mid-1930s with the introduction of the famous Red Hunter range of sporting ohv singles.

The Red Hunter name first appeared in 1932. As the Ariel catalogue put it: 'The Red Hunter is introduced to answer the demands of the sporting rider who wishes to combine fast road work or trials with the occasional racing.'

For 1932 the five-hundred Red Hunter (coded VH) featured a four-valve cylinder head with bore and stroke dimensions of 86.4 x 85mm, giving a displacement of 499cc. The power unit was also notable for having a vertical cylinder, instead of the more fashionable inclined (sloping) layout of many other Ariel singles of the period.

Unfortunately, the four-valve head was to give trouble, particularly when used in competition, with cracks developing between the valve seats, and so the factory switched to a conventional two-valve, twin-port head from 1933; later still the head became a single port affair.

As war approached in the spring and summer of 1939, so Ariel and other mainstream British manufacturers were requested to provide various bikes for evaluation by the military authorities. In Ariel's case these included the 497cc VA sv single, 349cc W/NG ohv single, 497cc VH (Red Hunter) ohv single, 347cc NH (Red Hunter) ohv single, 497cc VG ohv single, 347cc NG ohv single and the 598cc VB side-valve single.

Although small batches of VH, NH and VG models were acquired during 1939 and 1940 (the government effectively commandeering many civilian-produced machines in the early months of the war), it was the specialised W/NG that became Ariel's principal military motorcycle of World War Two. Production of the W/NG began in 1940 and it was to remain in continuous production until 1945. The work of Val Page, it was based on the successful trials bike campaigned by works rider Fred Povey in the 1938 Scottish Six Days Trial. A total of 47,599 W/NG models were built, making it the most numerous British military motorcycle of the conflict with an ohv engine.

Post-war, as part of the giant BSA Group, Ariel slowly lost its independence, but not before a new range of parallel twins with 500 and 650cc engines was introduced.

Ariel also enjoyed notable successes in the various branches of motorcycle sport – road racing, scrambling (motocross) and, most of all, trials. In the latter, Sammy Miller's exploits with his lightweight 500cc HT5 are the stuff of legend.

The most obvious difference, however, was to the mudguard: glass-fibre mouldings produced by the Watsonian Sidecar Company from Sammy's own moulds. The front 'guard dispensed with stays, while the rear one served also as the seat base. A much lower fuel tank mount had been adopted, so that the tank skirt now shrouded the engine valve gear.

Another change, this time not aimed at weight-saving, was Sammy's modification of the front fork lower yoke where, by cutting off the spectacle plate and re-welding it in place at a higher level, an additional ¾ in (20mm) of fork movement had been gained.

Seven Years' Development

Although in theory Sammy had taken seven years to develop his Ariel, when the machine was allocated to him following the factory's retirement from trials (in mid-1959) the really big changes had come since then. Right from the beginning he had carried out a weight-saving exercise; however, up to mid-1959 he had to work within the confines of the standard Ariel frame. But when he, in effect, went from being a works rider to a privateer, this was actually a big bonus when it came to future developments.

Sammy and the *Motor Cycle's* Midlands area journalist Bob Currie showing how the width of Ariel HT5 GOV 132 had been reduced to the bare minimum.

In preparing GOV 132 for the 1962 Scottish Six Days, Sammy had carried out yet more weight-saving measures. Here he lifts the machine clear of the ground to prove his point.

First of all he sat down to think. Engine weight a little more forward, perhaps…dispense with the oil tank…make a real job of the weight saving. And so Sammy set to and developed the machine, which reached the definitive form just prior to the Scottish Six Days in the spring of 1962.

The Engine

But what of the engine? Here Sammy had always kept the press and public in the dark. The flywheels were standard (although he had tried light and medium-weight wheels but found the heavier ones had the advantage of storing low-speed punch). However, the compression ratio had been upped from the stock HT5 5.5:1 to 6.6:1. The object, said Sammy, was to get more complete combustion, plus a shade more top-end urge.

When ridden in the 1962 Scottish Six Days the Miller Ariel tipped the scales at 242lb (110kg).

Official scrutineering of GOV 132 prior to the start of the Scottish Six Days, held in Edinburgh in May 1962.

The Scottish at Last

In one-day trials Sammy was almost unbeatable, but in the Scottish Six Days it had been a different matter, until May 1962. Then, after being very much in the hunt over the previous four years, he finally achieved the feat.

Sammy not only relegated his great rival Gordon Jackson to second spot, the position he himself had occupied in 1961 and 1958 when Gordon had scored two of his four wins, but he also did it in style, not only winning by a 10-mark margin, but also leading this most famous of all trials on each of the six days.

With only eight marks lost, Sammy, on his ultra-light Ariel, and Gordon Jackson (347cc AJS) on 18 were head and shoulders above the rest of the field.

The course covered 781 miles (1,256.6km), with 210 riders (all on solos) starting and 179 finishing – an unusually high proportion at that time.

Previously Sammy might have seemed edgy in the Scottish, but this time he seemed a changed man. Several commentators even described him as 'relaxed.' *The Motor Cycle* said: 'His path-picking was an education and his throttle control so precise that it reminded me of a surgeon on a delicate operation. Rarely was his Ariel anywhere except just where he wanted it. Never once did I see him in the throes of one of his famous phenomenal body leaning recoveries from a seemingly hopeless predicament.'

Besides his victory Sammy also won the Alexander Trophy for Best Performance and was a member of the winning Sunbeam club team. He also won the Best Over-350 award.

Scottish Six Days Trial – May 1962

1st	S.H. Miller (497cc Ariel)	8 marks lost
2nd	G.L. Jackson (347cc AJS)	18
3rd	M. Ransom (246cc Francis-Barnett)	29
4th	E. Adcock (246cc DOT)	30
	D.G. Langston (249cc BSA)	30
6th	J.A. Sandiford (249cc BSA)	31
	J.V. Smith (249cc BSA)	31

Gordon Jackson (347cc AJS) number 174 and Sammy number 173 in Edinburgh prior to the start of the 1962 Scottish Six Days.

The James Scrambler

The James factory in Greet, Birmingham, had recently launched a new scrambler with a square-barrel two-fifty motor, and due to his privateer status, Sammy could, in effect, consider any offer.

So, armed with the James (one of only two prototypes then in existence) he decided to make something of a return to this branch of the sport and thus entered a trio of meetings in early June. His first event on his new machine was on Sunday 4 June 1962 in the Birmingham 30 Club's Ragley Park Scramble. Despite some trouble with the air filter, which became quickly detachable during the earlier races, Sammy won his heat in the unlimited event and was third in the final behind John Harris and Bob Curtis. After saying that he 'had really enjoyed myself', he told reporters that he had two other scrambles lined up, both in the Lake District at Kendal and Bassenthwaite. These two meetings came the following weekend over the Whitsun holiday period.

In one-day trials Sammy had become virtually unbeatable, but in the Scottish Six Days it had been a different matter until May 1962, when he won with the loss of only eight marks, compared to the runner-up Gordon Jackson's 18.

As *Motor Cycle News* reported in its 13 June 1962 issue: 'Sammy Miller, making his first visit to the Northern Centre as a scrambler, provided strong opposition to the local riders in the Westmorland Motor Club's scramble at Kendal on Sunday.'

After winning his heat in the 250cc event, Sammy went on to finish runner-up in the final to M.J. Watson (DOT). After another second to Watson in the Atkinson Trophy race, Sammy ended the day by winning the main event, the Skirrow Scramble from Watson.

Then, the following day, on Whitsun Monday, Sammy was down to ride at Whittles, Cumberland, in the Bassenthwaite and District Motor Club's scramble.

All went well until the main event of the day, for the Sun Inn Trophy. Shortly after the start of the first heat, with Sammy disputing the lead with his friend Peter Fletcher, he hit a massive bump – taking off and being propelled high in the air. The James went one way, Sammy the other. His first thought was to remove himself from the path of the oncoming riders, but as Jeff Clew described in 1976: 'He would have made it too, had not another rider reached the same spot at the same time with a 500cc Gold Star BSA in full cry. Sammy felt as though he had touched a power line at the moment of impact, then it all went dark and he took no further interest in the proceedings.'

The 1962 Scottish Six Days Trial winners' presentation; a very special event for Sammy.

After being taken to the local Kenwick Cottage Hospital, where at first his injuries were not thought to be serious, it was subsequently discovered that not only had he broken his shoulder blade and four ribs, plus facial injuries, but he had also suffered a broken pelvis! In its 21 June 1962 issue *The Motor Cycle* reported that: 'He is expected to be in hospital for another 12 weeks.' This effectively knocked out his Thruxton 500-mile ride with Cecil Sandford on Arthur Taylor's Arrow.

Many thought that it would also mean that Sammy would be laid up for even longer; however, as with his slipped disc episode, they had not reckoned upon Sammy's speed of recovery from such setbacks.

In fact, Sammy was back in action during August, riding a 250cc James in the appropriately named James Trophy Trial. It is also worth recording that Alan Kimber of James was keen to sign Sammy, but after visiting the factory Sammy decided to stick with his Ariel.

Manx Two Day Trial

It was with his faithful Ariel GOV 132 that Sammy made a winning return to major trials action over the weekend of 1 and 2 September 1962, in the Manx Two Days. Finishing one mark in front of Scott Ellis, with six marks lost, it was Sammy's fifth Manx victory in five years.

The 1962 International Six Days Trial saw Sammy opt to ride his 'obsolete' Ariel as a privateer after the British selectors considered he was not fit enough (following a scrambles accident earlier that year). In typical Miller fashion Sammy not only won a gold medal, but was also third-best individual gold medallist!

Manx Two Day Trial – 1 and 2 September 1962

1st	S.H. Miller (497cc Ariel)	6 marks lost
2nd	S. Ellis (199cc Triumph)	7
3rd	D.C. Clegg (246cc Greeves)	10
4th	M.J. Andrews (347cc AJS)	14
5th	J.A. Sandiford (249cc BSA)	18
6th	A.J. Marvell (249cc BSA)	19

The ISDT

Sammy had been dropped by the ACU from the British ISDT Vase A team: 'Because of doubts concerning his fitness.' So he decided to compete on a specially prepared Ariel five-hundred as an individual entry, in the 1962 event held in West Germany. Sammy told *MCN*'s Peter Howdle: 'I definitely would not be going if I did not think I was fit enough for the Six Days. I had long enough in hospital to learn not to do anything silly and land myself back there. It's a great pity that I'm out of the team, but I suppose it's just one of those things.'

To prove to the selectors just how wrong they had been, he and his 'obsolete' Ariel not only won a gold medal, but he was also third-best individual gold medallist!

A Super Scott Result

Following the ISDT, Sammy returned to the one-day trials scene, with victory after victory. But it was the Scott which was his biggest success. Sammy was not the fastest man on the rain-soaked Yorkshire moors in November 1962, but he still won the most challenging of all one-day trials by an impressive 40-mark margin. Jeff Smith was fastest, setting standard time in 4 hours 15 minutes 21 seconds, but he sacrificed 65 marks on observation.

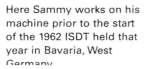

Here Sammy works on his machine prior to the start of the 1962 ISDT held that year in Bavaria, West Germany.

Sammy, who had won in 1958, finished 14 minutes later than Jeff, but riding his Comerfords-entered Ariel special with what *MCN* described as 'incredible skill', he lost only 18 marks on observation. Conditions for the Darlington and District club classic were so appalling that only 27 out of 185 competitors completed the 60-mile (96.5km) course!

Second fastest was Gordon Blakeway, while third best overall was Arthur Lampkin, winner in 1960 and 1961, who failed to make a hoped-for hat-trick.

Scott Trial – 10 November 1962

1st	S.H. Miller (497cc Ariel)	25 marks lost
2nd	J.V. Smith (249cc BSA)	65
3rd	A.J. Lampkin (249cc BSA)	79
4th	J.V. Brittain (246cc Enfield)	81
5th	J.A. Sandiford (249cc BSA)	89
6th	G.O. McLaughlan (347cc AJS)	94

By the end of 1962, Sammy had added another ACU Trials Star to his fast-growing awards collection, thus ensuring his status as British Trials champion for the fourth successive year. He had won no fewer than 19 outright trials of national status and seven class awards, including that ISDT Gold Medal.

At the Earls Court Show in London during November the managing director of Silver Knight Oils, Michael Matthews, not only signed Sammy on for another year of sponsorship, but also presented him with a large radiogram in appreciation of his efforts in what had been the company's first year of sponsorship.

Also during this period the Ariel factory in Selly Oak was axed and Ariel's manufacturing facilities were transferred to the massive BSA plant in Small Heath. This was an unsettling time for Sammy and the rest of the company's employees. And there is no doubt that the move was instrumental in his seriously considering his future.

Speculation began to grow as to what Sammy would do, but as time was to tell he was to stay with the Ariel company for several more months (some 24 to be precise).

Bad Weather

The winter of 1962–63 was one of the worst on record and several major events were postponed, with motorcycle classics such as the Vic Brittain and Exeter trials being postponed – the latter the first time this had happened

The winter of 1962–63 was one of the worst on record and several major events were postponed. This photograph of Sammy with his faithful Ariel is typical of the trials which did take place.

since 1927; however, those events that did take place, Sammy often won, including the Belgian Experts Trial at the beginning of February 1963, winning the event with the loss of 26 marks compared to his travelling companion Roy Peplow's 29. And although the annual Ulster Hurst Trial took place, with Sammy chalking up a seven-in-a-row victory, the weather meant that for the first time in its long history, the Cumberland club's national Alan Trophy trial was postponed.

Next Sammy won the Belgian Lamborelle Trial for the fifth time at the beginning of March. While at home, as *Motor Cycle News* reported in its 27 March 1963 issue: 'Sammy Miller goes on, and on, and on. On Saturday he won the Wye Valley Traders Trophy Trial – and has yet to be beaten in a National this year.' Then in April Sammy won the international Trosa Two Day Trial in Sweden. The event, near Karlskoga, was the first trial of its type to be held in that country.

The 1963 Scottish Six Days

Freak weather hit the first day of the 1963 Scottish Six Days Trial; a mixture of squalls and sunshine. For nearly eight hours of riding over some of the toughest trials country in Britain riders were lashed by rain, sleet and even hailstones. But, occasionally, dazzling sunshine bathed the snow-capped Highlands and, after a 170-mile (273.5km) trek from Edinburgh to Fort William, the 204 weather-beaten survivors gladly relinquished their machines for the night. Only three of them had finished that first day without losing marks – and Sammy was not one of them. Originally he had been docked 11 marks, but this was eventually reduced to six. He never really recovered, however, and at the end of the week his score was 38, compared to Arthur Lampkin (249cc BSA) with seven marks lost.

Scottish Six Days Trial – May 1963

1st	A.J. Lampkin (249cc BSA)	7 marks lost
2nd	M. Andrews (347cc AJS)	20
3rd	J.R. Sayer (199cc Triumph)	25
4th	D. Rowland (249cc BSA)	27
5th	G.O. McLaughlan (401cc AJS)	36
6th	S.H. Miller (497cc Ariel)	38

On a Greeves But Still Victorious

At the national Welsh Trophy Trial on Saturday 25 May 1963, Sammy rode a 246cc Greeves Scottish, loaned to him by the Essex-based factory. Although Sammy had briefly ridden a Greeves in the 1960 ISDT, this was his first appearance on the marque in a one-day event. But this seemed to make no difference because he won anyway!

Around the same time he visited Germany to run a trials training course, organised by the ADAC at the Bavarian resort of Garmisch-Partenkirchen.

One of Sammy's pupils on this course was none other than Gustav Franke, later to become European Trials champion, riding a Zündapp.

In the spring of 1963 Sammy visited Germany to run a trials training course organised by the ADAC at the Bavarian resort of Garmisch-Partenkirchen. One of Sammy's pupils was none other than Gustav Franke, later to become European Trials Champion.

Sammy with his Ariel during the Welsh three-day trial at Llandrindod Wells during summer 1963.

Winning on a BSA

On Saturday 27 July 1963 Sammy provided a surprise for spectators at the Neath club's scramble in South Wales. Riding a standard BSA C15S, he 'cantered home to an easy win' (*Motor Cycling*) in the 250cc race and then notched second place in the 500 and third in the unlimited event on the same machine.

A Czech ISDT

In September 1963 Czechoslovakia hosted that year's ISDT, with the main award, the team Trophy contest, going to the East Germans (mounted exclusively on MZs). Sammy was part of the British Silver Vase team which finished third. And he not only won another gold Medal (Ariel mounted), but was also the second highest-placed British runner.

A Third Scott Victory

Then, at the end of October 1963, Sammy won his third Scott Trial. But he was not without his problems. At one stage he ran out of fuel! But he was in luck, as he was saved by fellow competitor Eric Adcock – out of Eric's DOT and into Sammy's Ariel went a few pints of petroil mixture. Sammy was back in the hunt! This problem seemed to inspire him and he put in a display which Peter Howdle described in the following week's *Motor Cycle News* as: 'Sheer artistry.'

In September 1963 the Czechs hosted that year's ISDT. Sammy (riding his Ariel) was part of the British Trophy team which finished third. He not only won another gold, but was also the second-highest-placed British rider.

Scott Trial – 26 October 1963

1st	S.H. Miller (497cc Ariel)	76 marks lost
2nd	D. Rowland (249cc BSA)	88
3rd	A.J. Lampkin (249cc BSA)	93
4th	J.V. Smith (249cc BSA)	100
5th	W. Wilkinson (246cc Greeves)	101
6th	J.R. Sayer (199cc Triumph)	102

Once again the wins kept coming, and by the end of the year Sammy had chalked up yet another ACU Trials Star title. However, he did have to concede to Jeff Smith (249cc BSA) in the British Experts Trial at the end of November. Actually, both Jeff and Sammy lost 33 marks.

Into 1964

And so into 1964, and still the victories kept piling up. However, on Sunday 5 April, riding a two-fifty Butler (powered by a Villiers single-cylinder two-stroke engine) at the Central Wales AC's Knighton Trophy Trial, instead of his famous Ariel, Sammy once again proved his ability even on a strange machine. He was trying out the machine at the request of Chris Butler in order to find out what improvements could be made. Since he won, the answer was probably that Sammy could simply get the best out of any machine.

The Butler connection had begun when Sammy and Chris Butler had co-operated in producing new glass-fibre mouldings for the Ariel's tank, front mudguard and combined rear mudguard with tail fairing and seat base. Butler Mouldings was based in Hollands Road Industrial Estate, Haverill, Suffolk.

More Ariel Development

Towards the end of April 1964 Sammy debuted the latest, and final, development of his Ariel, in the Bemrose Trial (which he won), as a 'try out' for the Scottish Six Days the following month.

Impeccably prepared as usual, the machine now featured a slimmer, welded-up rear sub-frame. Detail modifications included new snail-cam rear wheel adjusters and a repositioned speedometer mounted in the plastic cover behind the cylinder. Also Sammy had tested a Reynolds front fork of the type originally designed for Geoff Duke's three-fifty Norton racer in 1958; however, even though Sammy spent some two weeks experimenting with various spring and damper combinations, he eventually decided to stick with the existing telescopic front-fork assembly.

Towards the end of April 1964 Sammy debuted the latest, and final, development of his Ariel. New features included a slimmer, welded-up rear sub-frame. He also extensively tested the Reynolds front fork shown here, but eventually decided to retain the existing teles.

The 1964 Scottish Six Days

Sammy was described as 'Superman' by *Motor Cycle News* in its issue dated 13 May 1964. This was in response, not so much to his third victory in the event, but to how he achieved it. The *MCN* report of the trial began: 'Sammy Miller breathed a sigh of relief when scrutineers docked him a final five marks for the condition of his Ariel. He had five stitches in his scalp. His battered five-hundred bore the scars of the toughest Scottish Six Days Trial in history. But he had won it after all – by eight marks.'

The story of Sammy's 1964 Scottish performance of incredible determination surpassed everything else which happened in this ultra-tough trial. And as *MCN* said: 'It is a tale that will become a legend in the annals of motorcycle sport; a success story of skill, resourcefulness and courage second to none.'

The weather was so bad that it came very near to wrecking the entire trial. As one period newspaper report stated: 'It rained continuously and made life a misery. Main roads were awash. Highland lochs, already brimful after three weeks of bad weather, reached bursting point. Mountain streams became raging torrents.'

The second day was generally agreed to have been the wettest and most disastrous in the history of the Scottish. Incredibly, it was also the only day that week when a rider came back without loss of marks, and the only one who completed Tuesday's 146-mile (235km) course without penalty was Sammy.

As the days passed he experienced machine problems (due to a titanium pivot bolt), a damaged rear brake cable, he ran out of petrol and even crashed after colliding with a sheep (and so ended up with a badly cut head, among other things).

Scottish Six Days Trial – May 1964

1st	S.H. Miller (497cc Ariel)	30 marks lost
2nd	M. Andrews (347cc AJS)	38
3rd	D. Smith (252cc Greeves)	39
4th	G.O. McLaughlan (347cc AJS)	44
5th	M. Davis (246cc Greeves)	47
6th	J.R. Sayer (199cc Triumph)	50

The ACU finally saw sense and invited Sammy to be a member of the British Trophy team for the forthcoming ISDT. This came following his excellent performance in front of all but one of the ACU's factory-backed riders (Johnny Giles, 649cc Triumph) who took part in the Welsh Three Days Trial which was held towards the end of May 1964.

An East German ISDT
The 39th International Six Days Trial was staged in East Germany for the 1964 event. The total distance of the trial was 1,087 miles (1,749km), ending with a speed test on a 2.5-mile (4km)-long concrete circuit at Erfurt, where the trial was based. Longest days were the first (7 September) and third, covering 230 miles (370km) in opposite directions. The last day was to be only 50 miles (80.5km). Most of the routes included over 50 per cent of cross-country going. Ten timed special tests, in addition to the speed test, consisted of two acceleration tests, one acceleration and brake test, three hill climbs, three cross-country runs and one combined cross-country and hill climb.

The British Trophy Squad
The British Trophy squad for the 1964 ISDT comprised:
Johnny Brittain (499cc Enfield)
Johnny Giles (649cc Triumph)
Ken Heanes (649cc Triumph)
Sammy Miller (497cc Ariel)
Roy Peplow (349cc Triumph)
Jim Sandiford (346cc BSA)

For the first time in two years a British Trophy team survived the first day of the ISDT without penalty, and although the East Germans won the Trophy for the second year running, it was, as the *MCN* front-page story told its readers, 'Hats off to Brittain, Giles, Heanes, Miller, Peplow and Sandiford. Six cheers for the first British Trophy Team in four years to put up a really good show in the International Six Days Trial.' It continued: 'Outclassed in the special tests, they finished second in the easiest ISDT on record. Only East Germany and Britain finished with clean sheets.' As runners-up the British team received the Watling Trophy, donated by the first Secretary General of the FIM. Sammy had another 'gold' to add to his collection.

International Trophy		Marks lost	Bonus points
1st	East Germany	0	3912.735
2nd	Great Britain	0	3793.093
3rd	Russia	309	3104.440
4th	Czechoslovakia	578	3240.247
5th	Poland	966	2742.062
6th	Austria	1,472	2435.280

Runner-up in the Scott

In November 1964 Sammy finished runner-up to Greeves rider Bill Wilkinson, and although he only missed victory by a single mark, afterwards he commented: 'I just wasn't in it.' In truth he was probably disappointed after failing to score only the second hat-trick in the history of the Yorkshire event.

Then came the rumours, with Sammy being linked to the Spanish Bultaco concern. Was it really true, they asked? And yes it was – although Sammy wasn't saying anything.

Winning the British Experts

Then, on Saturday 28 November 1964, came Sammy's last ride on the Ariel – at least in that era – in no less an event than the British Experts Trial. By now it was common knowledge that Sammy had signed for Bultaco.

With headlines such as: 'End of an Era' and 'Era's End', Sammy bowed out of the big-bike scene in a blaze of glory. By five clear marks he beat his nearest challenger Gordon Adsett (246cc Greeves) and so he and his famous Ariel bowed out, and took the British Experts Trial for the third time.

On Saturday 28 November 1964 came Sammy's last ride on the Ariel – at least in that era. The event was the British Experts Trial, and of course he won; with this he and his famous machine bowed out. A few days later he made his Bultaco debut.

British Experts Trial – 28 November 1964

1st	S.H. Miller (497cc Ariel)	30 marks lost
2nd	G.R. Adsett (246cc Greeves)	35
3rd	R.S. Peplow (199cc Triumph)	39
4th	S. Ellis (199cc Triumph)	40
5th	J.R. Sayer (199cc Triumph)	42
6th	P.H. Gaunt (246cc Enfield)	46
7th	D. Smith (257cc Greeves)	47
8th	M. Andrews (347cc AJS)	53
9th	W. Wilkinson (246cc Greeves)	55
10th	E. Adcock (252cc DOT)	58

As *Motor Cycle* said in its 3 December 1964 issue: 'there's a touch of sadness in the break-up of a perfect partnership. From now on, Sam-the-Ariel becomes Sam-the-Bultaco.'

So it was exit the Ariel – enter the Bultaco.

Chapter 5

Bultaco

As 1964 came to a close, Sammy was British trials champion once more, making it five in a row. His best achievements of the year were his Scottish Six Days victory and his gold medal in the International Six Days, where he was third-best British Trophy teamster.

Then, in the 14 October issue of *Motor Cycle News*, in his 'The Sporting Scene' column, Ralph Venables penned the following: 'Having taken orders for nearly 400 Metisse scramblers during the past two or three years, the Rickman Brothers are extending their New Milton premises for the quicker production of these machines. The hope of many mud-pluggers is that there may one day be Metisse trials models, and already the air is thick with rumours of a Bultaco-engined "bogwheel" designed in collaboration with Sammy Miller. Derek Rickman denies that the rumours have any foundation, and it is a fact that Metisse supply has never kept pace with demand. To market a trials machine would make matters worse, but the Rickmans have a knack of surmounting most obstacles. So has Sammy Miller.'

Front Page News

The Venables story was followed exactly two weeks later by a front page story in *MCN* dated 28 October 1964. Headed 'Rickman – Miller Bultaco Tie Up', this is what it said: 'Sammy Miller, British trials champion for the past five years with a 500cc Ariel, returned from Spain yesterday (Tuesday) after visiting the Bultaco factory. His visit was a prelude to an imminent change of British concessionaires for Bultaco two-strokes. At present imported and distributed by Anelay's of Blackburn, Lancashire, the Spanish machines will in future be handled by Don and Derek Rickman, the New Milton, Hants, riders and manufacturers of the famous Metisse scramblers. The changes will take place in the New Year when Miller's contract with the Ariel factory has expired. News of Miller's change of job, and machine, which first appeared in *Motor Cycle News* (October 14) led to considerable speculation. Now the cat is out of the bag.'

The truth was that Sammy had visited Spain following the Welsh Three Day Trial (which the British selectors used to select riders for the forthcoming ISDT) at the request of Francisco Bulto, head of the Bultaco factory near Barcelona.

As Sammy said himself: 'I took GOV 132 [his Ariel] with me, to evaluate the new 250cc Bultaco that was being developed in Señor Bulto's factory. The arrangement had been made during the previous year's ISDT in Czechoslovakia, when Bulto had agreed to construct a 250cc version of the 200cc model already in production. It was not my first visit to Spain, for at an even earlier date I had tested the 200cc model in secret on Señor Bulto's farm, as the result of an approach via Harry Lindsay [the Southern Ireland Bultaco importer and a close friend of Sammy's].'

As fellow author Jeff Clew explained in his own biography of Sammy first published in 1976: 'The original idea had been planned so that Sammy could meet Señor Bulto in his factory, but on arrival in Barcelona two whole days passed before he could make contact with the factory as it was fiesta time! Sammy had quite a job finding the factory, which was hidden away in the back streets, and was trying to make the reason for his visit understood when Francisco Bulto happened to walk in. Sammy was promptly whisked off to his private estate, Villa Nuevo, and given a 200cc Bultaco to try over some of the sections there. Without doubt the machine had distinct possibilities, provided it could be stretched to full-blown 250cc capacity and could be persuaded to handle less like a camel!'

The Development Process

The development of the new 250cc trials Bultaco, to be referred to as the Sherpa N, is detailed throughout this chapter, but suffice to say now that the engine unit was essentially a bored-out version of the existing air-cooled 196cc unit. By increasing the bore size from 60 to 72mm, the result was oversquare dimensions of 72 x 60mm. Also it is worth saying that the original two-fifty (actual capacity 244cc) came with a four-speed gearbox, like the 196cc version, and featured an alloy cylinder head (with radial finning and a cast-iron barrel).

When the 250cc-engined version was finally ready, Sammy returned to Spain to put in some very comprehensive testing, which was to take some 12 days to complete. By having his Ariel to compare to the new Bultaco two-fifty, Sammy was able to have a direct comparison at his fingertips. In truth, during this time the Miller treatment in effect created an entirely new motorcycle, different from the one which had begun the tests. As originally constructed, the new 244cc-engined bike was in effect little more than a rehashed and re-engined existing Bultaco ISDT-type machine. And in truth, Sammy had to create an entirely fresh, specialised trials mount. Towards the

The bike which Sammy essentially created in the amazingly short time of only 12 days; the 244cc Bultaco Sharp N trials mount. *Inset:* The earlier production 196cc Bultaco Sherpa, which Sammy was able to use as a starting point.

end of the transformation, Francisco Bulto himself was able to see that Sammy had built his works a truly competitive machine, and one that, like Sammy, was a winner.

The Contract

A contract to not only ride, but also to work on an ongoing development programme was duly discussed with Sammy. This included Johnny Grace, himself a road racer of considerable ability and experience, having previously ridden in the Isle of Man TT, and one of Señor Bulto's right-hand men. The contract was duly signed, with the agreement that the change-over would immediately follow the 1964 British Experts Trial.

Of course, Sammy's visits and the contract were kept well away from public view, with Sammy piling up yet more victories aboard his famous Ariel, GOV 132. As Jeff Clew was to comment: 'It was superb gamesmanship, right up to the brink.'

Exit the Ariel – Enter the Bultaco

As *Motor Cycle News* was able to report in its 2 December 1964 issue: 'Sammy Miller and his new Bultaco are winners first time out! After a superb win at Saturday's British Experts Trial, when he rode his 500 Ariel for the last time, he won his first event on a 250 Bultaco, on Sunday.' *MCN* continued: 'Miller made a surprise appearance as a last-minute entrant for a snow-bound Norton club trial in the Cotswolds. And despite being over-geared, he beat his nearest rival, Mike Winford (250 BSA), by 13 marks.' As Sammy jokingly told *MCN*: 'It's the greatest thing since sliced bread.'

As is detailed in the previous chapter, in Wales the previous day the maestro had capped eight-and-a-half glorious years with his legendary Ariel, winning the Experts Skefko Gold Cup for the third time by a margin of five points, from runner-up Gordon Adsett (250 Greeves).

The Doubting Pundits

That first Bultaco outing *had* to be successful, as not only were the eyes of the entire motorcycle world upon him, but there were also plenty of doubting pundits ready to see Sammy make the slightest error on his foreign machine; but in typical fashion he gave them no such opportunity.

One has to remember the background. Sammy's move from Ariel to Bultaco was a massive culture shock to the trials world when it took place. At this time British bikes still dominated the feet-up game. The Ariel, like most other successful, winning trials bikes up to that date, had featured a four-stroke engine, meaning that to many 'Sam was not merely now a heretic, but one who had also lost his marbles!' as one journalist later put it.

Also many of the so-called 'experts' in the media simply wrote him off with comments that it would take months, if not years, for Mr Miller to properly adapt himself to a two-stroke with half the engine size of his Ariel.

But that debut victory on his prototype four-speed two-fifty Bultaco (registration 669 NHO) made these doubting pundits eat their words.

Twice Runner-up

To finish runner-up in a major trial on a strange bike was a feat few riders could achieve, but, the weekend after his debut ride and victory on the Bultaco, this was exactly what Sammy achieved over Saturday and Sunday 5/6 December 1964. The first of the two events was the Drake and Gibb Trial, run by the Gloucester club, where our man lost to Scott Ellis (199cc Triumph) by a single mark. The following day at the national Knut Trial, run by the Bath and West club, he repeated this. And again Sammy had to be content with second place.

To finish runner-up in a major trial on a strange bike was a feat few riders could hope to achieve, but following his debut victory on the Bultaco the weekend before, Sammy achieved this over Saturday and Sunday 5–6 December 1964. The Sunday event was the famous Knut; this photograph was taken during the trial.

However, this came after he had finished dead level with winner Tony Davis (250 Greeves) on observation, but was beaten by the clock – losing four marks for lateness.

Will Sammy Set a Fashion?

Writing in the 16 December issue of *Motor Cycle News*, that doyen of the trials scene, Ralph Venables, headlined his piece 'Will Sammy Set a Fashion?' He went on to say: 'The Rickmans booked orders for more than £100,000 worth of complete machines at Earls Court last month. And a fat slice of this brisk business was accounted for by the Bultaco Sherpa.'

On Sunday 20 December 1964 Sammy had what *MCN* described as a 'Black Day'. While rival Don Smith (250 Greeves) capped an excellent year by winning his first-ever Southern Experts Trial, Sammy and the Bultaco seemed ill at ease and he was unplaced. Afterwards he remarked: 'It took me three years to master the Ariel and I reckon I'll take six months to get the hang of the Bultaco.'

Twelve in a Row

All this was soon forgotten when on Boxing Day, 26 December 1964, Sammy was on the ball once again. Home in Belfast for the Christmas holiday, he rode his 250 Bultaco in the Rusk Memorial Trophy Trial and won for the 12th year in succession. This event was also the last trial in which the Irish system of marks gained was used. Sammy gained a total of 568, his nearest rival being Benny Crawford (250 BSA) on 507. Thereafter Ulster adopted the English system of marks lost.

Next came a move from Birmingham to a new home near Barton-on-Sea in January 1965. Sammy realised that it was necessary to go south so that he could use the facilities at the Rickman works (situated in Gore Road, New Milton) to develop the trials Bultaco, although it should be pointed out that he was *never actually in their employ*.

The Southern Debut

Sammy's debut in the Southern Centre got off to a flying start when he won the Sturminster Newton club's New Year Trial during mid-January. This is how Max King (a trials rider himself) saw the action for *Motor Cycle News* in its 20 January 1965 issue: 'Sam seemed relaxed and confident – more so perhaps than at any time since taking over the Bultaco.' King's report continued: 'For its part the Sherpa responded well – it had plenty of power and did nothing unpredictable. It appeared to handle positively and found grip in places where it is difficult to come by. In short, Miller and the Bultaco looked a pretty formidable partnership.'

Then, in the 3 February issue of *MCN*, Ralph Venables viewed Sammy's progress so far – and also started an Ariel-Bultaco controversy: 'As anticipated, it took Sammy Miller no time to make his mark on the Southern Centre trials scene. "He would have won our first two events by even wider margins if he'd been on the Ariel" said a competitor at the Southern Centre Team Trial. I doubt it. The Bultaco is ideal for the shorter and trickier sections which characterise trials in that area nowadays. My impression is that Miller has not yet perfected the two-stroke technique – utterly different from that required for the Ariel. He'll need at least another month. Sam's superb Ariels [GOV 132 and 786 GON] are still on sale at Comerfords – price £375 each. The Bultaco Sherpa is listed at £268. Now, suppose some philanthropist

During the winter of 1964–65 Sammy had moved from Birmingham to Barton-on-Sea. He is seen here outside his new home in Farm Lane South, together with the author's much-missed friend, Alan Aspel. Alan (brother of TV's Michael Aspel) was a well-respected motorcycle journalist, and he sadly died in a motorcycle accident during an industry test day in the early 1980s. One of the then new 252cc Sherpas is in Sam's pick-up truck.

offered to give you one or the other of the vastly different trials models, which would you choose – the Ariel or the Bultaco? The reason for your choice could be of considerable interest to other *Motor Cycle News* readers – so why not put your thoughts down on paper and send to me (at my home address please – Old Manor Cottage, Treyford, Midhurst, Sussex). We will publish the best pro-Ariel letter and the best one in favour of the Bultaco.'

Exactly two weeks later, in *MCN* dated 17 February 1965, Venables revealed the result.

'What a fantastic state of affairs! A fortnight ago, I asked readers to imagine that someone wished to make them a gift of the ex-Miller 500cc Ariel or the 250cc Bultaco Sherpa – and I invited them to let me know which one they would choose (and why). I promised to publish the best two letters representing each school of thought. But the plan cannot possibly be put into operation! My scheme has been shot down in flames for the simple reason that out of 60 letters received, not one contained a preference for the Bultaco!' Ralph then went on to say: 'Quite honestly, in all my 30 years of motorcycle journalism I have never come up against anything quite so incredible. Even allowing for the fact that the Ariel is worth about £100 more than the Bultaco, I never expected such a one-sided response.'

So what did all this prove? The answers Ralph Venables received were that although the Bultaco would be easier to ride, the Ariel would be more fun, that the Ariel was a four-stroke and would provide more grip and that it would probably prove more reliable.

But, of course, all this was surmise. In truth none of those who wrote in had ridden a Bultaco, many were pro-British and just as many were four-stroke enthusiasts who considered they wanted, as one correspondent put it, 'a man's machine'.

Sammy's Reply

Not long after the Venables Ariel v Bultaco saga, the following letter from Sammy himself was published in *Motor Cycle News*:

'Regarding Ralph Venables' article this week and his comments over the last two months, I was wondering how much commission he is receiving from the BSA group. I think the only solution to his problem on which is the better machine, Ariel or Bultaco, is a meeting to clarify it. If Ralph cares to present himself with the Ariel on any "he-man" hills, I shall be only too willing to demonstrate the Bultaco. I will also ride the Ariel if he wants, but in case he thinks there is any rolling back of the throttle, he can provide a suitable jockey. If any of the readers who have sent letters care to attend they will be very welcome and, needless to say, Ralph will keep us all up to date on the venue and conditions of the challenge.

Sam The Bultaco Man! Barton-on-Sea, Hants.'

So what happened? Precisely nothing; and the whole episode was soon forgotten.

But, as history records, Sammy Miller and the Bultaco he developed changed trials forever. Today the proof exists in one simple sentence: pre-'65 events! I rest my case.

First National Victory on the Bultaco

But even before the second Venables piece appeared, the headline in the 10 February 1965 issue was quite clear: 'Miller Shatters All His Critics', with reporter Bob Light going on to say: 'Shattering the critics who said that he had not yet mastered the Spanish two-stroke completely, Sammy Miller scored his first National win on the Bultaco in Sunday's Colmore Cup trial with a six mark advantage at the finish over local hero David Langston (250 BSA).' For the 1965 event the Stratford club had taken over much of the fieldwork, while the Sunbac organisation handled the administration. The result was a tough 48-mile (77km) course over the rocks and tree-roots of North Gloucestershire. And a difficult course it was too, as witnessed by the *MCN* report: 'Right from the start on the Fosse Way near Shipston-on-Stour the solos were on trouble at Meakin's mount, where no-one mastered a super-steep climb and right-hand turn on a treacherous greasy surface. With no room for a fast approach, Miller and Langston spun to a halt in the first few feet while Tony Davis (250 Greeves) and Don Smith (250 Greeves) both struggled through for three. There were no cleans either at Warners King, where an elite half-dozen coped with single dabs, these being Miller, Langston, John Ashcroft (250 Greeves), Johnny Brittain (250 Enfield), Chris Leighfield and Mick Bowers (200 Enfield).'

And things didn't get any easier. For example, leading contender Don Smith suffered broken handlebars and a damaged wrist after falling backwards off some rocks. But he was able to continue after changing the 'bars.

The original four-speed Bultaco 250 trials engine, with radial finned cylinder head, chain primary drive, vertically split crankcases and a Spanish-made Amal carburettor.

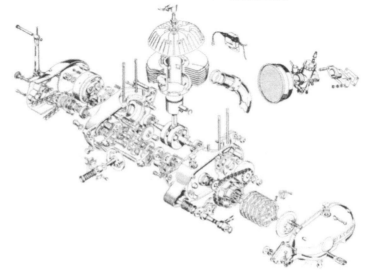

But Sammy was pressing on, and the remaining sections cost him just one mark.

Colmore Cup National Trial – 7 February 1965

1st	S.H. Miller (250 Bultaco)	16 marks lost
2nd	D.G. Langston (250 BSA)	22
3rd	S. Ellis (250 BSA	30
4th	D.R. Smith (250 Greeves)	31
5th	C.F. Dommett (250 Cotton)	33
6th	J. Brittain (250 Enfield)	34

And, of course, all the top six were mounted on 250s!

The following weekend, on Saturday 13 February, Sammy 'outshone formidable opposition' (*MCN*) to win his second National trial in six days, this being the St David's, by a clear 11 marks. But, as reporter Robin Miller (no relation!) wrote, another side of Sammy was shown that day: 'If there had been an award for tenacity, it should certainly have gone to Val Daly, the only woman competitor. Three times she and her Dot capsized in Keenan's. Each time she gritted her teeth and restarted. Then halfway up it stalled. At that moment a gentleman by the name of Miller was inspecting the section. Very kindly, he restarted her machine and gave her a push up the hill.'

And at the end of February 1965, Sammy returned to his native Northern Ireland where he completed his by now normal double over the weekend of 27/28th by winning the Hurst Cup Trial on Saturday before travelling to the Alan Trophy Trial in Cumberland the following day. In the Ulster event, riding his 244cc Bultaco, Sammy easily beat fellow countryman Benny Crawford in the Hurst for his ninth successive victory.

Run over a fresh course, the Alan was no less difficult than previously and the 'Bultaco Man', as *MCN* now called him, won by 11 marks from Mick Andrews (250 James) to record his seventh victory in eight years.

Road Racing Again
The arrival of March brought another road racing season. Somehow, as events had shown before (with his brief appearances on an Ariel in production racing), Sammy had not yet fully got the tarmac sport out of his system. So it came as no great shock when rumours began to surface that he was to make a return to this branch of the sport.

To begin with, the press reports rather jumped the gun by linking Sammy with the 50cc class, *MCN* saying that 'A works 50cc Suzuki' would be provided for not only Sammy, but also for Chris Vincent and the 1964 Irish 250cc champion, Chris Goosen. The front page story, published in the newspaper's 3 March 1965 issue, also said: 'He [Sammy] reached a provisional agreement with Terry Hill, the Belfast dealer acting on behalf of Suzuki (Great Britain) Ltd.'

However, the idea of his racing the Suzuki was a non-starter, as not only was there no 50cc class for the North West, but Sammy had accepted the loan of an air-cooled Bultaco TSS racer from the Rickman Brothers. In fact, Sammy rode this machine in the North West, the Leinster and Cookstown 100; however, his debut ride (in the North West in May) did not get off too well. After completing one touring lap in practice, to familiarise himself with the course after such a long lay-off, he set off on a fast lap to put the Bultaco through its paces. As he approached the left-hander just prior to the finishing line, Sammy went to change down and could not find the gear lever – it had fallen off! Glancing down to see what happened temporarily distracted his concentration, and at that precise moment the engine seized. He grabbed the clutch lever and as he looked up again he was heading straight towards a telegraph pole. Luckily, the clutch freed just in time and he missed the pole by a fraction. The need for an engine rebuild precluded any further practising and it was impressive that Sammy came home sixth in the 250cc event. All-in-all it was a brilliant meeting, with thousands thronging the 11-mile (18km) Portstewart – Coleraine – Portrush circuit, the fastest in Britain.

North West 200 250cc – 5 laps – 55 miles – May 1965
1st   T. Robb (Bultaco)
2nd   L. Ireland (Honda)
3rd   J. Blanchard (Aermacchi)
4th   T. Barnes (Moto Guzzi)
5th   R. McCullough (Greeves)
6th   S.H. Miller (Bultaco)

The North West was followed a few days later by the Leinster – in southern Ireland. Here Sammy showed he was back in the groove, finishing runner-up behind his old friend Tommy Robb, who was riding a factory-supported liquid-cooled Bultaco. Even so, Sammy led for eight of the 15 laps. But it was his third meeting, the Cookstown 100, where he really showed he had lost little of his aptitude for the hard stuff, finishing with a victory after a brilliant ride in wet conditions.

Not content with the above exploits, Sammy, as we will see later, also took in a spot of production racing on a Bultaco Metralla.

Victory in the Scottish

Before his outings in the North West 200, Leinster and Cookstown 100, Sammy made history in early May by winning the famous Scottish Six Days Trial for the third time. In the process he scored the first win by a two-stroke and the first win by a foreign machine.

Sammy took the lead on the third day, when Scott Ellis (BSA) retired following a big-end seizure. From then on he duelled with Arthur Lampkin (on another BSA) to win by 29 marks to 33. In fact, his victory would have been by a greater margin had Sammy's Bultaco not jumped out of gear on Loch Eild Path, as he reached the end cards. His subsequent protest against a five-point penalty was rejected.

Many pundits doubted Sammy's ability to successfully switch from large capacity four-stroke to small displacement two-stroke. His victory in the 1965 Scottish Six Days effectively silenced these doubters.

Routes totalled 802 miles (1290km) with 149 observed sections. Only 38 of the 200 starters retired.

Scottish Six Days Trial – May 1965

1st	S.H. Miller (250 Bultaco)	29 marks lost
2nd	A.J. Lampkin (250 BSA)	33
3rd	M.J. Andrews (250 James)	37
4th	M.G. Davis (250 Greeves)	39
5th	J.R. Sayer (200 Triumph)	43
6th	R.S. Peplow (200 Triumph)	49

ISDT Selection

June 1965 saw the selection process for the British team in that year's ISDT. Because the selection needed British riders on British bikes, Sammy was asked to ride a 350 BSA (a B40 unit single); even though earlier that month he had retired in the Manx Three Day event when his 440 BSA developed ignition and gearbox gremlins.

Of course, the summer months were the 'close season' for the trials world. This enabled Sammy to take in more racing; this time, although Bultaco mounted, it was aboard a 196cc Metralla sports roadster. At Castle

At Castle Combe on Saturday 24 July 1965 Sammy shared this 196cc Bultaco Metralla with Peter Buswell. The pairing finished seventh in their class of the annual 500-mile (805km) race for production machines. Sammy later won on the same bike at the international Silverstone Hutchinson 100 meeting in August that year.

Combe on Saturday 24 July 1965, the Southampton club organised their annual international 500-mile (805km) endurance race. The club had been forced to switch from its traditional home at Thruxton, due to the latter's deteriorating track surface. The Castle Combe venue had a smoother 1.84-mile (2.95km) circuit.

Sammy was sharing the Metralla with co-rider Peter Buswell. A storm sent rain cascading down for some 30 minutes after the midday start (I know, I was one of the spectators at the Wiltshire track that day), bringing the usual crop of soaked brakes and ignition problems. But then out came the sun, with the track surface drying rapidly, and for the rest of the day the conditions were fine.

Sammy and Peter Buswell finished seventh in their class, completing 237 laps; this compared with the 250cc victors, Peter Inchley and Derek Minter, riding a works Cotton Conquest, with 259 laps.

The National Red Rose Trial

As the 11 August 1965 issue of *Motor Cycle News* reported: 'Sammy Miller's Bultaco must have felt really at home in Sunday's minor heatwave as it carried the maestro to his fourth outright win in the national Red Rose Trial held over a typical north country moorland mixture.' Postponed from March, when 4ft snowdrifts blocked the course, the trial took place over three laps of a much modified 15-mile (24km) course, which started from Shawforth, near the Lancashire town of Rochdale.

The going was extremely rugged and no fewer than 24 of the 78 starters packed up with machine trouble of one sort or another. *MCN* reported: 'Toughest of the 21 observed sections was the fourth sub at Robin Hood's Clough, a frightening mixture of rocks, mud and water.' The report continued: 'Miller really shone on this section.'

Red Rose Trial – 8 August 1965

1st	S.H. Miller (250 Bultaco)	15 marks lost
2nd	N.S. Eyre (200 Triumph)	22
3rd	J.A. Sandiford (350 BSA)	26
4th	W. Wilkinson (250 Greeves)	30
5th	P.H. Gaunt (250 Enfield)	35
6th	S. Ellis (350 BSA)	40

A Silverstone Victory

Exactly six days later, on Saturday 14 August, Sammy took part on the 196cc Metralla in the race for production machines at the 33rd International Hutchinson 100 meeting. Unlike his Red Rose Trial outing, the Silverstone production event was held amid a constant downpour of heavy rain. To make matters worse, Sammy was almost last away after his Spanish machine refused to start. However, displaying all his old verve, he set about carving his way through the field, ultimately going on to win the 250cc class after the long-time leader Reg Everett (Cotton Conquest) was forced to retire after the lead from his ignition coil came off.

Suzuki

At the beginning of September 1965, Sammy was pictured with a new 125 Suzuki single-cylinder ISDT machine, with disc-valve two-stroke engine and twin exhaust ports. Sammy teased the press by saying, in reply to their questions about what the connection was: 'you'll find out soon enough.' *Motor Cycle News* said: 'Our tip is that the Ulsterman will be leaving Bultaco's shortly and setting up business.'

The 1965 ISDT

In the week running up to the 1965 ISDT, clerk of the course Geoff Duke made the fatal error of forecasting: 'The first two days will be fairly easy but we'll hit 'em right between the eyes from the third day onwards.' Geoff was summing up British prospects in the Isle of Man where the trial was to be staged.

His forecast – made in good faith – was based on the skill of Britain's teamsters in really difficult cross-country conditions. But if Ken Heanes (500 Triumph), Arthur Lampkin (440 BSA), Roy Peplow (500 Triumph), brothers Bryan and Triss Sharp (both 250 Greeves) plus Sammy Miller (350 BSA) were to bring home the International Trophy, the highest team award in motorcycle sport, they would have to beat the history books. Previously, although Britain had won the award 16 times since 1913, the last time had been in 1952.

And what of the opposition? East Germany had been winners for the last two years. West Germany had been winners three times since 1953. Czechoslovakia had been winners six times in the same period. Austria had been winners in 1960, when special tests were introduced, plus Russia, Poland and Spain.

Since 1953, Britain's best showing was in East Germany in 1964, when only Britain and East Germany finished unpenalised, with Britain being beaten on the special tests.

The 40th ISDT was the first-ever staged in the Isle of Man. The four previous post-World War Two events staged by the ACU had all been in Wales.

The six-day routes in the Island totalled over 1,000 miles (1,600km) of roads, tracks, moors, mountains, rivers, bogs and beaches.

The Trophy Team

When Britain's Trophy team assembled at a final briefing at the BSA factory in Birmingham during early September, it was the riders' machinery which caused the most concern, as we already know from Sammy's earlier problems during the selection process. But BSA's Brian Martin, who was also the British team manager, had, it was said, 'gone over the 350 and 440 BSA team bikes with a fine toothcomb and the BSAs now had emergency ignition circuits.'

The trial began on Monday morning, 20 September. At the end of that first day Great Britain led with 0 marks lost and 700.79 points; East Germany and Czechoslovakia also had 0 marks, but with fewer points.

On days two and three Britain remained in the running, occupying the runner-up position behind East Germany. However, on the last of these two days both Greeves were late; Bryan Sharp lost 45 marks after ignition coil trouble, while his brother Triss had lost six marks. Then everything went wrong. First Alan Lampkin's 440 BSA, already sporting wired-up suspension, ran out of sparks. Next Sammy's 350 BSA began misfiring and, as *MCN* reported, 'finally conked out.' To cap it all, Bryan Sharp came off, blinded by mud from a guardless front tyre; completely dazed, he attempted to press on but got hopelessly lost. Britain's team was now down to half strength. The following day Triss Sharp, who had gone to bed red-eyed from the previous day's ordeal (it poured with rain for almost 24 hours), was so demoralised that he did not bother to get up. This was to cause a storm of bad publicity, mostly via the national media.

Only Ken Heanes and Roy Peplow finished, with Roy being Britain's only Trophy teamster to gain a gold medal (no marks lost).

As one press report stated: 'Mountain mist and torrential rain played havoc with man and machine. Out of 299 starters, only 82 finished. Of these, a mere 18 riders won gold medals. The FIM should strike them in platinum.'

The following month *MCN* published a full-page article headed 'The Six Day Trial Britain Should Have Won? What Went Wrong?' A caption to a photograph of Sammy studying his broken-down machine read: 'Tragedy in the Isle of Man. Trophy teamster Sammy Miller stopped in the Manx Three Day ISDT selection tests, when he rode a 440 BSA. Ignition trouble recurred on a 350 he rode in the Army Three Day, when he retired with a broken frame. Mysterious ignition failure caused his retirement, when still unpenalised, on the fourth day of the International. Three rides on BSA. Three retirements.'

Yes, that *MCN* caption told it as it was. Quite simply, even if you have the finest rider in the world, he still needs machinery with which he can complete the event...

It is also worth saying that when the misfire first set in, Sammy attempted to contact the Lucas and BSA representatives so that they could help him keep going. No one turned up and the misfire simply got worse and worse, even though he managed to coax his by now very sick machine a further 50 miles (80.5km) before it finally expired. What particularly annoyed Sammy was the knowledge that at no point on the Island was it necessary to travel more than 8–9 miles (13–14.5km) before reaching the coast. As he told Jeff Clew in 1976: 'Yet no one cared in the least about my misfortune – or the fact that I was representing my country in this important international event.' In fact, as Sammy (and the other riders) battled in the awful wet and cold conditions, the so-called 'trade barons' continued to frequent the hotel bars, turning a deaf ear to those who needed their help.

A week after the end of the ISDT Sammy and the then 21-year-old Mick Andrews (250 James) tied on 34 points each in the national West of England Trial on Saturday 20 October 1965; however, the Best Solo Award was eventually given to Andrews as he had conquered most observed sections without penalty.

Victory at Last

It was at the Ringwood club's national Perce Simon Trial on Sunday 7 November that Sammy finally got back to winning ways, after a run of seven successive runner-up awards in earlier events which had no fewer than seven different winners!

Instead of bemoaning his fate, Sammy had taken these defeats in good humour – though in typical Miller fashion the will to win had never waned. As *MCN's* Max King related: 'Not even the deluge which swamped Hampshire's New Forest throughout the Saturday night and during the trial on Sunday could deny Miller the victory he deserved – and needed so much. And make no mistake, this was a tough event – with the plain fact that only 63 of the 120 starters finished.'

Perce Simon Trial – 7 November 1965

1st	S.H. Miller (250 Bultaco)	16 marks lost
2nd	D.J. Adsett (250 Greeves)	30
3rd	G. Farley (200 Triumph)	32
4th	A. Dovey (250 Bultaco)	35
5th	P. Fletcher (500 Enfield)	40
6th	M. Whitlock (250 Enfield)	45

The French visit

A highlight of the 1965–66 trials season for Sammy was to come in France, where at the St Cucufa Trial, held in the Versailles Forest near Paris, Sammy not only won, but also had the satisfaction of besting his greatest adversary at that time – Don Smith – by five marks to eight.

St Cucufa Trial – 14 November 1965

1st	S.H. Miller (250 Bultaco)	5 marks lost
2nd	D.R. Smith (250 Greeves)	8
3rd	G. Blakeway (250 Bultaco)	13
4th	D. Thorpe (200 Triumph)	17
5th	A. Davis (250 Greeves)	17
6th	R. Bjorck (250 Husqvarna)	19

7th	R. Peplow (200 Triumph)	21
8th	K. Sedgley (250 Bultaco)	22
9th	S. Lundgren (250 Husqvarna)	22
10th	J.A. Sandiford (350 BSA)	23

Then, during the Severn Valley Trial which followed, Sammy beat Scott Ellis, the winner of that season's Victory Trial. The season was ended with another ACU Trials Star (this being Sammy's seventh star in seven years!). As with other awards, these were mounting up as the years rolled by.

Venables's view

MCN's trials scribe Ralph Venables was back in print on the Miller theme in the newspaper's 17 November 1965 issue.

Headed 'Sammy is Still Supreme', Ralph's piece is worth reproducing here as it reflects how attitudes were changing now that Sammy was established on the Bultaco.

'Great play has been made of the fact that Sammy Miller was runner-up in seven trials on the trot. "Is the Miller era over?" asked some. But the way I see it is, Sam's consistency was never more apparent. In those seven trials, he was second to six different people (Mick Andrews, Colin Edwards, Scott Ellis, Don Smith, Arthur Lampkin and Derek Adsett). In all seriousness, I would say that Sammy's superb ride in the Perce Simon was less impressive than was his achievement in occupying runner-up spot seven times in succession. And now that he has won the St Cucufa there can surely be no lingering doubts about Sam's supremacy.'

Runner-up Again

Sammy's bid to clinch his fourth British Expert's title at the end of November 1965 ended on the boulders of Bongham in the closing stages of the 70-mile (112.5km) course from Llandrindod Wells, Radnorshire. Until this point he was three marks up on the eventual winner, Scott Ellis (250 BSA), having taken the lead a few miles previously. As Peter Howdle wrote for *Motor Cycle News* in its 1 December issue: 'Scott Ellis crowned his first year as a BSA works rider by winning the British Experts Trial for the first time, in Wales on Saturday. After a titanic struggle, during which he twice lost the lead, Scott finally overcame Sammy Miller, beating the Bultaco man by two marks. Their scores, after one of the toughest events in the history of the Birmingham club's trade supported classic, were 64 and 66 marks lost.'

British Experts Trial – 27 November 1965

1st	S. Ellis (250 BSA)	64 marks lost
2nd	S.H. Miller (250 Bultaco)	66
3rd	G.R. Adsett (250 Greeves)	77
4th	D.R. Smith (250 Greeves)	78
5th	P.H. Gaunt (250 Enfield)	82
6th	A.J. Lampkin (250 BSA)	84

Going to Greeves?

The big front page story in *Motor Cycle News* dated 8 December 1965, with the headline 'Going to Greeves' with a picture of Sammy, read: 'There is a strong possibility that Sammy Miller, the world's top trials rider, may quit Bultaco to join the Greeves competition team. Tentative negotiations, associated with an agency for his new motorcycle business, are under serious consideration by both parties.'

Sammy was not available for comment, as he was in Spain visiting the Bultaco factory in Barcelona, with whom his existing agreement was soon due to expire.

Sammy Stays With Bultaco

Any confusion over Sammy's plans for 1966 was soon resolved by Bultaco's export manager, ex-racer Johnny Grace, the following week. He confirmed that Sammy would continue to ride for the Spanish factory, telling *Motor Cycling*: 'Sammy has made an arrangement to stay with us for another year. He has collected two new trials machines from the factory and our joint plans for the 1966 season have been completed.'

Before leaving for home, Sammy had given a demonstration ride in a trial organised by the *Pena Motorista* club of Barcelona.

And why wouldn't have the Miller-Bultaco partnership continued? Quite simply, since joining them a year earlier Bultaco had sold over 600 replicas of the 244cc Sherpa trials machine which the Ulsterman personally helped to develop. In that 12-month period, the British importers, Rickmans, had themselves sold 250 and another 100 were due to be delivered from Spain in January.

At this point it is important to point out that Sammy had already severed his link with the Rickman Brothers. Although they retained the Bultaco concession, he preferred to work independently on his own machines, with everything under his own control. To this end, and to open his own motorcycle business, he had begun trading at 85-

87 Christchurch Road, Ringwood, Hampshire. And it was here that he – and his customers – first benefited from his unrivalled experience in the sport. Additionally, he was often called upon to answer readers' questions from the varying motorcycle magazines. Typical was one regarding what he recommended riders wearing for trials. His reply was 'fireman's boots (or the Hawkin's slip-on type), Belstaff two-piece waxed suit, cloth cap, Octopus goggles and Kett's wrist-length gloves. Trousers are strapped to boots, not kept watertight by rubber bands.'

Machine of the Year Contest

At the end of 1965, *Motor Cycle News* published the results of its Machine of the Year competition. This showed just what an excellent job Sammy had done of promoting the Sherpa trials mount, as it was the first foreign bike in the poll, the only other being the 250cc Honda CB72 in ninth of the top 10 placed.

The results were as follows:

MCN Machine of the Year 1965

1st	650cc Triumph Bonneville
2nd	650cc BSA Lightning
3rd	440cc BSA Victor scrambler
4th	250cc Greeves Challenger scrambler
5th	250cc Bultaco Sherpa trials
6th	500cc Velocette Thruxton
6th	250cc Royal Enfield GT
8th	650cc Norton SS
9th	250cc Honda CB 72
10th	250cc Greeves Silverstone racer

'Millerised!'

'Millerised!' read the headline in *MCN* dated 22 December 1965. The report went on to say: 'Cool, calculating, craftsman Sammy Miller struck twice in the Southern Experts Trial at Ashford (Kent) on Sunday, and that was the end of the massed might of the opposition.' Even Don Smith, the previous year's winner, could not match the Miller tactics, finishing five marks adrift of Sammy. Seldom, since the Sunbeam club started the series back in 1931, had there been a tougher 'Southern'; only seven soloists were in the under-80-marks bracket at the end of a hard day's work.

Southern Experts Trial – 19 December 1965

1st	S.H. Miller (250 Bultaco)	46 marks lost
2nd	D.R. Smith (250 Greeves)	51
3rd	D.J. Adsett (250 Greeves)	56*
4th	A.L. Dovey (250 Bultaco)	56*
5th	G.J. Farley (200 Triumph)	58
6th	P.T. Stirland (250 Greeves)	76

*determined by special test

Sammy's Ulster Holiday

As had happened every year since 1954, Sammy spent Christmas with his parents at home in Ulster, and for the 11th year running he won the Rusk Trophy at the Conlig lead mines near Belfast. He was back in England for the New Year, when he had a runaway victory in the Sturminster Newton club's trial at Dorchester on the first day of 1966.

The first three months of the New Year were to witness victory after victory for 'Sam the Bultaco Man', as the press had now nicknamed our man.

A European Championship

During early 1966 both the ACU and the FIM, the sports governing bodies for Britain and internationally respectively, came under attack from both Sammy and his biggest rival in the trials world at that time, Don Smith, for their failure to organise an official European Trials Championship.

At the time Sammy commented: 'This country is supposed to be the most trials-minded in the world. But the ACU has given no leadership in pressing for an official Championship and has shown no interest in promoting a British round.'

Both Sammy and Don were pressing for a Championship based on five rounds – in West Germany, France, Belgium, Holland and Britain – with the rider's best four performances to count.

The Henri Groutars Trophy, initiated in 1962 as a team competition and changed two years later to an individual contest, had never advanced beyond the status of an unofficial European trials title with no recognition from the FIM.

Vic Brittain Trial

The first major trial of the new year resulted in an *MCN* headline: 'Sam Starts the New Year Right', continuing: 'Does Sammy Miller make New Year resolutions? If he does, then he should resolve to flatten the opposition as he did in Sunday's Vic Brittain Trial, first national of 1966.' This was because Sammy had led right from the very start of the 60-mile (96.5km) figure of eight course in the Shropshire hills south of Bridgnorth.

Vic Brittain Trial – 9 January 1966

1st	S.H. Miller (250 Bultaco)	36 marks lost
2nd	G. Farley (200 Triumph)	50
3rd	N.S. Eyre (250 Bultaco)	53
4th	S. Ellis (250 BSA)	57
5th	P. Gaunt (250 James)	60
6th	P. Fletcher (500 Enfield)	64

A Tribute Victory

When the national St David's Trial took place at Neath in South Wales on 12 February 1966, Sammy was a non-starter. Instead he was home in Ulster, where his father had died the previous day. And perhaps it was to be a fitting tribute that Sammy should turn out a few days later in his homeland to win the Hurst Cup for the 10th time in succession at the Clandeboyne Estate. Heavy overnight rain had turned most of the 16 sections into uninviting mud-pits, but Sammy, watched by his brother Freddy, a church minister in Canada, managed to find a key to the most tricky situations. Sammy's brother had been in Canada for 18 years and had never seen him in action.

Victory in the Victory

With what *MCN* described as: 'The fantastically low loss of only nine marks', Sammy eclipsed his rivals in the 1966 Victory Trial, held on Saturday 26 February. It was his third win (1959, 1963, 1966), the first win by a foreign machine and the first two-stroke 'Victory' since 1920. As *MCN's* Peter Howdle described: 'At his brilliant best on a rain-soaked Welsh course, Sammy Miller beat Greeves runner-up Don Smith by seven marks. The entry was dominated by two-strokes (92 out of 155 solos), but BSA third placeman Dave Rowland helped clinch a narrow four-stroke win in the manufacturers team contest.'

Victory Trial – 26 February 1966

1st	S.H. Miller (250 Bultaco)	9 marks lost
2nd	D.R. Smith (250 Greeves)	16
3rd	D. Rowland (250 BSA)	18
4th	M.J. Andrews (250 Bultaco)	19
5th	D. Jones (250 Sprite)	20
6th	P.T. Stirland (250 Greeves)	22

In the special colour 10th Anniversary Supplement given away free with *Motor Cycle News* dated 23 March 1966, Sammy Miller was referred to as 'Admiral in Chief of the Spanish Armada.'

The 252 Sherpa

By mid- April, when he won the national Mitchell Trial at Merthyr Tydfil, South Wales, Sammy was aboard his new 252cc Sherpa. A week later Sammy was taking part in a three-day British ISDT training session in mid-Wales. But instead of the problem-stricken unit BSA singles, he was aboard a 490cc Triumph twin.

Next came the Scottish Six Days, in early May. And just a year since Sammy had scored his first win in the event by a foreign machine, there were more Bultacos than any other make of machines. Out of 206 entries, there were 60 of the Spanish bikes, and, as *Motor Cycle News* commented: 'Sammy Miller has ensured a late number by entering the 350 class on a bored-out 252cc Bultaco.'

At the end of the first day, six riders retained clean sheets – Sammy, plus Mick Andrews (250 Bultaco), Stan Cordingley (250 Greeves), Paul England (200 Triumph) and Peter Fletcher (500 Royal Enfield).

But it was not to be Sammy's week. Young Syd Lampkin became the first man in history to win with a brother having already won the event.

After one of the closest battles for many years, and actually losing the lead on the fifth morning, Syd beat Sammy by four marks – final scores being 23 and 27 respectively. Mick Andrews was third, for the second year running.

Sammy in ISDT action during September 1966 with his 504cc Triumph twin. He was the highest British scorer in the special tests.

Scottish Six Days Trial – May 1966

1st	A.R.C. Lampkin (250 BSA)	23 marks lost
2nd	S.H. Miller (252 Bultaco)	27
3rd	M.J. Andrews (250 Bultaco)	31
4th	A.J. Lampkin (250 BSA)	40
5th	S. Ellis (250 BSA)	44
6th	W. Wilkinson (250 Greeves)	49

A week after the end of the Scottish, Sammy became the second rider to score a consecutive hat-trick of wins in the national Red Rose Trial. Riding his 250 Bultaco, he lost only 11 marks and finished 10 marks ahead of runner-up Bill Wilkinson (250 Greeves).

It was the Ulsterman's fifth win in the North Western Centre's big national, his previous successes having come in 1960, 1961, 1964 and 1965. First to win the event three years in succession was Johnny Brittain in 1957, 1958 and 1959.

At the end of May it was announced that the entire six-man British ISDT Trophy team would be mounted on Triumph-engined machines – the squad named, after tests the previous week, was: Johnny Giles (350 Triumph), Roy Sayer (350 Triumph), Roy Peplow (500 Triumph), Sammy Miller (500 Triumph), Ken Heanes (504 Triumph) and Arthur Lampkin (504 Triumph-engined BSA).

In mid-June Sammy, riding a 504 Triumph, won a gold medal in an ISDT training event – the Isny Three Day Trial – held in the Stuttgart area of West Germany.

Bultaco Modifications

In the early summer of 1966 Sammy travelled to the Bultaco factory once again. There he made a number of modifications to a machine that he intended riding in Poland's Tatra Trial in mid-July. While in Spain he also agreed alterations to the 1967 Sherpa model, which it was hoped would be available by the Earls Court Show in November. On the Tatra Trial machine the steering head angle had been changed to give more trail, and a longer swinging arm had been fitted to accommodate a 4.00 x 18 scrambles-type tyre (legal for the Tatra and ISDT). The sub-frame had been lengthened to provide more support for the rear mudguard and facilitate lifting. Accessories included a prop stand, chain oiler and lights.

However, after driving over 2,000 miles (3,218km) to take part in Poland's time and observation Tatra Three Day Trial, both Sammy (Bultaco) and Jim Sandiford (Greeves) retired with ignition failure. Both Britons began well, but Sammy's machine unfortunately stopped with condenser failure before the second section of the first day.

Sammy (in bowler hat) enjoying a rest period during the 1966 International Six Days staged in Sweden.

Another view of Sammy in ISDT action during September 1966.

Top Points Scorer in the ISDT

Sammy was the highest British scorer in the ISDT special tests when the event took place in Sweden in September 1966. He ended up scoring 643.76 points out of a possible 660. In an exclusive article published in *Motor Cycling* shortly after the end of the trial, and even though Great Britain finished runner-up behind the East Germans, Sammy was not impressed, saying: 'England might have won the World Cup this year, but 1966 was not the year that Lady Luck smiled on us in Sweden. For a change our Trophy machines were 100 per cent reliable, but, let's face it, they are now outdated compared to the products of MZ, Husqvarna, CZ and other continental manufacturers. One thing this year's event proved is that our factories will have to have a rethink before next year's. Our big bikes may, at last, be capable of finishing but they are not the machines for scoring high bonus points.' Sammy continued: 'To stand a good chance in Poland next year we will have to either enter different capacity classes or revamp our machines for more speed. It's most embarrassing on a speed test not to be able to out-ride an overbored 250 MZ.'

RAFMSA

After the ISDT, Sammy was involved – as the instructor – in the Royal Air Force Motor Sports Association (RAFMSA) four-day trials school at the Army Motor Transport School, Bordon, Hampshire. In addition to using their own machines, most of the pupils tried the sections on Sammy's Bultaco, a works Greeves and a Sprite, which were taken down by Chris Leighfield. Beside riding techniques, Sammy also gave advice on machine preparation. The school concluded on the final day with an RAF Championship Trial won by Jon Tye (brother of the former BSA works rider, David).

Back in the Winning Groove

In October 1966, after a disastrous ride in the West of England Trial the week before, Sammy stormed back into the winning groove when he won the Bristol club's national John Douglas Trial by a six-mark margin from Malcolm Davis. The well-known Gloucester scrambles star was using a Villiers-engined Cotton, having been unable to secure the use of a Bultaco.

Then, the following day, Sammy scored a John Douglas and Dick Farquharson national 'double' when, after his resounding Bristol victory, he was still in unbeatable form the following day at the Shaftesbury event.

After the 1966 ISDT Sammy was involved – as an instructor – with the RAFMSA (Royal Air Force Motor Sports Association) when it held a four-day trials school at the Army Motor Transport School, Bordon, Hampshire.

Sammy on his way to victory in the 32nd British Experts Trial on 26 November 1966. The *Motor Cycle News* headline simply read, 'Miller the Greatest'. Just study that concentration!

The following weekend it was 'Sammy Again!' (*MCN*). This was in response to another victory, this time the national Welsh Trophy Trial near Rhayader, which many competitors said was 'just like a little British Experts.'

These victories set in motion a string of successes throughout October and November, culminating with what *Motor Cycle* dated 1 December 1966 headlined: 'Wizardry in the Hills' in response to Sammy's winning performance in the British Experts Trial. The report began: 'Tossed into the torrents and mashed into the mud of mid-Wales last Saturday went the hopes of two dozen trials top-liners, imprinted with the tyre marks of Sammy Miller's 252cc Bultaco. This was Miller at his unstoppable best, fighting every inch of the way through the toughest hazards the Birmingham club could devise, to romp home triumphantly as the first four-time solo winner of British Experts' Trial laurels.' *Motor Cycle News* simply said: 'Miller the Greatest.'

Sammy's score was truly impressive – 22 marks dropped – less than half the total of the next man, Mick Andrews (Bultaco), and almost two-thirds less than third-place man Derek Adsett (Greeves). Sammy's score was a new record and he won by 28 marks, the biggest margin then in the history of the trial.

British Experts Trial – 26 November 1966

1st	S.H. Miller (252 Bultaco)	22 marks lost
2nd	M.G. Andrews (250 Bultaco)	50
3rd	D.J. Adsett (250 Greeves)	60
4th	D.R. Smith (250 Greeves)	61
5th	P.A. England (200 Triumph)	71
6th	J. Ashcroft (250 Greeves)	77

All in all 1966 had been, with the exception of his runner-up spot in the Scottish, a fantastic season for Sammy. And shortly after the 'Experts' he left for Spain to discuss prospects for a contract for 1967; although at that time he said he was considering a move back to the Midlands after receiving what he called 'an exceptionally good offer' from the Norton-Villiers concern.

Then 32, Sammy was at the height of his trials career, and as *MCN* said in its 7 December 1966 issue: 'The undisputed king of the trials game.' Interestingly, *MCN's* Peter Howdle went on to comment: 'Ask Sammy how long he can remain at the top and he'll remind you that Stanley Matthews played League football at 50, that Archie Moore and Sugar Ray Robinson won boxing titles in their mid-40s, that Hugh Viney won the British Experts at 41 and that Luigi Taveri is nearly 40 and still one of the fastest men in grand prix racing.'

A Three-Year Bultaco Contract

In late December came news that Sammy would not be riding a British machine in 1967 – after having approached him Norton-Villiers sent a telegram that they were 'unable' to offer him a contract. Sammy arrived at the Bultaco factory on 3 January and returned with a longer, three-year contract from the Spanish company. Bultaco export manager Johnny Grace said: 'We are delighted that Sammy had agreed to stay with us. The long-term contract was a mutual idea.'

In late December 1966 Sammy signed a longer, three-year Bultaco contract. He is seen here with one of the latest Pursang models.

Francisco Bulto

There can be few of the world's motorcycle marques which owe their origin to the events of another company's board meeting. None, perhaps, except Bultaco.

In May 1958 a meeting of directors was called at Montesa, then the largest of Spain's motorcycle factories. There had been heated disputes for some time over a single, central issue – to race or not to race – and this meeting was to prove the final straw.

The two key figures at the centre of the disagreement were the factory's founders, both of whom were not only directors but also major shareholders. Francisco Xavier Bulto and Pedro Permanyer were men whose partnership had seemed ideal when they had founded Montesa in 1945. Now they found themselves on opposite

Bultaco founder and owner Francisco Bulto (with coat and hat) chats to Barry Sheene and his father Frank at Brands Hatch, October 1969. The machine is a works three-fifty Bultaco.

sides of completely irreconcilable views. Permanyer, the majority shareholder, was backed by the other Montesa directors; in his opinion the factory should withdraw completely from racing for the same economic reasons that had influenced foreign competitors, including Norton, AJS, Gilera, FB Mondial and Moto Guzzi. To Bulto, however, racing involvement and reputation was all-important and without it he saw no future for Montesa.

The meeting proved a watershed for Bulto. Now aged 46, he quit Montesa, intending to devote his time and energy to other business interests; a textile plant and a piston manufacturing concern. But it was not to be. Learning of Bulto's departure, most of Montesa's competitions department followed suit and within a few days the 'old man' received an invitation to dinner with several of his former technical staff, mechanics and riders. There, Bulto's former employees pleaded with him to start a brand-new motorcycle company – one which could share their combined love for the sport.

Impressed as much by their enthusiasm as by their logic, Bulto agreed to set about the huge task of creating a completely new name within the Spanish industry at a time when so many others were floundering and when even mighty Montesa were struggling.

Despite their love of racing, all those at the meeting were only too aware that they would only survive if their machines were commercially viable – and that meant that they had to build series production roadsters.

And so in June 1958, one month after Francisco Bulto quit Montesa, the embryonic company moved to a farm owned by Bulto at San Adrian de Besos on the northern outskirts of Barcelona.

Conditions there were spartan in the extreme, especially for an engineering-based company. The offices were in the farm outbuildings, many of which were crumbling with age and disrepair. Engineering facilities were even more primitive; for example, the lathe and other machine tools were set up with only a roof to cover them so far as was essential for production purposes.

It took four months for the design team, headed by Francisco Bulto himself, to conclude its work and so turn the initial design sketches into metal. Himself a keen and active motorcyclist, Francisco Bulto often rode the prototypes to assist with the road test programme.

By February 1959, development work on the first design had been completed and a press day was planned to launch the new marque's first product. Only one detail was lacking – a suitable name for the farmyard company. Johnny Grace, works rider and engineer, was the man who supplied the answer by using a combination of 'Bulto' and 'Paco' (a Spanish nickname for Francisco) – hence Bultaco. The origins of the famous 'thumbs-up' symbol on the company's badge were equally fortuitous. Bulto himself conceived the logo after he witnessed British rider David Whitworth giving a thumbs up to his pit crew. Asking what this meant, he was told that it signified that all was well. From that moment on, it appeared on all Bultaco machinery.

As we know, Bultaco not only went on to build roadsters and racers, but were equally famous for their off-road machines, in trail, trials and motocross forms. And as the main text reveals it was the subject of this book, Sammy Miller, who was responsible for the huge success garnered by Bultaco in the trials world, where the Spanish company truly rewrote the history books. But, of course, it was very much a combination of two men's efforts – Sammy Miller plus Francisco Bulto.

Political change in Spain during the 1980s forced the closure of the factory.

1967

During 1967 Sammy seemed to simply carry on where he had left off the previous year – in other words scoring win after win. A few typical headlines read: 'Miller's Victory Again'; 'The golden boy of trials takes fourth win'; 'Miller conquers Welsh "impossible"'; 'Sammy's non-stop Bemrose'; 'Miller's 35 magic' and so it went on.

Ralph Venables was even confident enough to predict: 'Miller's a cert for the Scottish.' And Ralph was spot on. Even at the beginning Sammy was clearly dominant, with *Motor Cycle News* saying: 'Sammy Miller (Bultaco) established a commanding lead on Monday's first stage of the Scottish Six Days Trial. He completed the toughest and coldest first day for years with a loss of only five marks – 10 fewer than his nearest rival, Gordon Farley (Triumph).'

He went on to win the Scottish – leading from start to finish. As *Motor Cycling* said: 'The Bultaco ace romped from day to day with an ever-increasing lead, beating runner-up Dave Rowland (175 BSA) by a staggering 16 marks.'

But the last word on his 1967 Scottish victory must go to the editorial written by Harry Louis, editor of *Motor Cycle*: headed 'Miller The Magnificent', it went on to say: 'No title could have been more fitting than the one used last week to head our first report on the Scottish. Sammy Miller certainly meant business right from the start. He was way ahead of the rest all week. He rode with the knife-edge brilliance that recalled the years of the other great post-war winners, Hugh Viney and Gordon Jackson. With wins in 1962, 1964, 1965 and this year, Miller has four in the bag. That puts him level with Viney and Jackson but he has yet to match Viney's hat-trick, 1947 to 1949.'

A 5-speed Pursang

Sammy built a five-speed Bultaco Pursang 250 for the Welsh Three Day Trial, which started on Wednesday 24 May 1967. He was the only member

of the previous year's ISDT British Trophy team to compete in the Welsh training event. Modifications to the Pursang scramblers included: a quickly detachable rear wheel, enclosed final drive chain, wide ratio gears, Metralla 7in (180mm) front brake, alloy front mudguard (in place of a glass-fibre one), folding footrests with return springs and a new exhaust system.

However, after finishing third and fourth in the Welsh Three Days, both Sammy and Mick Andrews (Ossa) were referred to as the 'black sheep' of Britain's ISDT candidates. Both riders had been offered AJS singles as members of the Trophy team, but neither relished the prospect of riding them in Poland. And Sammy soon made it abundantly clear that as the top British scorer in Sweden he was simply not prepared to drop to Vase team status on his Spanish Bultaco.

The 'Super Sherpa'

What *Motor Cycle News* referred to as 'Sammy's Super Sherpa' arrived in Britain during the summer of 1967. *MCN* commented: 'If anyone other than Sammy Miller used a five-speed trials bike they would be laughed out of every section in the country from Weavers Down to Loch Eild Path.' This machine was to be the forerunner of the 1968 Sherpa – a working prototype in fact.

When Peter Fraser tested the newcomer for *Motor Cycle* in its 23 August 1967 edition, he said: 'Bultaco's five-speeder is no gimmick machine.' And 'Gimmick or gain? If that is your query about the extra cog of the first five-speed trials machine on the scene, the 244cc two-stroke Bultaco Sherpa, forget the gimmick part. The bike is for Sammy Miller and he has no time for gimmicks. The more functional his machinery the better. It was no surprise to me, then, to find when I galloped the latest Sherpa last week, that the extra ratio brings a big bonus. In fact, it is not just an extra ratio added to the existing four.'

New Ratios

In fact, Sammy, after a lengthy session in Spain during April that year, had evolved a new set of ratios which he considered 'will meet just about any situation.'

The new five-speed ratios (with the four ratios in brackets for comparison) were as follows: bottom 34.1 (29.5); second 26.5 (24); third 20 (15); fourth 13 (9); top 9.

Fraser found that 'bottom gear is so low, in fact, that there should never be any need to use the clutch, even on dry, nagery going.' And that 'second will serve in all but the tightest sections,' while 'third meets those occasions which most riders must have feared, when a section needs more speed than second will provide, yet third is too high. Between section cross-country going is where fourth features, with fifth there for roadwork.'

But while the additional cog might well have been the main talking point, it was by no means the only new feature.

A Revised Engine

For a start the engine had been brought up-to-date, being a detuned version of the Pursang scrambler/Madador trail models. Instantly noticeable was the cylinder-head finning which was now longitudinal, not radial as on the original four-speed Sherpa, while fin area on the barrel had been increased and the spigoted barrel and head were attached to the crankcase by thru-bolts instead of flange studs as previously.

An additional ball-race, making three in all, had been adopted for the drive-side crankshaft. Power output had been raised by 2bhp to 20.

A cam gear selector replaced the fork change and it was housed inside the main gearbox case, not in the characteristic bulge at the rear of the unit. This change had made it necessary to relocate the speedometer drive to the offside (right) of the rear wheel hub.

First ride over a car (a Volkswagen Beetle), on his 252 Bultaco, c.1967.

Except for altered mounting to suit the new power unit, the frame was unchanged from the 1967 model.

More Changes

Still in glass-fibre, the fuel tank had been restyled to reduce its overall height and this helped lower the centre of gravity. Another modification (used by Sammy himself for the past year) was the fitment of a 5in (130mm) diameter front brake (normally found on the Lobito roadster). This not only saved weight, but was also still up to the job of providing adequate stopping power.

The Miller Mods

Additionally, Sammy had fitted some of his own Bultaco SM accessories. These included Girling rear shocks; light-alloy front mudguard stays (standard stays were steel); a handlebar 3in (75mm) higher than standard; the rear chain oiler, which had proved a big seller since he introduced it; and his own silencer (claimed to provide an additional two horsepower).

The Debut Ride

Sammy made his debut ride on the five-speeder in the national Clayton Trophy at the very end of August 1967. Even though he finished runner-up with 20 marks to Malcolm Rathmell (200 Triumph), who lost 18 marks, he still described it as 'a deplorable start.'

The following weekend in early September, Sammy not only won the Manx Two Day Trial, but also registered what was his sixth win in the event.

At the end of the first day Rathmell had looked like repeating his previous week's victory, dropping 11 marks to Sammy's 12, but while the Bultaco man excelled himself on Sunday's course, adding just one more mark, Rathmell failed to maintain his form and finished third, behind the eventual runner-up Gordon Farley (200 Triumph), who dropped 18.

Manx Two Day Trial – September 1967

1st	S.H. Miller (250 Bultaco)	13 marks lost
2nd	G.J. Farley (200 triumph)	18
3rd	M.C. Rathmell (200 Triumph)	23
4th	L.C. Telling (250 Bultaco)	27
5th	D. Jones (250 Greeves)	31
6th	C. Leighfield (250 Sprite)	32

A Record Breaking Scott

On 28 October 1967 the Ulster trials ace made history in the Scott Trial on the Yorkshire moors when he rode his Spanish machine into best overall position on time and observation to give a foreign factory victory for the first time in this classic event, the 41st in the series, which had begun way back in 1914 on the very eve of World War One.

Chris Carter, reporting for *Motor Cycle*, described the action: 'While youngsters, such as Yorkshireman Bill Wilkinson (250 Greeves), who set standard time with a lap of the 65-mile [105km] course in 4hr 30m 25s and finished third overall, Malcolm Rathmell (200 Triumph) and Chris

Sammy lifting the front wheel of the latest 252 Bultaco at the Lightweight Motorcycle Club's Trial, autumn 1967.

Hemmingway (250 Sprite), rushed along in an effort to make up for marks lost on the observed sections, Miller gave a superb feet-up display to lose only 39 marks on the 60-odd sections. This was 57 fewer than the next best, Jim Sandiford (254 Greeves), who finished second overall.'

Scott Trial – 28 October 1967

1st	S.H. Miller (252 Bultaco)	47 marks lost
2nd	J.A. Sandiford (254 Greeves)	99
3rd	W. Wilkinson (250 Greeves)	101
4th	G.J. Farley (200 Triumph)	108
5th	M.C. Rathmell (200 Triumph)	109
6th	C. Hemmingway (250 Sprite)	118

European Champion

Next Sammy became the first official European trials champion when he took first place in the Clamart Trial near Paris. Having already won all four Championship events held up to then, he could not be beaten. The first round – the Swiss Alpine Trial – had taken place on Sunday 1 October 1967. As in the other rounds, this was a truly European affair with riders not only from Great Britain, but also Germany, France, Belgium and Switzerland, filling the first 10 places.

The fifth and final round of the European series was held in England near Ashford, through Kentish woodland. Organised by the local Ashford club, it was chosen not only as a suitable trials ground, but perhaps most

During 1967–68 Sammy became European (read World) Trials Champion. Here he is seen during the Lamborelle Trial in Belgium on 4 February 1968 with his Bultaco Sherpa, which now sported a five-speed gearbox.

importantly for its closeness to the Channel ports. And here Sammy Miller made it a five-in-a-row sweep of victories; truly he was 'Trials Master of Europe'. Runner-up in the European series, and at Ashford, was the German works Zündapp rider, Gustav Franke.

Final result of the European Championship 1967–68
(five meetings in Switzerland, West Germany, Belgium, France and Great Britain)

1st	S.H. Miller (Bultaco)	40 points gained	24 to count	(8,8,8,8,8)
2nd	G. Franke (Zündapp)	20	15	(3,6,3,2,6)
3rd	W. Wilkinson (Greeves)	15	14	(6,4,1,4,0)
4th	G.J. Farley (Greeves)	14	14	(0,0,4,6,4)
5th	P.H. Gaunt (Suzuki)	8	8	(0,2,6,0,0)
6th	D.R. Smith (Montesa)	7	7	(4,0,0,0,3)
7th	C. Rayner (Montesa)	6		
8th	J. Atzinger (Zündapp)	3		
9th	D.J. Adsett (Greeves)	2		
	R. Bjorsk (Bultaco)			
11th	J. Crossett (Bultaco)			
	J.A. Sandiford (Bultaco)			
	H. Wolfgruber (Zündapp)			

British Champion a Ninth Time

Sammy once again won the British Trials champion series – just how dominant he was that year can be seen in the results: 93 points, with Gordon

Farley second on 53 and third-place man Scott Ellis with 30. Sammy had been British Champion for the past nine years!

Breaking the Scottish Record

The *Motor Cycle* headline said it all: 'Fifth Victory By 20-Mark Margin. Sammy Rides into Scottish Six Days History.' *Motor Cycle News* were able to report: 'Sammy Miller (252 Bultaco) broke yet another record when he became the first man to win the Scottish Six Days Trial five times.'

Taking the lead on the third day, he forged ahead to finish with a loss of 17 marks – 20 fewer than runner-up Gordon Farley (250 Greeves).

The trial, although tough, enjoyed above-average weather. Of the 213 starters, 120 finished; 43 won special first-class awards, 64 first-class and 13 second-class.

A Bultaco team, spearheaded by Sammy, made history by becoming the first foreign make to win the manufacturers class (Sammy, plus Jim Sandiford and Alan Dovey).

Scottish Six Days Trial – May 1968

1st	S.H. Miller (252 Bultaco)	17 marks lost
2nd	G.J. Farley (250 Greeves)	37
3rd	M.J. Andrews (250 Ossa)	39
4th	R. Edwards (250 Cotton)	60
5th	H.M. Lampkin (250 BSA)	60
6th	D.R. Smith (250 Montesa)	62

The North American Tour

For six weeks, starting on 20 July 1968, Sammy toured North America in a coast-to-coast trials epic, during which he not only competed in six trials events, but also instructed at the same number of trials schools.

The tour had come as a result of discussions between Sammy, Francisco Bulto and the American trials clubs. These events took place in New England, Detroit, St Louis, Seattle, San Francisco and Southern California, and they proved a big hit.

Cycle World, who promoted one of Sammy's schools, said: 'English-style trials are gaining recognition in the US as a sport involving little danger and minimal financial outlay, but requiring great skill and determination.' When he returned to Britain Sammy said: 'I have never seen such enthusiasm before. There is no question about trials catching on over there. They regard it as the sport of the future.'

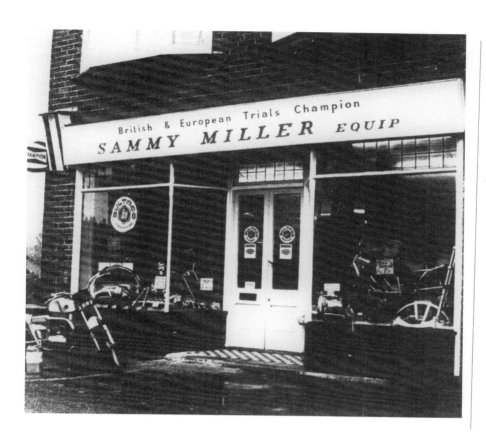

The Sammy Miller 'Equip' shop at Highcliffe was now able to use the 'British and European Champion' title.

During the late 1960s, with business at his Highcliffe shop expanding, Sammy built this trials special using a Bultaco chassis and 246cc Villiers 36A engine. But power unit supply problems were to bring this interesting project to a close after only a few machines had been completed.

Sammy being interviewed by Charles Deane at Highcliffe in 1969.

The Miller Frame

Weighing only 19lb (8.6kg), compared with 26lb (11.8kg) of the stock Bultaco frame, and available from Sammy's newly relocated shop (at 466 Lymington Road, Highcliffe, Hampshire), the Miller business – now known as Sammy Miller Equip – moved into a new phase.

The new frame, manufactured in T45 tubing by Colin Whites and suitable for both four- and five-speed Bultaco Sherpa engines, featured a strengthened swinging arm pivot, while the swinging arm had been lengthened by ¾in (19mm) to improve handling. It had a bright nickel finish and accepted all standard Bultaco components.

Also in September 1968 it was revealed that Sammy (together with Gordon Farley) faced a dilemma as a dates clash between national trials counting towards the ACU Trial Championship and the winter's European Trials Championship existed. And Sammy chose the domestic championship over the European.

A Fifth Scott Win

At the end of October 1968 Sammy notched up his fifth Scott Trial win, thus equalling fellow Ulsterman Billy Nicholson's record. As *MCN* said in its 30 October issue: 'Third fastest, and by far the most skilful over the obstacles of a 70-mile [112.6km] course, Miller (Bultaco) was eight minutes slower than Gordon Farley (Greeves).'

Scott Trial – October 1968

1st	S.H. Miller (250 Bultaco)	48 marks lost
2nd	C.J. Hemmingway (125 Sprite)	79
3rd	G.J. Farley (250 Greeves)	93
4th	P.H. Gaunt (125 Gaunt-Suzuki)	94
5th	R. Edwards (125 Sprite)	95
6th	D. Jones (125 Gaunt-Suzuki)	98

By now Sammy had become so dominant in the trials world that a *Motor Cycle* reader, P. Crossley of Birmingham, even wrote a letter in which he said: 'It seems to me that the most straightforward way of injecting a degree of life into the trials game is to outlaw Sammy Miller!' In the same week a headline read: 'It's Sammy yet again', this in response to his 'cakewalk' victory in the British Experts' Trial at Llandrindod Wells, in mid-Wales. This latest win put the Bultaco rider two victories ahead of any other solo rider in the history of the event. And when one considers that he had to ride with sore ribs following an earlier collision with a barrier at the Perce Simon Trial, his victory was truly demoralising for the opposition.

A 10th Successive British Title

By mid-November 1968 Sammy had secured his 10th successive British Trials Championship title, with three rounds still to go. With 72 points from seven wins and two second-placed in 10 rounds, his nearest challenger Gordon Farley had to accept defeat.

And thereafter the successes just kept coming. In late 1968 he added the Greeves agency to his other dealerships at his Highcliffe shop.

Scott Trial

Up to the end of the 1970s Sammy Miller had gained a record-breaking number of victories (seven up to the end of 1977) in what many reckon to be the most difficult of all trials, the legendary Scott.

Up to that time Sammy had competed 14 times, chalking up five second places to those record-breaking seven victories. His only failure was caused by a broken wheel spindle after he had drilled too much titanium out of his famous five-hundred Ariel, GOV 132, and his non-finish in his debut appearance in 1955.

The Ariel carried Sammy to three Scott wins, and when he switched to Bultaco he won four years in succession.

Winner of the first post-World War Two Scott was fellow Ulsterman Bill Nicholson, who won the event five times between 1946 and 1951. Sammy's reign spanned the period from 1958 to the end of the 1970s.

Named after Alfred Angus Scott, the pioneer two-stroke motorcycle manufacturer, it was in January 1914 that three Scott workers produced the spark of an idea which was to become as famous as the motorcycles bearing the same name.

And so the Scott Trial was born, with the first such event being run on Sunday 15 March 1914, with Alfred Angus Scott as the judge and Eric Myers, a Bradford motorcycle dealer, as chief observer.

A mere 14 competitors took part, with Frank Philipp being eventually declared the winner, both his machine and himself carrying an assortment of battle scars over a 90-mile course which included the notorious climb of Park Rash, near Kettleworth, and getting his bike (a Scott of course!) waterlogged crossing the River Nidd, at Angram, a place which has since vanished beneath a reservoir.

After the war, the trial was thrown open to anyone and although Scott employees featured prominently, the 1919 event was won by Geoff Hill, piloting a DR (Despatch Rider) 550cc Triumph.

The 84-mile (135km) course eliminated over half the 74 entries. A significant innovation was the adoption of arrowed cards for route marking, with blue for left turns, red for tight turns and black for straight on.

During the 1920s the trial evolved, and by the end of the decade saw the arrival of out-and-out competition machines, when, as one commentator remarked: 'Organisers were faced with the problem of striking a fair balance between a test of machine reliability and the stamina of the rider.'

The 1930 Scott included a match race between six-man teams representing the North and South. The 1930 event also marked the end of an era. The organisation had become a task of such mammoth proportions that the venue was switched to a more compact course around Blubberhouses. It was cheerio to Airedale, Coverdale, Nidderdale and Wharfdale.

Although the 1932 event was a two-lap affair totalling only 50 miles (80.5km), Allan Jefferies made history by becoming the first rider to achieve the double of setting standard time and being best on observation. Ironically, he was also the last man to win the Scott on a Scott machine.

When Jefferies next won, in 1937, he was mounted on a Triumph, a marque for which he was to become a legend in his own right.

The organisation changed hands again in 1938, when the Middlesbrough and Stockton club ran a two-lap, 20-mile course in the Cleveland Hills of East Yorkshire. Then after World War Two the Darlington and District Motor Club took up the reins, their first event coming in 1949. This paved the way for future competitions, with the Scott starting from the outskirts of Richmond, with a national entry often in excess of 200 competitors negotiating a 70-mile (113km) course among the disused lead mines of Swaledale.

Compared to a conventional one-day trial, the Scott is an unusual event with contenders often setting a fast pace. As falling off or getting stuck in a bog wastes valuable time, the niceties of normal one-day trials riding tend to give way to a far more cut-and-thrust riding style. For example, when Martin Lampkin won the Scott for the first time in 1977, he overtook all but two of the 130-odd riders who had set off before him.

Perhaps the best way of describing the aura of the event is to say that many of the riders who, year after year, were heard to comment: 'Never again!', for some obscure reason always came back; that's the magic of the Scott Trial for you.

Sammy's World Tour

As 1969 dawned it was announced that Sammy was to tour the world in a bid to boost interest in one-day trials. The Bultaco rider had recently visited the Barcelona factory, where plans for the trip were finalised.

Upon his return to Britain, Sammy had said: 'The idea is to run a series of two-day trials training schools in eastern and western USA, Canada, New Zealand and western Australia. I will ride a standard production Sherpa provided at each of the venues.'

A sequel to the previous year's successful visit to America, which was to lead to Americans and Canadians competing in the 1969 Scottish Six Days, Sammy's trip was to be sponsored by the Bultaco factory and the US magazine *Cycle World*. The first stage of his trip would be at Pittsburgh, USA, on 5 and 6 July, but he would be home in time to compete in the Manx Two Day Trial (30 and 31 August).

Before leaving on the 'tour' Sammy experienced the disappointment of not winning the 1969 Scottish Six Days and thus not equalling Hugh Viney's triple in three years.

The tour, which took in several countries, was of real benefit, not only to Bultaco, but also to the whole trials game.

After finishing runner-up to Paul England (200 Triumph) in the Manx Two days, Sammy went on another winning run to score several successes, including the Red Rose, John Douglas and Mitchell trials.

A Record-Breaking Sixth Scott

As *Motor Cycle* said in its 29 October 1969 issue: 'Miracle-Man Sammy Miller capped his incredible career with yet another record on Saturday. Scoring his third-successive Scott Trial victory on his 252cc Bultaco, he became the first man ever to notch six wins in the rugged Yorkshire classic.' It continued: 'It completed a shattering succession of firsts in Britain's four top trials series – disregarding the scores of lesser events in which the 33-year-old Ulster ace has set targets which are unlikely ever to be approached, let alone surpassed.'

Besides having pipped that other post-war Irish trials star, Billy Nicholson, with his latest Scott win, Sammy now topped the list in the Scottish Six Days Trial and the British Experts' Trial, with five victories in each. And barely a fortnight before, he had scooped his 11th successive crown in the British Solo Trials Championship!

But as the *Motor Cycle* concluded: 'To anyone else, that might look like more than enough laurels to rest on. To the indomitable, indefatigable Mr Miller it is probably just another springboard to yet more fantastic feats.' And do you know, they were dead right!

Scott Trial – 25 October 1969

1st	S.H. Miller (252 Bultaco)	68 marks lost
2nd	G.J. Farley (250 Greeves)	92
	D. Thorpe (250 Ossa)	
4th	M.C. Rathmell (250 Greeves)	106
5th	C.J. Hemmingway (120 Alta Suzuki)	111
6th	G.S. Butterfield (250 Montesa)	114

Comerfords Take Over the Bultaco Concession

1969 had also seen new British importers for Bultaco, the Thames Ditton, Surrey, concern of Comerfords. Director John Comerford had concluded the deal after the Rickman Brothers had asked to be relieved of the agency.

Comerford's sales manager Don Howlett commented: 'Our main aim will be to promote the sales of scrambles machines,' while the existing stock of some 50 Sherpa trials machines held by the Rickmans were to be distributed by Comerford's in co-operation with the Rickmans. The latter firm would also continue to handle the spares business before officially handing over stocks in mid-November 1969.

It took Sammy only six of the eight rounds counting towards the 1969–70 title series to regain the European Trials Championship crown.

Regaining the European Title

It took Sammy only six of the eight rounds counting towards the 1969–70 title series to regain the European Championship title he had held in the 1967–68 season. After being overshadowed by Montesa the previous year, when Don Smith took his undefended title, Sammy had stormed back to regain his crown.

Interestingly, when interviewed by Peter Howdle in the 13 May 1970 issue of *Motor Cycle News*, Sammy revealed that winning the European Championship meant little more than a gold medal from the FIM and the honour of being supreme individual in a difficult and exacting job. He went on to say: 'I get a straight salary from Bultaco. They pay all my expenses. I would get the same if I stayed in England. I have never received a penny in starting or prize money, but Castrol pay me a good bonus.' He

Sammy in vivid action with his 252 Bultaco at the Hurst Cup Trial, 14 February 1970.

continued: 'Trials have always been a poor man's sport. It would be a nice gesture for the FIM to accord world status to the Championship, specially in view of the tremendous interest in the USA, but I deplore the apathy of British manufacturers towards trials.'

Finally, once more Sammy reminded readers: 'As soon as Japanese factories like Yamaha, Kawasaki and Suzuki cotton on to the potential of this comparatively cheap sport, trials will come into their own.' This, of course, once more showed that as far as the sport of trials was concerned, Sammy Miller had his finger on the pulse.

Sherpa Updates for 1970

Bultaco had updated the production Sherpa for the 1970 season. It now had bigger flywheels and lower compression ratio (from 10 to 9:1), which the factory claimed improved bottom-end power. The clutch had been modified, while its operating arm was now situated on top of the gearbox casing instead of underneath it as formerly. Restyled light-alloy primary chaincase and magneto covers were fitted and a new-shape gear pedal tucked in closely to the unit. Rear suspension top mountings had been repositioned and a front mudguard mud-flap was now a standard fitment.

Back to British Action

Having spent much of the summer touring abroad, Sammy returned to Britain in the latter half of 1970. What was probably his major success came when he won his fourth successive Scott Trial at the end of October – and his seventh victory in the legendary Yorkshire event. His victory was by a single mark, from Gordon Farley.

Scott Trial – 24 October 1970

1st	S.H. Miller (250 Bultaco)	62 marks lost
2nd	G.J. Farley (250 Montesa)	63
3rd	M. Lampkin (250 Bultaco)	91
4th	A.R. Lampkin (250 Bultaco)	96
5th	B. Hutchinson (150 Sprite)	98
6th	G. Chandler (250 Bultaco)	104

A week later Sammy virtually lost the chance of retaining the British Championship title he had held for the past 11 years when he retired with ignition trouble at the Perce Simon Trial in Hampshire's New Forest. The winner, Gordon Farley, who had tied with Sammy before the ninth Championship round, was now clearly in the lead with 101 points to Miller's 86. And with only one more round to go, only a miracle could now save Sammy from surrendering the crown he had held for so long.

The *Motor Cycle News* headline said it all: 'Sammy Miller out in a Blaze of Glory.' The report went on to say: 'Sammy Miller lost his British Championship in a blaze of glory when he won a fantastic war of nerves at Sunday's Knut Trial, near Bath, Somerset. Gordon Farley took the title with a lowly seventh place, "I didn't enjoy myself one little bit" the new champion confessed after a nerve-wracking battle in the 10th and final round of the 1970 season. Superbly confident after 11 years at the top, 36-year-old Miller shattered his successor by winning the event for the third year running and the eighth time in 12 years.'

Knut Trial – 5 December 1970

1st	S.H. Miller (250 Bultaco)	21 marks lost
2nd	R. Edwards (250 Montesa)	24
3rd	I. Haydon (250 Montesa)	31
4th	L. Telling (250 Montesa)	33
5th	P. Dunkley (250 Bultaco)	37
6th	C. Leighfield (125 Sprite)	39

Scottish Six Days

In 1977 *On Two Wheels* called it 'the ultimate Test,' and if this is true then Sammy Miller has certainly left his mark on the event, which is, of course, the world-famous Scottish Six Days Trial. From the end of World War Two to the end of the 1970s – in other words what we now call the 'Classic Era' – five men dominated the event: Hugh Viney, Gordon Jackson, Mick Andrews, Martin Lampkin and Sammy Miller.

The Scottish began in 1911, when a trio of Edinburgh clubs amalgamated to form the Edinburgh and District Motor Club, the body which has organised the Scottish Six Days Trial ever since.

Until 1933 the event was open to solos, sidecars and light-cars; however, as motorcycle development evolved so more difficult sections were incorporated, which were to prove impassable for four-wheel vehicles and so from that year the class was abandoned. Eventually, sidecars were to experience precisely the same problems and they were axed by the beginning of the 1960s.

In 1938, the organisers decided to start the Trial in Edinburgh and to finish in the same city, but otherwise the base would be at Fort William, a town on the very edge of Loch Linnhe, and in the shadow of Scotland's highest mountain, Ben Nevis.

Fort William was an excellent choice, located as it was in spectacular countryside, and from 1977 onwards the Edinburgh Club decided to locate the entire event there, rather than start and return to Edinburgh.

And in fact, May had become universally known as the 'Scottish month' in the trials world.

During the immediate post-war period the AJS marque was the dominant force in the event, with Hugh Viney winning in 1947, 1948, 1950 and 1951; while the same rider was runner-up in 1953. Then Gordon Jackson took over winning in 1956, 1958, 1960 and 1961. Jackson was also runner-up in 1953, 1959 and 1962. All these successes were gained on 348cc AJS single-cylinder ohv machinery.

Sammy Miller's first visit to the Scottish came in 1954, when he rode his home-built SHS (Sammy Hamilton Special) to an amazing fourth spot – what a debut! This and Sammy's other results in the event are detailed in the main text, but suffice to say these were simply outstanding.

After scoring a final victory on his famous Ariel GOV 132 in 1964, Sammy shocked the trials world by riding a Spanish Bultaco in the 1965 Trial. Four-strokes had previously dominated the Scottish since its inception. Although two-strokes had often been used, they had never seriously challenged, but six days later Sammy had changed all that. He rode his 244cc Sherpa model to record two notable firsts – a two-stroke victory, and the first for a non-British manufacturer.

Even when first the European and later the World Trial Championship was introduced, many still viewed the Scottish as *the* trials event.

In 1976, Martin Lampkin completed a unique family hat-trick when he won the Scottish. His brothers Alan and Arthur had each won the event some years earlier.

> As the years went on the Scottish Six Days Trial became ever more a truly international gathering, and apart from the many European countries being represented, by the late 1970s entries were coming from as far afield as America, Canada, Japan and Australia.
>
> So what makes it so appealing? As one journalist described the Scottish during the 1970s: 'The terrain is certainly demanding and the Highland weather fickle, warm sunshine one moment, heavy rain and even snow the next. Those changes of conditions are a feature of the trial, but they have never proved to be a deterrent to a determined trials rider.' The piece continued: 'Completion of the event brings satisfaction to even the lowest-placed rider, for he is sure to covet the little bronze medal he will receive as a souvenir of his participation in the event.'
>
> As for the victor, well not only will he receive immediate stardom in the trials world, but perhaps more important and long-lasting will be his inclusion in a list which contains many of the greatest names in the sport.

End of an Era

The front page of *Motor Cycle News* carried the main headline in two very simple words: 'Miller Quits'. It went on to say: 'Sammy Miller, the greatest trials rider of all time, has decided to retire'. Sammy told *MCN*: 'I will be 38 next birthday and it is becoming a bit of an effort'. This came after he had returned from the Bultaco factory the previous week. Sammy continued: 'I am retiring from national and international trials but I shall continue to compete in open-to-centre trials.'

The winner of nearly 500 trials since he quit big-time road racing in 1957 (although he still rode for the CZ and Ducati factories for part of 1958), Sammy told *MCN* that: 'I made up my mind at the 1969 Scottish Six Days. I knew then that I was not riding as well as I should be, but a lack of serious opposition persuaded me to continue for another year.'

Of his previous week's visit to the Spanish factory, Sammy had this to say: 'Mr Bulto was taken aback. He wants me to remain contracted to Bultaco. I will continue to help with development of the Sherpa.' He revealed: 'I shall visit the USA again in June and July. We hope to assist Bultaco riders as much as possible and reach an agreement for the future management of the Bultaco team.'

Sammy also said he would now be concentrating on improving the range of accessories at his Highcliffe business and that he would remain on the Belstaff (clothing) payroll as a consultant. He had already begun the process of collecting and restoring old motorcycles – which eventually was of course to lead to the creation of Sammy's now world-famous museum.

If anyone had expected Sammy to be taking it easy on the trials riding front, however, they would have been sorely mistaken. As a typical extract from *Motor Cycle* dated 3 February 1971 proves: 'Riding to his sixth consecutive win in five weekends, Sammy Miller (252 Bultaco) showed that, despite retirement from the big-time, he had lost none of his edge.'

He had also taken over management of the official British Bultaco team from importers Comerfords. In the future, Malcolm Rathmell, Paul Dunkley and Geoff Chandler formed a Sammy Miller Bultaco UK team, Sammy saying: 'We have trade support from Castrol, Belstaff, Dunlop, Champion and Renold.'

May 1971. Sammy with his official Bultaco UK team. He was in the process of taking over the management from importers Comerfords. Riders shown, left to right: Martin Lampkin, Syd Lampkin, Jim Sandiford, Geoff Chandler, Malcolm Ruthmell and Paul Dunkley.

A 325 Sherpa

Sammy was largely responsible for the next development in the Sherpa story, a 325cc version. And he had the first prototype, which he would ride in British (non-Championship) events, with the idea of Martin Lampkin, Yorkshire's Pinhard Prize winner (awarded annually for the top under-21 motorcycle achievement) riding it in the following year's European Championship.

However, Oriol Bulto said there were no immediate plans for production. The additional 81cc had been achieved by increasing the bore size from 72 to 83mm; the stroke remaining unchanged.

ISDT Return

In September 1971 Sammy, riding a Comerfords-entered 244cc Bultaco Matador, contested the ISDT (run that year in the Isle of Man) after a five-year lay-off. He was one of the 22 British riders to win a gold medal.

Channel Islands

In November 1971 Sammy added the Jersey Two Day Trial to his list of successes, when he paid his first visit to the Channel Islands.

As *Motor Cycle News* reported: 'The ex-trials king lost 15 marks on Saturday and 13 on Sunday. It was a devastating performance which beat Jersey's Archie du Feu by the enormous margin of 60 marks. Totals were: 28–88.

Sammy had flown over by charter plane from Southampton's Eastleigh airport, with a party of 27 riders and 11 friends.

Jersey Two Day Trial – November 1971

1st	S.H. Miller (250 Bultaco)	28 marks lost
2nd	A. du Feu (250 Bultaco)	88
3rd	M. Diggle (175 Greeves)	96
4th	D. Jeremiah (250 Bultaco)	100
5th	M. Raplay (250 Montesa)	102
6th	J. Luckett (170 Cotton)	109

325 Sherpa Debut

As the 23 February 1972 issue of *Motor Cycle* said: 'Sammy Miller roared the 325cc Bultaco to a great British debut on Sunday, when he beat Chris Watts (250 Bultaco) by eight marks to take the Bristol MCC's regional restricted Don Mountstevens Trial at West Harptree, Somerset.'

Don Mountstevens Trial – 22 February 1972

1st	S.H. Miller (325 Bultaco)	12 marks lost
2nd	C.J. Watts (250 Bultaco)	20
3rd	R. Shepherd (250 Montesa)	25
4th	M.C. Rathmell (250 Bultaco)	26
5th	B. Shuttleworth (250 Bultaco)	28
6th	L.C. Telling (250 Montesa)	29

Sammy displaying his skills on the 325 Bultaco to a throng of spectators in March 1972.

Just to prove that this was no fluke victory, Sammy and the 325 followed it up a week later with a fine six-mark victory at the Sudbury club's national East Anglian Trial. The Miller Bultaco trio of Sammy, plus Tony Davis and scrambles star Dave Bickers, won the team prize.

East Anglian Trial – 1 March 1972

1st	S.H. Miller (325 Bultaco)	11 marks lost
2nd	A.J. Davis (250 Bultaco)	17
3rd	D.J. Adsett (250 Ossa)	19
4th	A. Collier (250 Hubbard Bultaco)	30
5th	K. Rowbotham (250 Bultaco)	30
6th	D.G. Bickers (250 Bultaco)	31

The Old Magic

On 27 August 1972 Sammy grabbed the headlines when he returned to the big-time trials arena on his 325 Bultaco and turned on 'a display that he alone could perform' (*MCN*) to win the Wood Green DMC's 37th annual Clayton Trophy Trial with the loss of a single mark.

For the seventh year in succession the trial was run over one lap of six sections near Brecon, Mid-Wales, and for once the club was blessed with excellent weather conditions for the 170 riders.

Clayton Trophy Trial – 27 August 1972

1st	S.H. Miller (325 Bultaco)	1 mark lost
2nd	R. Shepherd (250 Montesa)	3
3rd	G. Galloway (250 Montesa)	10
4th	E. Legg (250 Montesa)	11
5th	D.J. Adsett (250 Ossa)	12
6th	I. Haydon (250 Montesa)	14

In fact, by the end of 1972 Sammy had competed in 40 trials, winning 26 of them and scoring six seconds; these included several nationals, notably the Manx Two Day.

1973 – A Year of Change

With the arrival of 1973 came a year of change for our man. For example, the front page story of *Motor Cycle News* dated 9 May was headlined: 'Miller-Honda?' going on to say: 'Honda want Sammy Miller to quit Bultaco and develop their trials machine of the future. But Miller, the greatest trials rider of all time, is under contract to Bultaco until 1974. Last week, he flew to Spain to discuss plans for the future. His Bultaco contract is the same as when he was at the height of his riding career in 1965. On Monday, 40-year-old Miller was not prepared to comment, but he did not deny the possibility of joining Honda. Will Miller switch to Honda? Now that Gordon Farley has signed for Suzuki, Mick Andrews for Yamaha and Richard Sunter, Mark Kemp and Jack Galloway for Kawasaki, Miller could land the biggest plum in the trials game.'

The truth was that Sammy was ready to quit Bultaco, but as he said at the time: 'I'm all ready to go but my contract with Bultaco has over a year to run' (he had signed a five-year agreement just four years previously). To be fair, the Bulto family and Sammy had always had a close and friendly relationship, and Juan Soler Bulto told *Motor Cycle*: 'We understand why Sammy wants to go, he has had a good offer, but this is a business matter and it will probably take us two weeks to reach a decision.'

Actually, the whole process concerning Honda was to take much longer than anyone at the time could have imagined.

March 1972. Sammy's new showrooms in Gore Road, New Milton, under construction, adjacent to Stem Lane Industrial Estate.

The Gore Road premises following their official opening by Lord Montague on 14 June 1973.

A Business Move

Opened by Lord Montague on 14 June 1973, the new showroom of Sammy Miller Equipment marked the move of the organisation specialising in competition motorcycles and equipment from a modest shop in Lymington Road, Highcliffe, to a new and specially-built and designed complex in Gore Road, New Milton, adjacent to Stem Lane Industrial Estate.

Work had begun on the new site in August the previous year. The staff of the new premises numbered seven, including general manager Chris Lees and chief engineer Bob Stanley.

Lord Montague accepted from Sammy, as a memento of the occasion, a 1949 998cc Vincent-HRD Rapide for his motor museum at Beaulieu, where it would join Sammy's famous Ariel HT5 trial bike GOV 132. A display board in the new showroom proudly boasted Sammy's 159 outright and 500cc wins, all on the machine he developed.

The new premises occupied an area of 4,000 sq ft and the single-storey building was divided into three approximately equal areas: showroom and office, stores and workshop.

At the time Sammy Miller Equipment were distributors for Bultaco, Ossa and Montesa motorcycles and spares, and also manufactured and distributed a wide range of Sammy Miller Products – including accessories, tools and spare parts – marketed in transparent bags carrying the Miller name.

At around the same time Sammy had restored a Brough Superior SS100 (registration VX 3333) for Charles Stanley (then 89 years old). Charles Stanley, who manufactured the Stanley motorcycle in Aylesbury, Bucks, from 1901 to 1909, was by now long since retired and living near Sammy in Bournemouth. His grandson, Bob Stanley of New Milton, had earlier joined the Miller organisation working as an apprentice at Sammy Miller Equipment. As I write this book in the summer of 2009, Bob is still with Sammy (his longest-serving employee), and he is now his right-hand man in the restoration of both museum exhibits and customers' machines.

Still Waiting

At the end of 1973 Sammy was still riding his 325 Bultaco and Ralph Venables had this to say, with a headline which read: 'Still waiting for that invasion' (the invasion meaning the Japanese!). Ralph forecast: 'Next year should see the war between Spain and Japan develop into a titanic struggle.' This was even though Honda's offer to Sammy to help the Japanese giant with the development of a trials machine was only open until 1 December 1973. And Bultaco had not finally agreed to terminate his contract. There is absolutely no doubt that Bultaco were reluctant to let Sammy go. Later,

Riding a Whitehawk (powered by a 175cc BSA Bantam engine) at RAFMSA trials training school, Hayling Island, near Portsmouth, in 1972.

director of Comerford's, the British importers, Don Howlett said: 'We are sorry to end the tie-up but Sammy wanted to go. We thank him for all the help he has given the factory in the past.' The Bultaco contract, which was valid until August 1974, had proved a stumbling block in Honda's attempt to gain Sammy's services.

When Sammy was finally 'released' he said: 'I now have an awful feeling that, because of the international economic crisis [the OPEC oil price issue], Honda may drop the project.'

The Phoney War

Something akin to the Phoney War during the winter of 1939–40 now took place. In *Motor Cycle News*' 'Feet Up' column, Peter Howdle had this to say: 'Sammy Miller never allows grass to grow under his feet. He has broken his Bultaco contract but that doesn't mean he'll go to Honda. And that is going to start a lot of speculation.' As for Sammy himself, he told Peter Howdle: 'If the Honda job falls through, I shall not be out on a limb. I have another good proposition, nearer to home, to speculate.'

And as Howdle went on to say: 'He hints at an alternative but gives no further clues. But my bet is that the booming Italian motorcycle industry could be receptive to Miller's specialised skill. It must be a sore point among Italian manufacturers that feet-up trials are growing in popularity on their doorsteps but that all the top Italian riders have Spanish machines.'

As for Honda, there was what is best described as a 'wall of silence'. When approached by the British press, Maurice Rolls, general affairs manager of Honda UK, commented: 'There was a suggestion that Miller might help Honda on a trials project, but because he was not free to leave Bultaco the whole thing was washed up. We have now informed Tokyo that he is available but we are only acting as post office in the matter.'

So as 1973 became 1974 would it be Honda or Italy? As for Sammy, all he could say was: 'Bultaco have cancelled my trip to the USA next month, when I would have competed in the first round of the FIM's World Trials Championship.'

A Decision is Finally Reached

Finally, at the beginning of April 1974, Sammy put his signature to a two-year contract with Honda. His brief from the Japanese company – the last of the big four to sign a British rider – was to produce a trials machine and run a team of riders in top-class events.

A new and exciting chapter in the Sammy Miller story was about to begin.

Chapter 6
Honda

After months of waiting caused by the indecision of Bultaco after Sammy's request to be released from his contract with the Spanish firm, following an approach by Honda he finally signed a two-year contract in London with the Japanese giant during early April 1974. After he had finally completed the Honda deal, Sammy commented: 'It will be nice to break new ground; it's a new challenge.'

As recorded in the previous chapter, it had taken virtually a whole year for the matter to be finally resolved. To begin with, in spring 1973 Sammy had flown to Spain to meet Bultaco management to request that they cancel his contract (which was not due to expire until mid-1974); however, it was to be many months before, finally, Bultaco agreed, although this was *after* Honda's 1 December 1973 deadline had expired. So, effectively, Sammy was left in no-man's land.

In reality he had quit Bultaco in the hope of a Honda contract. Although Honda were the last of the 'Big Four' Japanese manufacturers to enter the trials scene, Sammy had forecast a Japanese trials invasion long before a Yamaha, Suzuki or Kawasaki bog-wheel appeared on a trials course.

Things Move Quickly

Once he had signed on the dotted line for Honda things moved quickly. The Japanese company was keen not only for Sammy to develop a trials bike, but also to promote the brand name around the world in this new area (for Honda) of motorcycle sport.

The company also had other plans for Sammy, including setting up a permanent trials course in Japan.

The Japanese Visit

As Jeff Clew was to recall in his 1976 book: 'After everything had been signed and sealed in London, arrangements were made for Sammy to visit Japan and shortly afterwards he found himself flying to Tokyo over the North Pole route, via Alaska and Anchorage. It was quite an experience to look down on the desolate, frozen wastes and to see Eskimos at the stop-off points.' Sammy flew out from Heathrow on Tuesday 16 April 1974.

Sammy's initial test riding during his visit to Japan in April 1974 was with either the TL125 or XL250 (one of the latter is shown here).

But it was Japan itself which really captured Sammy's attention. On arrival, he was given the red carpet treatment, including a small entourage of Honda personnel – who followed him everywhere from the moment he touched down on Japanese soil. And at the same time he was given a detailed timetable for his six days' stay, which was carried through 'to the letter and with great punctuality.' Sammy says: 'If I was to be awakened at 7.30am, they would patiently wait outside my door, eyes on watches, then at the precise moment it was 7.30, they would hammer on the door to make sure I woke up on schedule!'

The Honda Research and Development complex was some 15 miles (24km) outside Tokyo, in what Sammy described as an 'outlying suburb.' On his arrival, Sammy discovered the Union Jack flying alongside the Japanese flag, with a horde of photographers lined up to record this historic occasion. There followed a tour of the facilities, and he noted: 'The one thing that struck me most was the sheer dedication of the entire staff. Everywhere it was a case of test and re-test, check and re-check. Not that this was a put-up impression either; it was a permanent feature of how Honda operated.'

As Sammy described: 'The R&D workshops were some one and a half miles from the main site, this requiring transportation of the bikes in closed vans. There was a high level of security everywhere, and unless you had the correct badge for a designated area, there was absolutely no chance of entry, whoever you were.' He continued: 'They had constructed trials sections at the rear of the workshops, where large quantities of rock and earth had been dumped to create a selection of hazards.'

One definite weakness with this plan that was immediately obvious to Sammy was that if any work needed to be done to a machine during these tests it had to be transported by van to the workshops, 'even if a change of carburettor jet was needed. Imagine climbing into a van with the bike every time a modification or change was required, then waiting in the reception area in trials riding gear for the return journey!'

The Machinery

The initial test riding was carried out with either the TL125 or the XL250. The former, known in Japan as the 'Bials', had been launched at the 1972 Tokyo Show and had been Honda's first attempt to build a pukka feet-up trials iron. This employed the 121.9cc (54 x 49.5mm) two-valve sohc engine from the existing SL125 trail bike.

However, it was the XL250 on which Sammy was to concentrate his attention. To begin with, he focussed on the engine, even though, in his opinion, the existing unit was 'too long and too wide.' Low-end torque was his main requirement, but without loss of top-end power. Once the engine had been sorted out, his efforts could be directed to the chassis.

As the author knows from personal experience, having owned and extensively ridden a 1974 XL250 in the period, although an excellent

Honda's first trials effort was the TL125 'Bials', which had been launched at the 1972 Tokyo Show.

machine, it was certainly no trials mount; it was, in fact, a machine designed for the Stateside green-lane/trail market. And there is a lot of difference between trail and trial.

As Sammy says: 'It was no easy task to get the engine right for the purpose needed. I had meeting after meeting with the R&D team which had been placed at my disposal – until it dawned on me that they were placing too much faith on computers to the extent that they were in danger of being completely misled. The computer can only analyse data that is fed into it, assuming it is programmed correctly.' Sammy knew, however, as the result of over 20 years' practical experience in the field, that a totally different approach would have to be adopted. But rather than upset his hosts, Sammy 'played it cool' and concentrated his efforts on slimming down the engine assembly and reducing excess weight.

'There were far too many variables in danger of receiving attention at one and the same time, so that it was becoming virtually impossible to establish a definite line upon which progress could be evaluated.' Sammy cited carburation as an example, going on to say: 'It was terrible on the test machine and no amount of juggling would give the machine the clean pick-up that is essential to trials riding.' While 'clutching at straws', the R&D personnel started examining the exhaust system, adding 'yet another variable.' Finally, as Sammy himself admitted, he blew his top. As Jeff Clew says: 'This had the desired effect, even if he couldn't speak the language [which is probably just as well].' From then on, the Japanese accepted that Sammy knew something about development, without having to retreat to the computer.

Sammy also realised that it was very important to keep on the 'right side of the development team, even though I sometimes knew they were running in the wrong direction.' Of course, it would have been all too easy to play the 'Mr Big' and to have alienated the Japanese. Instead, Sammy took the trouble to learn a few words of Japanese, so that he was able to offer the 'basic courtesy of saying yes, no and thank you in their native language.'

Back Home
Although the engine assembly was beginning to improve, carburation glitches continued, so it was finally agreed that this should be left to Sammy, on his return to Britain, to sort out in his New Milton workshop. This was to result in a new type of carburettor, providing 'clean' carburation throughout the rev range.

The Honda frame and cycle parts were also in need of a major rethink, for in Sammy's opinion, the 'Hi-Boy' frame which he had designed for the

Bultaco trials machine was 'infinitely superior.' Quite simply, there was only one remedy: a new frame closely resembling the Hi-Boy was designed and built at New Milton, especially for the Miller-modified XL250 engine assembly. Weighing-in at 22lb (10kg), this featured a smart chrome-plated finish and was equipped with the existing Honda leading axle front forks, but using an upper yoke of Sammy's own creation. The Honda brake hub assemblies were also utilised, apart from the fitment of alloy wheel rims as a means of further reducing the weight. A special mention should be made here of suspension units. Sammy used Girling-made dampers, but his speciality was the springs. He had a tame spring winder who could produce springs of any desired poundage. And this is an example of where his great experience came into real use: Sammy knew instinctively what poundage was required to produce the optimum handling qualities.

Although Sammy won in most cases, the Honda computer did score one important 'victory'. The Honda development team had created no fewer than three separate silencers in the exhaust system; the middle one being of what is best described as a triangular shape akin to a small competition-style toolbox. Looking to save weight, Sammy chose to discard the one described – only to discover that it performed a vital function in terms of low output

The Honda frame and cycle parts were simply not up to the job at hand. So, upon his return to New Milton, Sammy created a purpose-built machine using a new frame resembling his existing Hi-Boy and a Miller-modified XL250 engine.

Sammy's own prototype TL250, still in its development stage.

combined to maximum engine efficiency. Sammy was to recall: 'The computer was correct on this occasion and the definitive TL250 exhaust system had three silencers.'

The Publicity Machine

Honda informed Sammy that they were sending a team of cameramen from Japan to film his bid for his 800th trials win on Sunday 21 July 1974.

Back from Japan, Sammy said: 'I hope to receive a new 250 engine this week, it still has a magnesium crankcase [not an ideal situation on a trials bike] but the motor is shorter, without an oil sump.'

Due to the urgency of Honda development work, Sammy had declined an invitation to compete in an international trial in America, at Colorado Springs, later that year. But he said he had decided to make his national debut on the Honda at the Manx Two Day Trial, an event which he had previously won on eight occasions.

The Miller Team

April 1973 had also seen the launch of Sammy's new Miller trials team of Brian Higgins (250 Bultaco), Geoff Parkin (325 Bultaco), Bob Stanley (325 Bultaco) and Mick Whitlock (250 Ossa), the quartet having made their debut over the Easter weekend.

Pending arrival of Honda engines, as Sammy was now contracted to the Japanese factory, the teamsters would be campaigning the three Bultacos and the solitary Ossa. The quartet had new-styled bikes featuring Sammy's Hi-Boy-type frame, conical hubs, alloy fittings and Girling rear units. Entered as Millers, the bikes were to act as a stand-in for the new generation of trial bikes which 'were planned for the future'.

Central to this future plan was a prototype cantilever frame designed by Sammy and constructed by specialist Mick Whitlock. Sammy had tried a cantilever a year previously and sent a prototype to the Bultaco factory. But they decided not to develop it, so Sammy decided to press ahead himself.

The frame was constructed in Reynolds 531 tubing with a 2in (51mm) diameter main down tube holding a damping unit adapted from part of a Formula One car. Roy Topp, of Ken Tyrell's F1 team, had helped with advice over the unit and adaptation for a 200lb (91kg) rate spring. Adjustment of damping in both directions was through a threaded top piece on the top of the damper and an adjusting nut at the bottom. A 1½in (38mm) movement at the unit became 3½in (89mm) at the rear wheel.

The 800th Victory

Good as his word, Sammy rode the prototype 250 Honda to a 16-mark victory over Geoff Chandler (250 Ossa) in the Somerton club's times and observation trial at Sparkford, Somerset, on Sunday 21 July. The event, which was staged in two parts, counted towards the Southern Counties Timed Trials Championship.

Somerton Trial – 21 July 1974

1st	S.H. Miller (250 Honda)	40 marks lost
2nd	G.C. Chandler (250 Ossa)	56
3rd	M. Strang (200 Cotton)	80
4th	B.J. Higgins (250 Miller)	87

Earlier, Sammy had made his debut on the Honda at the Heath Cup Trial on 2 June (when he finished runner-up), and then he had scored his 799th victory and had his first Honda victory at the Shaftesbury Cup Trial a week later on 9 June.

Master Class

In the 17 August 1974 issue of *Motor Cycle*, Sammy put the newspaper's editor, Peter Kelly, through trials school. While Sammy was riding his 250 TL Honda (registered SAM 1N), the pupils – including Peter – rode the XL125 'Bials' model. The following is an extract from what was a comprehensive, two-page article, and came after Peter readily admitted getting things wrong:

'Have another go, and don't worry too much about the rocks once you've got your first turn right,' said Sammy, 'Just treat them as if they're a tarmac road and use the throttle a fraction more.' Peter Kelly takes up the story: 'It took half a dozen attempts before I got it right, then I cleaned it three times in a row. When you follow to the letter the instructions of the greatest trials rider of all time you are unlikely to put a foot wrong, after all.' Peter continued: 'Sammy poured hot, sweet coffee from a vacuum flask and offered me a jam scone. We sat on a concrete pillar surrounded by the sandy shingle of acres of wasteland near the Esso refinery at Fawley, Hants, where Sammy guides the weekly trials school run by the Esso Fawley club. He had taken the full afternoon off work to teach me the basics of trials riding before going on with the evening school.'

Sammy told Peter: 'The beauty of this sport is that you don't need to be a born natural.' He continued: 'It can be learned, and if you're willing to think about it seriously enough you can master it in the end.'

This feature showed two definite sides of Sammy which the reader or even other trials competitors may not have noticed. Firstly, an unbridled enthusiasm to teach others the sport of trials riding (which he continued to do for many, many years) and that in trials, practice could really make perfect.

Victorious Honda

Besides the results already recorded, Sammy scored nine other wins on the Honda in 1974, these beginning with the Minety Vale Time Trial on 8 September and finishing with the North Berkshire Trial on 28 December. Besides winning the Jersey Two-Days over the weekend of 8 and 9 November, Sammy also finished runner-up in the national Perce Simon Trial on 3 November and third in the Southern Experts' on 15 December. But, without doubt, above all there was one event, victory in the Somerton Time Trial, which represented Sammy's 800th trial win. As one commentator said: 'A truly remarkable record in any sport, let alone motorcycling.'

Latest Developments

Sammy's first victory on the second version of his prototype Honda, a machine which bristled with magnesium and titanium and weighed 198lb (90kg), came in the Sturminster Newton Trial at Gillingham, Dorset, on Sunday 6 October 1974, when he won with the loss of only eight marks, compared to G. Guy on 37 and D.J. Rickman on 41.

The machine, with a displacement of 248.6cc (74 x 57.8mm), had an alloy cylinder barrel with chromed bore, four-valves-per-cylinder and the oil reservoir for the engine in the five-speed gearbox. Carburation was taken care of by a 24mm Keihin instrument. It featured transistorised ignition with an automatic advance of 20 degrees at 1,000rpm. Maximum torque came in at 4,500rpm, but the motor, which weighed 73lb (33kg), peaked at 9,000. Compression ratio was 8.8:1, with overall gearbox ratios of: 42.0, 32.2, 22.3, 14.5 and 10.5 to 1. Minus the previous oil sump, the engine was an inch (26mm) shorter and stood 16½in (419mm).

Geoff Parkin, a member of Sammy's Honda team (the riders having now switched to Japanese machines – riding bored out TL125's – with 61mm instead of 56mm making 150cc), won the re-equipped team's first national award at the West of England Trial on Saturday 5 October, winning the 200cc class cup.

The *Motor Cycle* dated 28 September carried a photograph of the latest development TL250 (officially coded RTL – R standing for Research). Entitled: 'The shape of trials to come?' it went on to say: 'Featuring a brand-new engine with numerous internal modifications, Sammy Miller's latest development Honda trials bike looks much closer to production reality than its predecessor. More ground clearance is achieved by employing a Hi-Boy frame, and by containing oil in the gearbox. The flat-sided fuel tank, in unit with the side cowling gives a smoother appearance. Note also the louvred chain cover. Of course, this one keeps the famous (already!) number plate SAM 1N. Sammy's first ride was in Sunday's International Bognor Regis trial at Goodwood.'

Interestingly, the event was based on the car race circuit at Goodwood, Sussex, with the one-lap course including nine different areas, where the hazards varied from tricky turns among trees to ultra-steep ascents on solid chalk or loose sand.

Sammy finished joint third with R. Whitebury (325 Bultaco) with a loss of 16 marks, compared to winner Geoff Chandler (250 Ossa) with 12 and runner-up Dave Thorpe (also Ossa mounted) on 13. There were nearly two dozen overseas competitors, and easily the most successful were the German riders Felix Krahnstover (250 Montesa) and Helmut Stanik (160 Montesa). The former took the award for best foreigner, his loss of 29 marks putting him ninth among the 45 starters in the international category.

Goodwood Trial – 19 September 1974

1st	G. Chandler (250 Ossa)	12 marks lost
2nd	D. Thorpe (250 Ossa)	13
3rd	S.H. Miller (250 Honda)	16
	R. Whitebury (325 Bultaco)	16
5th	M. Kemp (250 Montesa)	17
6th	C. Harris (250 Yamaha)	21

In truth, much of 1974 since signing for Honda had been spent on development of the two-fifty Honda trials project. Then, in 1975, just when everyone expected Honda to emerge with a winning machine, just the reverse happened as the whole project stagnated. Questions were asked: was it Sammy, Honda or a combination of both? This was a most frustrating time for Mr Miller. He was, of course, a very 'hands on' individual and a perfectionist at that – Honda's endless committee approach, to say nothing of its love affair with computers, was, in the author's view, a major stumbling block to progress at this time.

Another American Tour
During the spring of 1975, Sammy made another of his American tours, this time to Charlottesville, North Carolina. The occasion was Honda's Expo 75, staged at the Charlottesville Speedway. Attracting large crowds of spectators, Sammy managed to perform four or five trials demonstrations each day, on the specially laid out trials course. He also performed a number of stunts, including riding over old cars.

Development of the experimental 250 trials model continued, both in Japan and at Sammy's New Milton workshop. And by 1975, the development programme had led to Honda being able to market a production TL250.

This was *not* an exact replica of Sammy's working development model. And although a well-built, reliable machine, it was considerably heavier. As for Sammy's own business, he began selling a 150cc version of the TL125, which featured, among other changes from the stock Japanese market TL125, a version of the Miller Hi-Boy frame. As we know, examples of the Miller Hi-Boy TL150 were also campaigned by Miller team riders.

One of the very first tests of the production TL250 was published in the April 1975 issue of the American magazine *Cycle World*. Without the weight-saving advantages of Sammy's development model, the production TL250 was both heavier and a shade less powerful than the two-stroke opposition; essentially it was not an experts' machine, capable of winning major events.

Sammy aboard a standard TL250 production model riding over an ancient Studebaker car at the American Honda 'Expo 75' Festival, Charlottesville, North Carolina, on 20 April 1975.

Over the years Sammy cut down several cars to create a purpose-built vehicle for transporting his trials mounts. This one is from a Mazda 1800 car, circa mid-1970s.

Sammy with his own Honda trials machine, SAM 1N. This cherished number now adorns his (current) car.

A Larger Displacement Engine

The works development TL250 was followed up by the TL301 with bore and stroke dimensions of 74 x 71mm – which in Honda terms could almost be described as 'long-stroke'. The new engine was also lighter in weight than the 250 unit, helped by reverting to a two-valve head.

There were many other changes too, including smaller and lighter flywheels, revised ratios for the five-speed transmission, and a new exhaust system. It seemed, at last, that the Honda R&D department had begun, after much persuasion by Sammy, to adopt the compactness and lightweight design priorities which had played such an important role in hoisting the Spanish machines to the very top of the trials tree.

Other engines followed, in which the stroke was finally reduced to only 58mm, with a bore size of 82mm. The object of this was to get rid of the top-end heavy bogey which had dogged Honda's trials effort. At the time of its arrival in April 1976, commentators said the latest engine was not much higher than a two-stroke.

Sidecar Use

Another engine, for sidecar use, had its displacement increased to around the 400cc mark. The Miller Honda team for the 1976 season comprised Nick Jefferies and Brian Higgins, plus sidecar man Bob Colein; in 1975 Sammy used Peter Gaunt and Geoff Parken. In both seasons Sammy also did a considerable amount of riding himself.

Also, by supporting Paul Dunkley, Arthur Dovey and schoolboy Rob Downey (on the TL150 machines), Sammy was certainly doing his bit to spread the Honda gospel further.

In 1976 the TL301 not only finished third in the British Experts' and fourth in the Irish Experts', but Brian Higgins also won the national Lyn Traders Trial. Besides the British effort, Bob Nicholson's six-man team in America, led by US number one Marland Whaley, showed that at last Honda was beginning to make progress in the feet-up game.

That same year Sammy was quoted as saying of the TL301: 'If I could shed 10 years of my age, I'd have no fear of any opposition now. The bike is the best tool for the game.' He continued: 'We have the weight down to just under 200lb [90.75kg], we have reduced the height and width of the motor, and improved the carburation and torque. It will pull anywhere in third gear.'

A New Rider

Towards the end of 1976 several riders, including Yrjo Vesterinen, came into the frame as possible Honda signings. But at the end of the year it was confirmed that the new man for the 1977 season would be Rob Shepherd, who would join Nick Jefferies; Bob Colein and sidecar passenger George Matthews completed the line up. But prior to the start of the new season Colein/Matthews retired and were replaced by Adrian Clarke and passenger Mike Bailey.

Rob Shepherd celebrated the arrival of 1977 by chalking up his first win on the Honda, but he then went home to nurse a sprained muscle in his back. He had pulled the muscle as he strained to heave his Honda out of a boggy patch at the end of a muddy section in the Eboracum Trial. This success was soon followed by a hat-trick of national wins, including the Cotswold Cup. All these had been achieved with the 'old' Mark 1 long-stroke TL301; which Shepherd said he preferred to the later short-stroke.

Next, in early 1977, came the latest variant of the '301', which featured compression releasers, and was known as the Mark 3.

This picture, taken in the spring of 1976, shows Sammy talking to his rider Nick Jefferies; the machine is one of the works 305cc trials models which Sammy had largely been responsible for.

The Sammy Miller Honda Trials Team for the 1976 Scottish Six Days. Left to right: Arthur Povey (90), Geoff Parkin (98), Nick Jefferies (163), Brian Higgins (177) and the Japanese rider Hiroshi Kondo (169). Nick Jefferies put up the best performance, finishing ninth overall.

Marland Whaley

Towards the end of July 1977 came news that the American Marland Whaley was to contest the final four rounds of the World Trials Championship for Honda. The young Stateside star had only ridden in his home round thus far, when he finished runner-up to Frenchman Charles Coutard. But now he would be campaigning a TL301 prepared by Sammy in Sweden, Finland, Czechoslovakia and Switzerland. Whaley, who was the clear leader of the American trials series, arrived on 17 August from America with Honda US manager, Bob Nickelson.

Also flying in to bring the Honda squad up to strength was Japanese rider Hiroshi Kondo. Diminutive Kondo was to have ridden a 301 like the American, but at only 5ft (1.5m) he found the model too big, and so opted to ride a new 200cc machine.

The Honda team for the final four rounds comprised Rob Shepherd, who was then leading the British Championship, Whaley, Kondo and reserve Nick Jefferies.

British Champion

Rob Shepherd had taken the British Championship series by storm at his first attempt. Wins in the Cotswold, Cleveland, Wye Valley and Alan Trophy trials had left him needing just two points from the Hoad Trophy Trial to clinch the top spot. This was achieved when he beat Martin Lampkin by six points to finish equal on points at the top of the table. Shepherd won the Championship because he had the most wins, a result that provided a nail-biting finish to the Championships.

A Bitter Pill

Then came the bombshell. As the 12 November 1977 *Motor Cycle News* headline read: 'Honda pull-out chokes Miller.' The article went on to say: 'Today, Sammy Miller's world is shattered. Honda's decision to pull out of trials competition has left the Ulster-born, all-time king of trials choked beyond words. With it has gone Miller's dream of a four-stroke trials revival inspired by machines he helped to design.'

So just why had the Japanese factory decided to pull out, which was puzzling to say the least? Obviously, Honda's involvement in trials over a three-year period had cost them an amount of money; however, this would have been peanuts when compared with their outlay in road racing and motocross.

The pull-out occurred at precisely the time when everything was slotting into place. With Rob Shepherd they at last had a rider who was getting consistently good results at both national and international level. This had generated excellent publicity, not only in Britain, but also on mainland Europe, culminating in Shepherd's World Championship win in Finland, home of world champion Yrjo Vasterinen.

Yes, Shepherd had preferred the older Honda engine. But as one commentator put it: 'So what? Maybe Honda were ahead of their time.'

As *Motor Cycle* pointed out: 'Not even the most ardent four-stroke enthusiasts can know the hollow feeling Miller has now, after shaping his life around the Honda project. With Japan insisting the machines must go back, there is not even the chance that Miller can carry on with outside sponsorship. Much of the magic of the national trials scene, inspired by the cracking sounds of these ohc motors will disappear and trials will be the poorer.'

Interviewed by *Trials & Motocross News* Sammy said: 'I wouldn't like to tell you how I feel. After three years we've won – and lost.' He continued: 'The bike has been developed to a state of perfection, but now I'm picking myself up off the floor after a right to the jaw.'

During his time with Honda, Sammy organised trials schools in Japan. Here he demonstrates techniques to members of his class. All of his pupils rode Hondas.

At the same time Sammy declined to comment on the release date for the long-rumoured production version of Honda's works trials bike. But, said *T&MX News*: 'They [Honda] are widely believed to be ready for marketing – and its sales potential is certainly enormous.'

Sammy told *Motor Cycle News*: 'Honda's decision is not good for the sport. We've proved a four-stroke is the best bike. Everybody was waiting for a production version. I was informed three weeks ago that Honda would not renew any contracts for next year. We'll just have to pick ourselves off the floor and go on from here.' And that was precisely what Sammy did. Not one to mope around, he simply put the Honda business behind him and got on with the rest of his life.

The Esso Fawley Southern Centre Trial at Hythe saw the last appearance of the Miller-Honda works effort. And it was Sammy, of course, who took the opportunity to bow out with a victory. His performance was described as 'masterly' (*T&MX News*).

And so as one venture ended, so another was to begin. First it had been Great Britain, then Spain and finally Japan. What country would it be this time?

Chapter 7

SWM, Hiro, Armstrong, Aprilia et al

Sammy's break with Honda meant that he was a free agent as regards commitments to a manufacturer for the first time since he had quit riding the legendary Ariel GOV 132 in late 1964 to join the Spanish Bultaco concern.

Cliff Holden

Even before the end of 1977, however, stories began to surface of negotiations between the SWM importer Cliff Holden of Ossa UK with a view to Sammy managing an SWM team in the UK the following year.

Cliff Holden, the existing British Ossa importer, had only just concluded an agreement with the SWM factory at the Milan Show in late November 1977 to handle their trials, motocross and enduro models for the British market. And the question arose, in the press at least, of whether SWM could afford a top-line British rider and Sammy Miller as development manager. This was because the Italian factory had already signed the leading French trials star, Charles Coutard (also concluded at the Milan Show) to campaign an SWM in the 1978 world championship series.

SWM Manager and Development Rider

In mid-January 1978 news finally broke that Sammy had joined SWM. *Motor Cycle* reported: 'After several weeks of talks with the new British SWM importer Cliff Holden, the former Ariel, Bultaco and Honda ambassador agreed last week to take up the reins as UK development rider and team manager.'

Sammy's own contract was given 'an enthusiastic approval' (*Motor Cycle*) by the Italian factory.

In mid-January 1978 news broke that Sammy had joined SWM. The following month on 5 February he scored SWM's first major success when he won the Southern Centre Team Trial.

Announcing the news, SWM importer Cliff Holden said: 'After trying for so long to get Sam, I'm really pleased he has agreed to join us. There isn't a better development man anywhere, and with him on our side, we should start to create a few headaches for other people.'

After agreeing terms, Sammy commented: 'My job will be basically the same as it was with Honda – except that with SWM I will be dealing with a family concern, instead of getting decisions made through committees and computers. I met the SWM people at the Milan Show, and they immediately wanted to show me their machine rooms and workshops. I've been very impressed by such a friendly attitude.'

SWM said it planned to produce some 3,000 trials bikes in 1978, with the first 50 machines being delivered to Cliff Holden's Ferndown, Dorset, premises in time for the London Racing & Sporting Show later in January.

Motor Cycle's Dave Wilcock's feature in his 'Trials Spot' column said: 'The day of the £1,000 trials bike has arrived. With an expected selling price of £1,068, the Milan-built 320cc [actually 280cc] SWM, a totally new and as yet unproved machine, will be on sale in Britain from mid-January.'

The 320 (the model number, not engine size) SWM featured an Austrian-made Rotax two-stroke disc valve engine, with Bosch flywheel ignition, housed in a twin down-tube cradle frame, with Italian Marzocchi front forks and rear shocks. The five-speed 320, which also featured a quickly detachable rear wheel, and weighed in at 185lb (84kg), was to be followed by a 125cc version in April 1978.

The following is an extract from an interview by *Trials & Motocross News* in its 13 January 1978 issue, in Sammy's own words: 'I have signed for Cliff Holden and SWM (UK) for a year at the moment. I will ride the machine and hope to clock up my 900th win on it. I will also do some development work and assist Cliff with team management. It's quite an interesting project and the Italians came down to my place during the week to have a look and to talk. I think the bike and the factory have great potential, and although the bike is not fully developed, the company is a big one and has the necessary resources.'

By then news had also filtered through of Honda UK's surprise move, which had seen the Japanese firm stay in British trials – and with Rob Shepherd, the rider Sammy had signed for them. When pressed about his reaction to the news, Sammy simply said: 'There are a lot of things which I could say, but I don't think it would do any good.' But he did go on to reveal: 'I'm glad Honda Britain have signed Rob. He is one of the best, if not the best, trials rider in the world.'

Finalising the Team

Things moved quickly, and by the end of January came news that Colin Bell, the 20-year-old Irish trials champion, had been signed by Sammy to ride in the SWM squad. Three works SWMs were being flown in from Italy. One was for 19-year-old John Reynolds, the other for Sammy.

Regarding Bell, this is what Sammy told *Motor Cycle News'* Norrie Whyte: 'He'll be able to use my practice patch and the workshop facilities of Ossa UK.' He went on to say: 'Bell and Reynolds will do the first five rounds of the World Trials Championship. They will contest all rounds of the British Championship. I would have liked to see their debut at the Colmore [national] but I had already entered the Frome Valley club trial on the same day. I shall be with the boys at the Hurst Cup on 11 February.'

First Major Success

It was the SWM's team boss who hit the headlines first, when Mr Miller made the headline in *Trials & Motocross News* dated 10 February 1978 with: 'It's A Knockout for SWM Sammy.' The report continued: 'Not even Sammy Miller visualised winning Sunday's Southern Centre's team trial, but the maestro not only scored SWM's first major success, but also led the XHG Tigers team – comprising Paul Dunkley, Roger Johns and Tony Cheney – to victory in this annual team contest.'

Southern Centre Team Trial – 5 February 1978

1st	S.H. Miller (280 SWM)	54 marks lost
2nd	P. Dunkley (350 SM Bultaco)	58
3rd	R. Moxon (250 Yamaha)	58
4th	L. Hutty (250 Gollner Kawasaki)	61
5th	M. Maskelyne (348 WCS Montesa)	63
6th	G. Chandler (350 WCS Bultaco)	64

Sammy getting some very muddy action during the 1978 Tor Timed Trial with his Rotax-engined SWM.

Throughout the first half of 1978 Sammy went on to chalk up a number of victories on his new bike. But he had decided that approaching 45 years of age he would no longer compete in two-day events. And so, instead of contesting the Isle of Wight Two Days, which he had won nine times, he contented himself by finishing runner-up to Mark Kemp in the Bristol Club time trial at Lair.

Even though Sammy was doing well on the SWM, the same could not be said of Colin Bell, who immediately quit SWM after the Scottish Six Days Trial, where the young Ulsterman had finished a disappointing 39th.

Besides winning the annual Greybeards Trial run by the Sunbeam Motor Cycle Club in Sussex, Sammy also found time to smash his own world record for the number of cars he could climb – on the SWM he managed 27, two more than his previous best achieved on the Honda. By then he was just six short of the 900 trials win mark.

Aprilia

Yet another marque which Sammy Miller was involved with developing and riding was the Italian Aprilia concern.

Now, at the beginning of the 21st century, Aprilia is the very epitome of Italian motorcycling, with its exciting range of machines from trendy 50cc scooters right through to 1000cc superbikes.

Aprilia began trading in 1956, when the company was created by Alberto Beggio, but at that time it made pedal cycles, not motorcycles.

Four years after Aprilia was formed, in Noale, near Venice, in the north-east of Italy, production of the first powered two-wheeler began, in the shape of a ride-to-work commuter model. Like thousands of other Italian ultra-lightweights, this was powered by a bought-in Minerelli two-stroke engine.

Although Aprilia's moped range expanded during the late 1960s and early 1970s, it was still the pedal cycle which dominated the company's thinking during this period.

Aprilia had become a limited company in 1962 and, throughout that decade, production had grown year-on-year. As the 1970s began, everything seemed to be going well. Then, during 1973 and 1974 the OPEC crisis hit western industry, with the oil-producing countries effectively blackmailing the industrial nations and forcing them overnight to pay a much higher price for crude oil. The effects were widespread. Many factories had to cut their working week to three days, and, in some cases, even two days. Plants were closed, jobs were lost, there were power cuts and large gas-guzzling cars became unfashionable. Rather surprisingly, the bicycle industry went into free-fall.

Somehow, motorcycles remained largely immune to this potential industrial meltdown. A faction within the Aprilia organisation, led by the founder's son Ivano Beggio, was behind the decision that now was the time for those with technical expertise to innovate and apply new technology. Niche markets had to be identified and exploited, so Aprilia totally ceased bicycle manufacture and put all its energy into the motorcycle and moped sector.

The management also realised that it would be taking a major financial risk if it undertook design and manufacture of its own engine units. So the policy of buying-in from outside suppliers was therefore continued, leaving the Noale facilities free to concentrate upon the design of the chassis, styling and assembling the best possible component parts. In fact, virtually the entire product was assembled from bought-in parts. This meant that the purchasing department was a vital cog in the Aprilia operation; not only ensuring the supply of components in the correct quantities, at the correct time, and at the most competitive price, but also, most importantly, seeking out the highest quality.

During the mid-late 1970s Aprilia had no fewer than four engine suppliers. Besides the German Sachs firm, the three others were all Italian: Minerelli, Morini-Franco and Hiro.

Another vital factor in Aprilia's success at this time was its correct choice of niche markets – mopeds, children's motorcycles, plus dirt bikes in the shape of motocross and enduro mounts. It was to be the off-road machinery which was first to bring to the public attention the Aprilia brand name, both in Italy and the export markets.

Having established themselves in the motocross and enduro fields, Aprilia saw the trials market as their next step, and their first model, the 340TR, made its debut at the international Milan Show in November 1979.

As we know from the main text, the subject of this book, Sammy Miller, had been deeply involved in the development of the Hiro engine and its use in trials. So it will come as no surprise therefore to learn that Sammy's expertise was extended to the Aprilia trials project.

The 340TR was powered by a Hiro 310cc (78 x 64mm) air-cooled single-cylinder two-stroke engine with conventional piston-port (featuring five ports) induction, featuring full unit construction, with a five-speed gearbox. Maximum power output was 19bhp at 5,000rpm, while the machine tipped the scales at 195lb (89kg). This was to signal Aprilia's involvement with trials, which was to last some 15 years.

It should be pointed out that Sammy had a vested interest in the Hiro-engined Aprilia trials effort, as the Ulsterman received royalties on all engine sales of the Hiro unit under his original development contract for the firm.

During 1981 Sammy rode the Aprilia (now with engine capacity raised to 320cc) to several wins that year. The British Aprilia importers at that time were the Birmingham-based pairing of Ken Sedgley and Pete Edmondson. The TR320 was joined by a smaller trials mount, the TR50, but this featured a six-speed Minerelli engine.

By the mid-1980s Aprilia had phased the Hiro engine out in favour of an Austrian Rotax unit, displacing 276.6cc; this employed disc valve rather than piston-port induction. The newcomer was coded TX311, which later became the TXR312. Later still, at the end of 1989, Aprilia introduced the Climber, the world's first liquid-cooled over-the-counter trials bike.

The final production variant of the Climber appeared in 1994, and with the demise of the model, Aprilia bowed out of the competition dirt-bike arena (having already quit motocross). From then on it concentrated its efforts on production and sales of its series production street machines – from scooters to high-performance sports bikes. From the mid-1980s it had also entered the Grand Prix road racing scene with considerable success, winning several World Championship titles. Valentino Rossi won his first world crown aboard a 125cc Aprilia in 1997.

Today Aprilia is part of the massive Piaggio group of companies.

Victory Number 900

The *Motor Cycle News* headline of Wednesday 12 July 1978 said it all: 'Sam's 900', Norrie Whyte saying: 'Miller makes a trials milestone', continuing: 'Samuel Hamilton Miller, that 44-year-old living legend of a trials rider, scooped his 900th trials victory in Sunday's XHG Tigers inter-club team trial at Bovington Heath, Dorset.'

And, as Whyte went on to explain: 'Immediately after he took his 280cc SWM to a four-mark win ahead of Roger Johns (Ossa), Sammy announced that he would be riding in fewer events in the future, saying "To win a centre event nowadays, I have to put in as much effort as I used to do to win the Scottish Six Days years ago."'

But which of those 900 wins did he remember best? His answer in July 1978 was: 'The 1962 Scott, when I finished on 21 and my nearest rivals, Jeff Smith and Arthur Lampkin, were in the 80s.'

In July 1978 Sammy scooped his 900th trials victory, riding the SWM, at the XHG Tigers inter-club event at Bovington Heath, Dorset.

After his 900th win, Sammy told Norrie Whyte that he: 'Planned to take three or four weeks off', something he had not done for 26 years! After that he insisted he would 'only ride in selective events I particularly enjoy.'

Not one to miss a commercial opportunity, Sammy was soon marketing components for SWMs, notably an extra flywheel for the Rotax engine. Weighing almost 3lb (1.4kg), this helped bottom-end torque and cost £10.88 – including VAT and post/packing charges.

No SWM Contract for 1979

In the week before Christmas 1978 came the news that Sammy's contract to develop SWM trials machinery would not be renewed. The Italian marque's British importer Cliff Holden revealed at the Bristol Dirt Bike Show that he was slashing his promotional budget to the bone the following year in a bid to peg the cost of SWMs at a time when they were just becoming good. He told *Trials & Motocross News*: 'If we carried on next year as we have like this it would add something like £200 to the bikes.' And: 'We are looking for a cutback of £20,000 on our international budget and will make any effort to peg out prices next year.'

Although Sammy and Cliff were long-standing personal friends, as *T&MX News* said: 'The old maestro was an early casualty of the sweeping economies. His contract had another year to run on option, and it is not going to be renewed.'

Sammy Joins Hiro

At the London Racing and Sporting Show in January 1979 Sammy signed a contract with Italy's Hiro factory. He had agreed a deal with Andrea Mosconi and his father, owners of the Origgio manufacturing concern based near Milan, to develop an engine for trials use.

The capacity of the prototype engine was given at 310cc, with bore and stroke dimensions of 78 x 64mm. It was of conventional piston-port two-stroke design with a six-speed gearbox. The factory produced between 600 and 700 engines a month. The bottom end of the proposed trials unit was essentially the same as the Hiro 250 motocross unit, but with an additional flywheel on both sides. The ignition was by normal contact breaker points, instead of transistorised, to save costs. At that time Sammy said he hoped to have complete prototype machines for himself and sponsored rider Geoff Parken 'by the first week of March.'

At the London Racing and Sporting Show in January 1979 Sammy signed a contract with the Italian Hiro company. He agreed to assist Andrea Mosconi and his father, owners of the Origgio manufacturers based near Milan, to develop an engine for trials use. The photograph here shows another of the firm's products, a 125cc motocross engine, with reed valve induction.

Sammy also revealed that the previous week he had reached an agreement with Ossa-SWM importer Cliff Holden for both Parken and himself to continue to ride SWM machinery until a competitive Hiro-engined machine was available.

In addition, Sammy had renewed his contract with Belstaff – meaning that he had been with the same clothing company for 21 years. Belstaff, whose two-piece Trialsmaster was still a best-seller, had no objection to Sammy having recently announced his own brand one-piece lightweight suit, because they did not make one themselves.

A Two-Year Deal

Sammy's contract with Hiro was for two years, the task being to develop a competitive engine and to build a bike to go round it. Sammy said 'I want an engine that's easy to work on and simple to maintain – something aimed at clubmen, in fact. We'll be using existing crankcases and I've started work already. What I find particularly interesting is that Hiro see themselves as a latter-day Villiers, making a competitive trials engine and supplying them to other manufacturers.' He continued: 'Andrea Mosconi, the Hiro boss's son, is an ex-trials rider himself and he sees this as a good opportunity to break into the trials field.'

With the mention of Villiers, it should be pointed out that during the late 1960s Sammy had produced around 45 complete trials machines powered by Villiers engines, before the supply dried up and this particular project came to an end.

Sammy's development work would be carried out at his New Milton premises and manufacturing undertaken in Italy. It was planned that the frame would be made at New Milton, 'using the best proprietary cycle parts.'

Founded in 1972, the Hiro company had emerged by the beginning of 1979 as a prolific supplier of engines to the off-road sector, with customers including Aprilia, Ancillotti, TMG and CCM. The trials project would join the already successful engines used in motocross, enduro and karting uses. And Sammy would receive royalties on all trials Hiro engine sales.

Motor Cycle News dated 27 December 1978 had carried a story entitled: 'Parken joins Hiro Sam.' In this it was stated that: 'Sammy Miller will ride in some nationals next year to help evaluate the [Hiro] motor,' and that he 'will sign Geoff Parken, the Wessex rider who gave SWM its only national win of the year.' But most controversially of all Sammy, referring to the SWM, said: 'I don't think a disc valve motor is the answer in trials. There is a funny power curve. The top and bottom ranges are OK, but it's very strong in mid-range. It'll be good to be back with piston-controlled trials motors.'

Sammy – the Development Engineer

As my old friend Bill Lawless stated in 1978 when he was the editor of *Trials & Motocross News*: 'As a rider, Sammy Miller has set the international trials world alight for a good part of his 25 years in the game. But in the final analysis, it could well be that his contribution to machine development has eclipsed his exploits on the footrests.'

And I, for one, can only concur with Bill's view.

Sammy began his development career with the SHS (Samuel Hamilton Special), a Matchless-framed, Villiers-powered machine back in 1953. It was not very long before the home-brewed bike was getting the better of many of the factory two-strokes, which were beginning to make an impact on the four-stroke dominated trials world.

Next Sammy waved his magic wand over a second-hand James Commando, and in doing so the combination gained much success between 1954 and 1956. Then came his first works machinery, in the shape of the now legendary Ariel HT5, GOV 132.

It was on that big British thumper that Sammy's very real, but completely untutored engineering genius really made its mark. In its final form, as Bill Lawless pointed out: 'It emerged with the magic vital statistics which, with only microscopic variations, are the norm on every serious trials bike since.'

These changes included steering head angle, 1½ degrees offset on the yokes, the same trail and a 52in (1320mm) wheelbase. In its final guise, the big Ariel was the most effective four-stroke trials bike of them all.

Then came the years campaigning the Bultaco, from 1964 to 1974. Again, Sammy created the design trend. The initial Bultaco he tried featured a 196cc engine and Sammy says: 'Handled like a camel.' At his insistence the cylinder was bored out from 60 to 72mm, thus setting the trend for the vast catalogue of successes of all Spanish-made quarter-litre bikes.

The Ariel's vital statistics went into the frame and steering areas, while Sammy and the Bultaco factory introduced the one-piece tank-seat unit, the leading axle fork legs, and the use of an aluminium sump shield which doubled up as the lower frame member. It is a little-known fact that Sammy attempted to patent this last feature, but dropped it because of the legal complications – and was later to admit he regretted that he did not go ahead.

His Hi-Boy frame started the trend, which by the end of the 1970s was a standard feature in the trials world.

In addition to insisting on a 250cc engine displacement, Sammy also opted for flywheel weight – some 22½lb (10.2kg) on the Sherpa – another two-stroke trend-setter.

When Sammy switched to Honda in 1974 he was back with four-strokes. But as Bill Lawless pointed out: 'Not that Honda were nostalgically inclined – it was just that the Honda computer after ingesting a mass of data, decided that a four-stroke offered more potential than a two-stroke.'

As the main text reveals, Sammy and the Honda computer usually differed...but somehow he gradually moulded the bike to near perfection. In the chassis stakes he constructed a kind of Hi-Boy replica frame to house the much-altered XL250 engine assembly; again following the Ariel/Bultaco template.

History records the unfortunate and untimely end to the Miller-Honda marriage – after winning the British championship title with Rob Shepherd in the saddle – Honda pulled out of trials, dropped Sammy, then came back in with Shepherd as their sole British works rider.

Shepherd's win on the Miller Honda was the first four-stroke championship win since Sammy had achieved this feat on the Ariel.

Then came SWM, Aprilia and Armstrong; plus, of course, Sammy's own Miller project.

Delay for the Miller-Hiro Project

Due to a strike at the Hiro factory, progress on the prototype trials engine was delayed so the Miller-Hiro machine was not ready until late spring.

After missing the Scottish Six Days for the first time in many years to visit the Hiro factory, Sammy's suggested modifications to the 310cc engine were incorporated in the solitary motor, which was subsequently dispatched a few days after Sammy had returned home.

Never a man to waste time, Sammy quickly slotted the revised engine in to the already completed cycle parts and, without attention to carburation or exhaust, initial testing confirmed his optimism in the project. At that stage he also commented that: 'I am to retail the completed machines below the price of current Bultacos and Montesas and one of the reasons why this will be possible will be that Hiro will not be hiring a highly paid Rathmell or Lampkin – a commitment which the general public pay for.'

Also in May Sammy had his final ride on the SWM, when he won an XHG Tiger Trial before returning the bike to importer Cliff Holden.

A Winning Debut

Then, on Thursday 1 June 1979, the completed motorcycle, ridden by Sammy himself, made a winning debut in an XHG Tiger's event held on his own land at Sway, Hampshire. At that time it was stated that the new bike: 'Will go into production later this year' (Motor Cycle Weekly). But no price had yet been decided.

Sammy competing in the
1979 Sunbeam
Greybeards Trial on his
Hiro-engined Miller
machine.

Although still 310cc, the Hiro motor now boasted Motoplat ignition, a 26mm Mikuni carburettor and a compression ratio of 9:1.

The chrome-finished frame was in Reynolds 531 tubing with Marzocchi front forks, while weight had been kept down to 190lb (86kg). Cycle parts were in white and black, with Pirelli tyres: a 2.75 x 21 front and 4.00 x 18 rear. Ground clearance was 13in (330mm), with a seat height of 31in (787mm).

Next it was Geoff Parken's turn to score first time out, when he squeezed home by the narrowest of margins during the Ringwood Championship Trial at Aldershot, Dorset.

One of the Miller-Hiro models. Badged as a '350', the actual capacity was 310cc (78x64mm). The engine was a conventional piston-port two-stroke with a six-speed gearbox.

Other Business

Besides the Miller-Hiro project, Sammy was more than ever engrossed in his business interests as the 1970s came to a close. For example, he was in the process of opening a new 1,500 sq ft workshop adjacent to his motorcycle operation at Gore Road, New Milton – Ted Evans and Dave Caines were the tenants and they would be manufacturing components for the SM business. Sammy had also concluded a deal to handle the distribution of replica 350cc AJS trials models constructed by Peter Pykett; while on the sponsorship front he had just agreed to field a two-John team of Parsons and Simmonds on the newly released Montesa Cota 349.

The Bristol Dirt Bike Show

At the Bristol Dirt Bike Show in December 1979 Sammy was very busy. First, as what was by now claimed to be the world's leading manufacturer of trials spares and accessories, the SM stand displayed a full range of Sammy Miller Products and the latest development of the Hiro-engined Miller 310 trials machine, which was 'to go into production during 1980.' On one part of the stand, customers were able to purchase most of the SM range of spares and accessories. This included Alpinestar and Dunlop trials boots, trials clothing, gloves and helmets.

Additionally, in Bristol Sammy had signed John Metcalfe to ride the Hiro-powered trials machine, as a replacement for Geoff Parken who had quit the team; however, this was something of an on/off deal, but eventually Metcalfe joined the Miller squad, his previous sponsor Comerford's waiving their own agreement so that Metcalfe could join Sammy on 1 January 1980; the Comerford contract should have run until April that year.

John Metcalfe had already tested the Hiro-Miller and was 'most impressed' with the Italian-engined machine. This signing also meant that Sammy could concentrate on preparation and development of the machine. In early 1980 Metcalfe debuted on the Hiro-Miller at an Esso Fawley MCC's trial, finishing second to southern star Geoff Chandler.

Gore Road

On 14 June 1980 Lord Montague performed an official ceremony to open a new, extended business complex at Gore Road, New Milton, which as *Trials & Motocross News* said, was: 'Without doubt the best-known address in the whole trials world.'

Expansion had been proceeding steadily for many years. The first big step (see Chapter 5) had come in 1973 when Sammy's Highcliffe premises became too small for the level of business then being experienced. So Sammy moved the operation to New Milton, where a much larger site offered him the room he needed to expand, with plenty of additional space for further developments.

Trials & Motocross News again: 'Sammy is now very big business indeed. It's hard to accept that any man can pack as many hours into the working day. These days the man occupies himself developing the Hiro-engined Miller trials bike, restoring classic machinery for his own museum, and chasing that unbelievable target of 1,000 trials victories which gets closer almost every weekend.'

Paul Dunkley

It was also revealed that Paul Dunkley, a former trials rider of considerable ability, would be taking over the day-to-day running of Sammy Miller Ltd. Paul, who had been with the company as manager for some four and a half years, would be taking over the administration of Sammy Miller Ltd wholesale and retail, to give Sammy more time to develop new products and set up a new development shop and museum complex with restoration facilities. Sammy commented: 'I am handing the reins over to Paul to concentrate on what we hope will be the country's leading motorcycle museum and restoration complex.'

It was also in 1980 that he first began riding in the newly created 'classic' events on both trials and road-racing machinery. This period of Sammy's life is covered in Chapter 9, but suffice to say that this ran parallel with Sammy's growing collection of old motorcycles. An example was the newly introduced *Classic Bike*-sponsored Cavalcade of TT history – one of the 1980 TT highlights. In later years this event was to become known as the TT Lap of Honour. Another facet of Sammy's life at this time was opening shows and presenting trophies at major sporting events.

During 1980 Sammy had continued to develop the Hiro trials engine, which by now was being used in Aprilia's 340 TR trials mount (which had made its debut at the Milan Show in late 1979).

Also, the Hiro engine development had seen the capacity upped to 320cc, by increasing the bore size 2mm to 80mm, while the carburettor had been changed to a Dell'Orto instrument; however, Sammy's own Hiro-Miller project had stalled, mainly due to the onset of a global recession from mid-1980 onwards. But Hiro were pressing ahead with the manufacture for other bike builders, including a new marque, Trans-AMA Maltry.

But the biggest customer for the Hiro trials engine unit (all of which now had 'Sammy Miller' stamped on the crankcases) was Aprilia.

Aprilia Developments

At the end of 1980 came news that Sammy was on the verge of obtaining a development and riding contract to boost the sales of the latest Aprilia trials model, which was now being marketed by the Venetian concern.

Sammy could clearly see the merits of riding a machine using the Italian Hiro engine to which he had devoted so much time over the last few months. At the same time it was revealed that a planned production run of the Hiro-Miller machine, which was entirely separate from the Aprilia project, had been shelved due to the enormous capital outlay required –

after a market survey had indicated that there was not enough demand to put it into quantity production. As we will see later, however, the project and general design was passed to Alan Clews of CCM, and ultimately the much larger Armstrong concern.

But Andrea Mosconi, boss of the Hiro company, had told Sammy that he was keen to see the Miller-Hiro relationship continue. And since Sammy received royalties on all engine sales under the original development contract, he was also keen.

Then, early in 1981, Sammy made his competition debut on the Aprilia 320 at the XGH Tiger's MCCs Club Championship Trial at Sway. Sammy finished third in an event easily won by Fantic works star Roger Johns.

On Thursday 21 May 1981 Sammy clocked up his 945th victory in the Ringwood MC and LCC Club Championship trial at Aldershot, Dorset. As *Trials & Motocross News* reported: 'Riding the ideal tool for the gripless conditions, the maestro lost 19 marks on the compact four-lap 10-observed section course.'

Ringwood Club Championship Trial – 21 May 1981

1st	S.H. Miller (320 Aprilia)	19 marks lost
2nd	S. Brett (350 Ossa)	24
3rd	K. Hitchings (156 Fantic)	25
4th	C. Taylor (349 Montesa)	25
5th	G. Vaughan (349 Montesa)	32
6th	P. Wesson (156 Fantic)	36

The Red Devil

Thereafter, Sammy proceeded to grab the headlines on the Aprilia, and when Roger Painter tested Sammy's own 320 model, he said the Italian was the: 'Forgiving Red Devil.' He continued: 'A winner within a month of being launched on the British market, the new 320 Aprilia imported by Pete Edmondson could capture a large slice of a market becoming increasingly oriented towards Italian bikes.' Painter revealed: 'As the test session progressed, and my confidence grew, my outstanding impression was that the Aprilia was working with me and not waiting to punish me for my mistakes. It is, above all, a very forgiving machine. Whether idling or attacking a climb flat-out in third or fourth gears the carburation remained spot on.' And: 'The gearbox is a six-speeder of truly superb action. I cannot remember using a better box or one with a more fine choice of ratios.'

Technique

In Sammy Miller's case 'technique' was replaced by enthusiasm, dedication and, quite simply, the 'will to win'. In fact, in the 'Meet the Champions' series, published in the *Motor Cycle News* issue of 6 March 1968, Peter Howdle began: 'Ask Sammy Miller what makes him so much better than other trials riders and he'll tell you: "It's just a question of having the will to win and keeping one jump ahead of the rest".'

There is no doubt that, unlike many others, Sammy revelled in adverse conditions, saying 'give me a winter trial any time. Tough conditions jolly things up. The Scott and Hurst are good examples. Perhaps it is all in the mind but I like a severe trial because I think it gives me an advantage over the other guys.' And: 'When I was road racing I preferred riding in the wet because I knew the weather was likely to slow the others down more than me.'

Why did Sammy quit road racing? His answer (given in the 1960s) was simple: 'I thought it was a waste of time trying to catch guys on faster machines. I remember thinking I was doing well during practice for the Belgian Grand Prix. I was on full noise, in top gear, and fully tucked in along the Masta straight, when my teammate Provini came past me like an express train. His Mondial was so much faster that I couldn't even get into his slipstream. I finished second in the race but I realised that, however hard you try you will always be beaten by a good guy on a faster bike. In any big trial there are at least 20 machines capable of winning. Preparation is still vital, but riding ability plus the will to win are more important. Any good engineer can prepare a trials-winning machine, but you can't say that in road racing.'

To the outsider – and probably other competitors – Sammy's will to win was not easy to define. But having got to know him, it's the combination of enthusiasm, dedication and a never-satisfied quest for perfection which has been his biggest asset.

He is certainly not one to suffer fools gladly. He once said: 'I find that when in business someone lets me down I realise that if I do the job myself, and something goes wrong, I have only myself to blame. This comes out in the way I prepare my machines.' And: 'To me, machine reparation is so important that nothing is too much trouble. Perhaps it is because I started in the sport by building my own trials bike (the SHS).'

In 1974 Dave Minton was comparing Sammy to Mike Hailwood, saying: 'Miller, too, is another one of the bike game's greatest personalities. Perhaps the two of them, Miller and Hailwood, rank as *the* greatest ever, the trial rider particularly because he has quite literally changed the sport's direction and is likely to continue to influence it for a long time yet. His success, too, you see, has solid foundations of practice behind it, born from the determination to not merely win, but to achieve satisfaction by reaching a level of skill beyond that of any other man.'

Sammy agrees with this, commenting: 'Even from my first days on trials bikes – as soon as I decided to make a career out of it – I've practised. Five sessions a week of 90 minutes each day and always alone. I don't want to worry about others when I'm practising. I set myself a task, something that yesterday had proved to be just a little bit too much, and I concentrate on doing it until it no longer worries me.' Certainly, in Sammy's view, practice really did 'make perfect'.

Motocross World Champion and fellow trials rider Jeff Smith, in *Motor Cycle News* dated 5 May 1965, confirmed this, saying: 'Miller's secret is ruthless determination to succeed, which drives him to practice harder and longer than any man in his particular sport has ever done before. This determination is the main spring of Sammy's character. He is one of those rare people who could probably do well in anything they put their hand to. Sam is not a born rider, he is a self-made one. Consequently his style is ugly, determination to succeed sticks out in every movement he makes while tackling a section.'

Finally, and I think it vital in being able to fully appreciate just why Sammy Hamilton Miller has achieved what he has, is also a quiet confidence in his own ability. This, I must add, is not over-confidence, but simply having the ability to know what is right for a given task. This you could apply not simply to his riding, but also to his machine preparation, development skills and business sense. As proof of this you need look no further than the Sammy Miller museum – which says everything about the man.

The 950th Victory

It was during the summer of 1981 that Sammy chalked up his 950th victory, beating Kevin Phillips and Mark Kemp at the North Somerset club's round of the Sun Life Time Trials Championship.

Sammy continued with the Aprilia into 1982, with yet more victories. Questioned about the prospect of reaching 1,000 wins, Sammy replied: 'I still have reservations. The Aprilia is going well but the Miller chassis is getting a bit rusty!'

Then, as the 27 February 1982 issue of *Motor Cycle Weekly* reported: 'Veteran Sammy Miller (320 Aprilia) moved nearer to his target of a thousand outright wins on Sunday. He scored an 18-mark victory over Mark Kemp (340 Bultaco) in the Sun Life Championship event at West Wilts club's Tanner Trudge timed trial, Lacock, Wiltshire.' It was his 10th success in the event.

Towards the end of July 1982 Sammy scored his 970th and final Aprilia victory with the loss of 13 marks.

Less than a month before his 50th birthday on 11 November 1983, Sammy chalked up an historic 1,000th trials victory riding a 310cc Armstrong. After deciding himself not to enter production with the Miller-Hiro, the project had been taken over by the Armstrong concern. But it was fitting that his landmark victory had been acheived on a machine of his own creation.

Joining Armstrong/CCM

Sammy's next move was to yet another manufacturer and, 19 years after switching from British to foreign machinery, news came that Sammy was to fly the Union Jack flag again aboard an Armstrong/CCM. At the time Sammy seemed excited by the switch, saying: 'The move came as a result of discussions between Alan Clews of CCM and Andrea Mosconi of the Italian Hiro engine factory, from whom I received royalties on all engines sold. It will be good to get full support again from a British concern.'

The Magic 1,000

Due to celebrate his 50th birthday on 11 November 1983, less than a month before, in mid-October, Sammy added the historic 1,000th victory to his long list of achievements, with a win in the Wells Club's President's Cup Trial at Emborough, Somerset, which was run in heavy rain. Soaked to the skin after his victory, he said: 'It's a relief to get it over.' In a neat twist of fate, this historic landmark was achieved aboard a machine he had been so closely linked with, the 310cc Hiro-engined Miller, which had been reborn as the Armstrong.

President's Cup Trial – October 1983

1st	S.H. Miller (310 Armstrong)	4 marks lost
2nd	A. King (240 Fantic)	14
3rd	R. Painter (250 Ossa)	15
4th	C. White (280 SWM)	21

Where Sammy was concerned, life really did begin at 50. He not only celebrated his half century, but also opened his new museum in New Milton *and* achieved his 1,000th trial victory.

These factors were obviously taken into account by the Guild of Motoring Writers, which in December 1983 voted him 'Rider of the Year'. The decision was announced at the Guild's annual dinner, which took place at Lord's Cricket Pavilion.

During 1984 Sammy appeared to lavish far more time on riding in Pre '65 trials than piloting the Armstrong. For example, in the Sunbeam Club's Greybeards Trial (for the over-40s trial rider) Sammy had experienced a remarkable run of success in the event, beginning in 1977 and having only missed out on the premier award once, in 1979. However, in 1984 he missed out again. But by the time the 1985 Greybeards arrived he had that meaningful gleam in his eyes and went home with the Len Heath Memorial Trophy once again, and he achieved this with a loss of only two marks, his mount being the Armstrong (now sporting the uprated 320cc Hiro engine).

By the spring of 1988 Sammy had chalked up his 1,100th victory, but by now virtually all of them were being achieved in Pre '65 events with his 497cc Ariel. And from then on the vast majority of his trials riding would be in this type of event, allowing him to rack up the truly amazing total of over 1,400 victories in the trials world!

Before finally retiring he switched from the Ariel to a BSA C15, saying: 'I've decided a lighter, smaller bike is more fun to ride.'

Another aspect of Sammy's trials career has been his help to other riders. For example, in 1993 he backed fellow Ulsterman Robert Crawford in his World Championship campaign with an Aprilia. Crawford said: 'Sammy has been good to me, not just with finance but with advice.' And many, many other riders have received sponsorship, help and guidance over the years on an array of machines.

But in the author's mind, Sammy's greatest achievement in the trials world has been his development work – which truly changed motorcycle design – and the manufacturers he was involved with over the years.

Chapter 8

The Museum

On Thursday 3 November 1983 Sammy invited well over 200 friends to New Milton, Hampshire, not only to be present at the official opening (by John Surtees) of his new museum, but also to celebrate his 1,000th trial victory. It was a memorable occasion in the career of a man who was 50 years old on the day of publication of an article on the opening ceremony, in the 11 November 1983 *T&MX News* by that doyen of the trials world, the late Ralph Venables.

Total Dedication

As John Surtees said in his introduction: 'Sam has shown total dedication to motorcycle sport throughout the past 31 years. Sam's sheer enthusiasm is as great today as it was when he started competing in 1952.'

Sammy's personal collection, *c.*1980.

Sammy shaking hands with John Surtees to officially open the museum at Gore Road, New Milton, on Thursday 3 November 1985. The machine in the background is an Aermacchi Ala d'Oro road racer dating from the mid-1960s.

At the official opening Sammy revealed that his decision to collect historical motorcycles had originally come from when he purchased his old Ariel GOV 132 from Ralph Venables (seen here on Sammy's left together with Lord Montague).

Sammy with the Moto
Guzzi five-hundred
Dondolino (rocking chair)
which he restored during
the early 1980s.

John Surtees, seven times World Road Race Champion, also congratulated Sammy on his new museum, which at that time contained some 100 historic motorcycles. Incredibly, it took a mere two months to build.

Thanking John for coming along to open the Gore Road Museum and unveiling the official plaque, Sammy revealed that his decision to collect historical machines had originally come from when he purchased his old Ariel HT5 GOV 132 from Ralph Venables in the summer of 1969. This was, of course, the legendary five-hundred Ariel which had carried Sammy to almost a decade of success before he made the switch to Bultaco during late 1964.

He welcomed his old Ariel teammates Gordon Blakeway and Ron Langston, who were present among many notables of New Milton on the afternoon of Thursday 3 November 1983. Others included Ken Heanes, Jim Sandiford, Gordon Jackson, Johnny Giles, Peter Stirland, Mark Kemp, Bill Faulkner and the Rickman brothers, Don and Derek.

As Ralph Venables said in his *T&MX News report*: 'A measure of Miller's popularity was the impressive number of friendly rivals in attendance.' As Ralph went on to say: 'Roger Maughfling had come from Wales, Melroy Youlton had come from Cornwall, grass-track champions Lew Coffin, Julian Wigg and Bernie Leigh were rubbing shoulders with road racers and enduro riders.'

On that day Sammy admitted that: 'My collection of old machines gives me great satisfaction – especially the thoroughbred British ones.' But John Surtees added that: 'The British motorcycle industry committed suicide.' It was then that Sammy, with a grin, had admitted it was: 'Go Spanish or I'd have been out of work!'

With the formalities completed, everyone moved outside into the sunshine to see and hear some classic competition bikes fired into life. First to be started was Sam's own 'personal favourite' the famous pre-war 500cc AJS V-four liquid-cooled racer, which had set the first 100mph (161km/h)

The Sammy Miller Museum, Gore Road, New Milton, in the early 1990s.

A view of the café during restoration.

The finished café.

The upper gallery of the museum before restoration.   The café before restoration.

The courtyard before work.

Before the racing gallery was constructed.

The racing gallery.

The courtyard on completion.

The new extension gets under way.

John Surtees opening the museum.

The new racing gallery complete with bikes.

Grand Prix lap at the Ulster in August 1939. This was followed by a couple of DKW twin-cylinder two-strokes from the same era (a 250 and a 350).

Millionaire Ron Amey was there to ride his 1927 AJS Big Port three-fifty single (the actual machine on which he had competed in so many grass-track events). There was a much more sedate 1933 five-hundred Sunbeam which was put through its paces, followed by the 1956 500cc Ariel which Sammy was still riding in pre-1965 trials, and finally a 1947 500cc Grand Prix Triumph racing model.

As the last of these machines were finally being put away, Brooklands and pre-war TT rider Noel Mavrogordato drove away in his fabulous 1914 Opel racing car – a fitting climax to 'what must surely have been the most triumphant day in Sammy Miller's career' (Ralph Venables); it certainly was up to that time.

A Real Love Affair

As Sammy admitted a few years ago, of his museum project: 'It's a hobby gone mad, but I get a lot of satisfaction out of the restorations we do there.'

In truth, collecting and restoring motorcycles from the past has become a real love affair for Sammy. You have only to study the machinery and the high standard of restoration carried out to realise that this is a true passion.

Although November 1983 had seen the launch of the museum itself, Sammy had begun collecting many of the machines from the late 1960s onwards.

Besides the actual collecting and restoration, to the author the most significant feature of the museum is the equal mix of road and competition machinery *and* the number of truly rare machines (often the only known surviving example) which Sammy has been able to unearth.

This is where, from a personal angle, I can appreciate the amount of detective work involved. It's a very similar ethos to the way in which I apply myself to researching my books. Again, for both Sammy and myself, second best is simply not good enough.

Another important factor in the birth of the museum was that Sammy was one of the first people to recognise the value of older motorcycles; at that time during the late 1960s and early 1970s these bikes were simply old and were being cast aside. At first Sammy had begun by purchasing motorcycles that had been linked to his past – a 1929 Francis-Barnett, identical to his first machine and a 1949 AJS 7R, a reminder of his first racing motorcycle, the ex-Charlie Gray 7R on which he had begun his road racing career in 1954.

Back in 1977 Sammy had been co-opted to the motorcycle advisory board of the Beaulieu National Motor Museum. In fact, Sammy's Ariel GOV 132 was on show at Beaulieu for several years, the machine having been purchased by Ralph Venables – a document having existed to the effect that the machine would never go out of Great Britain. Eventually the bike returned to Sammy's ownership and it is now a centre-piece of the museum.

Sammy with his fellow restorer and also longest-serving employee Bob Stanley, pictured with the four-valve Excelsior they had recently restored, 3 February 1996.

Old Bashley Manor Farm

By the mid-1990s the continued growth of the museum (there now being almost double the number of machines than at its opening in 1983) meant that Sammy was on the lookout for more suitable premises.

The venue chosen was Old Bashley Manor Farm, a manor house, land and farm buildings, all badly in need of considerable work to restore them to their former glory.

In November 1995 *Trials and MotoX News* told readers that his new venture 'should open in the new year,' and 'it's Sammy's intention to make his new project one of the most exotic collections of sports machines ever assembled in one collection.'

When the relocated museum was officially opened on 29 May 1996 (with John Surtees again performing the ceremony), most people were unaware of the considerable problems experienced by Sammy in his quest to restore the buildings for not only the museum, but also workshops, tea rooms, craft shops and the like.

On 29 May 1996 the museum was officially re-opened (again by John Surtees) after it had been relocated to a new site at Old Bashley Manor Farm. This is part of the Upper Gallery section.

The legendary Ariel HT5 GOV 132 trials machine on display at Bashley, together with the display board listing Sammy's successes on this bike.

Another of Sammy's most prized museum exhibits is the 1939 AJS supercharged, liquid-cooled V4 racer which, with Walter Rusk at the controls, became the first machine to lap a GP circuit in excess of 100mph at the Ulster in August 1939.

The Ernie Earles BSA-engined five-hundred A7 twin-engined racer of 1951 with aluminium frame; ridden by BSA employee Charlie Salt in the 1952 and 1953 Isle of Man Senior TTs.

The museum is full of exotic and rare motorcycles. Typical are two contrasting small capacity two-strokes, the 1967 Suzuki RS67/68 125cc V4 Grand Prix prototype...

...and the equally rare 1956 Triumph Cub twin-cylinder, two-stroke prototype.

Beside complete motorcycles the museum is full of many other exhibits, including this Wooler flat-four beam engine.

Yet another extremely rare machine to be found in the museum is this Redrup with 248cc three-cylinder power unit. It is the only one still in existence.

The Letter

The best way for the reader to appreciate exactly what transpired is to reproduce the following letter from a Maurice Hopkins, published that year in a local Hampshire newspaper:

'Sir. As an ex-New Miltonian I followed with interest, through the *Advertiser*, the planning battle between Sammy Miller and the planners concerning the scruffy old barn he wanted to convert. I recently visited this phoenix, risen from the ashes, now the Sammy Miller Motorcycle Museum, and the transformation was breathtaking.

'How could the planners, in their minds eye, not envisage the finished product – a building of beauty from something that nobody would have missed had it been bulldozed flat! I have known the site since my boyhood – in fact, I learned, strictly illegally, to ride a motorcycle in the old gravel and potholed Stem Lane in the early 30s! To see the site now should bring a flush of pride to all Miltonians. On your doorstep you have a one-off gem – a world-beater, reviving memories of when Great Britain was the world leader in this field of engineering. Sammy Miller is to be admired for his courage as a road racer, his skill as a trials rider, persistence against the brick walls of the planners and for the finished article, his motorcycle museum.'

However, it should be stated here that throughout all the planning wrangling, Sammy received constant support from the New Milton Town Council (Alan Rice). In due course he received a Certificate of Appreciation from the New Milton Town Council, which reads: 'Presented to Sammy Miller Museum for a sensitive development which has enhanced our community, bringing redundant farm buildings back into use in the process.'

In March 2005 a new extension was opened at the Old Bashley Manor Farm site, increasing the floor area of the museum by approximately one third. John Surtees once again performed the opening ceremony. How many other famous faces can you recognise?

The museum is very much a working one. Many of its exhibits are displayed at events during the summer months. Typical is this display at the Goodwood Festival of Speed in 2007. Motorcycles include: Gilera 500 four, FB Mondial 250 and an AJS Porcupine.

A New Extension

In March 2005 a new extension was opened at the Old Bashley Manor Farm site, increasing the floor area of the museum by approximately one third. John Surtees once again performed the opening ceremony duties on 17th of that month. Having now visited the museum several times since this extension has opened, I feel it has significantly increased not only the space, but also the overall effectiveness of the museum's displays.

In the 7 April 2006 issue of the local *Daily Echo* newspaper, Sammy was quoted as saying: 'I'll shut my museum for good.' This came in response to another planning problem, concerning a craft shop and beautician on the site; however, on 7 December that year the *Daily Echo* was able to report: 'Motorbike Museum wins fight.'

As Sammy knows only too well: 'No museum can stand on its own financially.' So the inclusion of other businesses on the site was of vital importance.

The Bashley Manor Tea Rooms are also an important feature of the museum – so there are the tea rooms, craft shop, children's play area, farm machinery and a wide selection of different animals for visitors to see up at close quarters. There is also a large (free) car park.

Normally open seven days a week, this is reduced (for the museum) to weekends only in the winter period (December, January and February).

The 1949 AJS Porcupine, ridden by Les Graham, shown here at the Sammy Miller Museum.

Sammy (Gilera) and Phil Read (MV Agusta) mixing it at the Bealieu Motorcycle World Show, 2007.

No wonder Sammy looks so happy posing for the author with one of his latest restoration projects. This is because ever since the 1950s he has admired the works DKW 350 three-cylinder two-stroke GP racer.

There are also Special Events Days, including autojumbles, steam rallies, marque and club days. Full details of the various events in the calendar can be accessed from the museum's web site www.sammymiller.co.uk.

Of course, several of the museum's exhibits can be seen outside the confines of the Bashley site itself. Besides various race circuits, Sammy can be seen at, for example, the site of the old AMC works in south-east London (Plumstead Revisited 2005) and as the Ducati Owners Club lead rider in the 2009 New Year's Day Parade around the streets of Landon (on a restored Ducati 900 SS bevel V-twin).

Sammy proudly shows the author his framed photographs of the unique McCandless four-cylinder prototype, dating from the early 1950s.

Finally, my own view of the museum is that this embraces all Sammy's attributes of determination, dedication and skill to perfection. It is also very much a lasting tribute to a true motorcycling legend.

Chapter 9

Riding Classics

Ever since the beginning of the 1980s Sammy has taken part in numerous historic sporting events – or as they are almost universally known – the classic scene. This has seen him travel worldwide riding a range of machinery in both trials and road racing events; the latter more often parades than actual racing.

Besides all four corners of the British Isles, he has visited New Zealand, Japan, the USA, Austria, France, Italy, Spain, Canada, Australia, Germany and Belgium.

Origins

During the late 1970s Sammy had purchased a 10-acre site at Mount Pleasant Lane, Sway, near Lymington, Hampshire. Commenting at the time of his purchase in 1977 Sammy said: 'It was too rough for agricultural or industrial development, but is absolutely ideal for trials.' He continued: 'It is not very far from the New Forest home of ISDT team manager Ian Driver. I plan to use the land for XHG club trials and possibly a school.' The Sway site was to become an integral part of Sammy's life for the next quarter of a century and witnessed his transition from active competitor and development engineer for modern-day trials to the classic scene – in not only the riding field on both dirt and tarmac, but also machine restoration and his museum project.

A year later in 1978 Sammy had the vision to commission a batch of frames similar to his famous Ariel trials mount, GOV 132; the 'do-it-yourself' frame kits with the oil in the top tube. Upon the launch of the Ariel kits the cost was £140, plus 8 per cent government tax. A total of 25 such Ariel frames were sold, these joining other 'Hi-Boy chassis' for Bultaco, Ossa, Yamaha and Sammy's own Miller (Hiro) trials model.

Cavalcade of TT History

In 1980 the VMCC (Vintage Motor Cycle Club) organised the Cavalcade of TT History sponsored by *Classic Bike* magazine at the Isle of Man TT in June of that year.

The VMCC had organised almost 100 machines, together with some of the world's most famous riders – including Sammy – who rode his restored 1939 supercharged AJS V-four.

Other celebrities included Stanley Woods (Velocette), Mike Hailwood (who acted as a travelling marshal on a 1978 860cc Ducati), Frank Perris (Suzuki), Percy Tait (Triumph), Alan Shepherd (AJS 7R) and John Cooper (Seeley).

But as *Classic Bike* themselves stated: 'The most outstanding machine was Sammy Miller's 1939 AJS blown V4. Appropriately, this engine was the first to cackle into life in the paddock, to be followed by the thunder of Norton and AMC singles. Fans who had not previously witnessed vintage or classic racing must have wondered why modern two-strokes are branded as noisy!' As the last bikes blazed out of the Governor's Bridge dip in Glencrutchery Road, people were already asking: 'Will you do it again next year?' *Classic Bike* said: 'We hope so.'

The TT Lap of Honour

Enthusiasts had their prayers answered, because 12 months later the first TT Lap of Honour took place on Friday 12 June 1981. There were certainly many famous names, including Sammy, this time piloting his fully restored, ex-Terry Hill dustbin-faired NSU Sportmax.

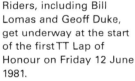

Riders, including Bill Lomas and Geoff Duke, get underway at the start of the first TT Lap of Honour on Friday 12 June 1981.

Others included the then 78-year-old Stanley Woods riding the 500cc Velocette he used in the 1939 Senior TT, Bill Lomas on a modern Suzuki instead of a promised Moto Guzzi V8, Geoff Duke on a four-cylinder Gilera and Tommy Robb on a screeching Honda six.

'A gentle amble around the TT course, as befits elderly gentlemen on elderly machines? Think again!' said Bob Currie. And there was certainly nothing sedate about the take-off of certain riders – notably Percy Tait on his three-cylinder Triumph Trident Rob North-framed machine.

Others, too, were in race mode, including the former Czech GP star Franta Stastny, who had been reunited with the three-fifty Jawa dohc twin on which he had garnered a couple of second places in the Junior TT during the 1960s.

For many a single lap was enough, but Percy Tait certainly wanted more, lapping in 22 minutes 43.1 seconds, or 99.6mph (160.25km/h) on his second circuit.

As *Motor Cycle Weekly* reported: 'So near the magic ton, but there's always another year. Like vintage wine, vintage racers seem to improve with age.'

Incidentally, Sammy had rescued the NSU, which had been found deteriorating in a Dublin wooden shed. Sammy commented: 'I found it there lying in a terrible state.'

Sammy with his 1955 NSU Sportmax during the 1981 TT Lap of Honour.

Pre '65 Scottish

Another feature of the classic sporting scene was the emergence of Pre '65 trials (and scrambles), the first Pre '65 Scottish being staged on a Tuesday afternoon in May 1984. The organising Edinburgh & District Club had finally yielded to pressure brought by pre-1965 trials enthusiasts who yearned for a contest of their own – which *Trials & MotoX News* described in its 18 May 1984 issue as: 'A light hearted affair where the actual results counted for less than the resultant atmosphere.' *T&MX News* commented: 'Quite simply it was out of this world.' It went on to paint the picture: 'With nearly 100 pre-1965 machines converging on Kinlochleven from as far afield as Bournemouth, Bristol and the Isle of Man – their riders eager to pit their skill against a total of 22 observed sections.' These hazards were situated in four areas – Mamore, Loch Eild Path, Pipeline and Grey Mare's Ridge. All of these were very much traditional, and familiar to thousands of Scottish Six Days Trial enthusiasts, and according to *T&MX News*: 'Ideal for classic British ironmongery.'

The earliest machine was Mike Vangucci's 1946 five-hundred Matchless, but most of the machines were from the late 1950s and early 1960s – many of which looked to be in showroom condition.

As Ralph Venables described: 'Hardly in the spirit of the event, a few sported Michelin "sticky" rear covers, and 1984 clothing was much in evidence.'

But wall-to-wall sunshine put everyone in high spirits, and the presence of former Scottish Six Days winner Jeff Smith (all the way from America) added additional glamour. As *T&MX News* commented: 'Smith dropped 35 marks out of a possible 110, but who cared? Certainly not the legendary JVS.'

From the start at Kinlochleven, competitors proceeded at once to Man Brec – something of a 'warmer-upper' (*T&MX News*), which cost very few marks. Then, a mile further on, the notorious Mamore was encountered, exactly as used in pre-war days.

Three dozen clean climbs of this rocky hill confirmed forecasts that Mamore was just right for the occasion. Gordon McLaughlin's 1961 350cc Matchless sounded 'very healthy' (Ralph Venables).

Loch Eild Path proved considerably more difficult. Pipeline was harder still – as *T&MX News* was to comment: 'So steep and rocky that not even the

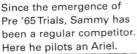

Since the emergence of Pre '65 Trials, Sammy has been a regular competitor. Here he pilots an Ariel.

mighty Miller accomplished a clean climb. Like Rathmell, he dabbed twice in the top section.'

However, Sammy simply waltzed his way up Grey Mare's Ridge, as effortlessly as he had when winning the 1962 Scottish on a similar machine (Sammy was riding a 500cc Ariel – although not the legendary GOV 132).

In typical Miller fashion, the 1984 Pre '65 Scottish was his by the end of play; his 1,014th victory. Afterwards Sammy told *Motor Cycle News*: 'The rocks were a bit loose, but fine weather made the event a big success.'

Pre '65 Scottish Trial   15 May 1984

1st	S.H. Miller (500 Ariel)	2 marks lost
2nd	M. Rathmell (200 Triumph)	4
3rd	M. Lampkin (250 BSA)	8
4th	B. Irwin (200 Triumph)	9
5th	J. Sandiford (350 BSA)	12
6th	N. Eyre (250 Greeves)	13

The Greybeards Trial

Launched on 3 September 1959, to mark the 20th anniversary of the outbreak of World War Two, the annual Greybeards Trial was another event upon which Sammy was to stamp his authority. The Greybeards became a yardstick by which all other events for riders over 40 were judged. And from the time he reached his 40th birthday, S.H. Miller was often at the head of the results sheet.

The Talmag

Motor Cycle News dated 30 January 1985 carried the headline: 'Sammy's Just Amazing!' Peter Howdle then went on to say: 'The amazing Sammy Miller made no mistake at Sunday's Talmag Trial for pre-1965 four-strokes at Hungry Hill, Aldershot, Hants. On his much modified 500cc HT5 Ariel, he was the only rider in the important class to complete two laps of the 15 old fashioned sections without penalty.'

Talmag Pre '65 Trial Class D (over 300cc springers)   January 1985

1st	S.H. Miller (500 Ariel)	0 marks lost
2nd	J. May (350 AJS)	1
3rd	G. Braybrook (350 Enfield)	2
4th	T. Wright (350 Enfield)	6
5th	M. Lakin (500 Ariel)	7*
6th	M. Barnes (350 Enfield)	7

* on test result

The Pre '65 scene has embraced events such as the Scottish, Greybeards and Talmag trials.

To catalogue all the outings Sammy has taken part in during classic meetings would require a book in itself. In fact, he could almost be described as an ambassador in this field.

Sammy has travelled worldwide to compete in historic meetings. This shot shows him with Siegfried Wunsche (DKW) centre and Walter Zeller (BMW) at the Österreichring, 1993.

Sammy and his wife Rosemary, together with the 1939 ex-Walter Rusk works AJS 500cc supercharged V4, during the Classic Racing Festival at the Österreichring, Austria, on the weekend of 31 July–1 August 1993.

The top three placed riders of the Goodwood Lennox Cup 500cc Group 1 British Built Motorcycles; Goodwood, 18 September 1999. First Barry Sheene (7), second Tim Jackson (11) and third Sammy Miller (6).

Sammy (Moto Guzzi V8) and John Cooper (BSA Rocket Three) at a Goodwood Festival of Speed meeting.

A Stand-out Performance

There have been – and continue to be – outstanding memories of Sammy's rides on classic machinery. But to the author the stand-out one must be at Goodwood on 8 September 1999, when at 65 years of age he finished third in the Lennox Cup race for 500cc Group 1 British-built motorcycles from 1948 to 1962.

Riding a Manx Norton borrowed at the last moment from his friend John Surtees (he was originally down to ride a G50 Matchless), Sammy stunned everyone by mixing it with the top riders of the classic movement, including Barry Sheene. Murray Walker admitted: 'Being in awe of Miller's abilities on the Manx Norton, when racing against significantly younger and more experienced track racers.'

Sammy being interviewed by the late Alan Robinson. The machine is the Dave Kay-built Gilera 500 four replica.

Goodwood Lennox Cup 500cc Group 1 British Built Motorcycles – 18 September 1999

1st   Barry Sheene (Walmsley Manx)
2nd   Tim Jackson (Matchless G50)
3rd   Sammy Miller (Manx Norton)
4th   Mick Hemmings (McIntyre Matchless)

Another vivid memory I have is of when Sammy crashed his Dave Kay-built 500cc four-cylinder Gilera replica in 2003 at the final Montlhéry Coupe de Moto Legendes meeting in terribly wet conditions. As the French ambulance left the circuit with its sirens blaring I feared the worst. But when I phoned Sammy a couple of weeks later he was back at work! And all this after breaking three ribs, a broken shoulder bone, a broken shoulder blade, a punctured lung and numerous cuts and bruises!

Actually he had left hospital after only 10 days. When compiling this book, and with certain other crashes throughout his riding career from which he had made particularly quick recoveries, I asked Sammy how he managed it. His answer was simple and to the point: 'I'm blessed with strong bones,' he said.

Even as I was writing this book in the summer of 2009, Sammy, then aged 75, was still just as busy riding. Quite simply amazing, and proof, if any was needed, of his continuing enthusiasm for motorcycling.

Chapter 10

A Place in History

For most people being good at something is quite an achievement. But in Sammy Miller's case this has been achieved several times over. As John Craig entitled a feature on Sammy in *Classic Legends* magazine during the late 1980s: 'The Man Who Never Wanted to be Second' sums up our man to perfection.

In the author's opinion Sammy is determined and dedicated – driven, if you will. Second best in anything is simply not good enough for Samuel Hamilton Miller. Another facet of Sammy's persona is confidence. As Frank

Sammy riding a 500cc Gilera at the Goodwood Revival Meeting, 2006.

Melling wrote in 1975: 'His natural good grace and charm do nothing to reduce the overwhelming sense of confidence he exudes in a ceaseless flood. Not arrogance, but rather a total belief that anything he chooses to do is possible – and often is.' Gordon Blakeway (himself a trials rider of no mean ability) commented: 'I only wish people would understand Sammy. Nobody will ever change him – and that's why he became the best trials rider we have ever seen.' To which that doyen of trials journalists, the late Ralph Venables, pointed out: 'To that I would add not only the best – but the most ruthless.'

Like his close friend John Surtees, Sammy is above all a perfectionist; second best is simply not good enough. Whereas both John and Sammy are multi-talented, so to speak, the large majority of other superstar names in

In 1995 Sammy was president of the TT Riders' Association (taking over from John Surtees). The two men are seen here with other members, including Geoff Duke (far left) and Nick Jefferies (centre, top, between Sammy and John).

The Ariel HT5 trials as modified by Sammy, which helped change his life entirely.

Just a small number of the hundreds of trophies gained in competitive events by Sammy over almost half a century.

motorcycle sport have restricted their talent to only the riding side of the sport, and then only a single discipline.

In Sammy Miller's case he has not only competed in virtually every form of motorcycle competition, winning countless events over more than half a century, but has also been equally successful in many other fields. These have included design/development engineer, test rider, team manager, sponsor, motorcycle dealer, motorcycle mail order operator, restorer and museum creator. In 1995 Sammy was president of the TT Riders' Association (taking over from John Surtees). Below is a list of Sammy's major motorcycle sporting achievements:

- 11 times successive British Trials Champion.
- Twice European Trials Champion (read World).
- 13 times successive Hurst Cup winner.
- 18 times successive Walter Rusk Trials winner.
- 5 times winner of the Scottish Six Days Trial.

Sammy and his second wife Rosemary enjoying a well-earned break in New Zealand, 2008.

Sammy is someone who values old friendships. He is seen here at an event with Pam Venables, widow of the late Ralph Venables.

- 7 times winner of the world's most arduous trial, the Scott, on the unforgiving Yorkshire moors.
- Winner of 1,226 trials events.
- 9 gold medals at International Six Days Trial.
- Irish Motocross Champion.
- Irish Sand Racing Champion.
- Winner of most Irish road races, including the North West 200 and the Leinster 200 three years in succession.
- Grand Prix World Championships on works FB Mondials: 1957 250cc third and 125cc fourth.
- Sponsor of the British Classic Trial Championships.
- Still rides today at retirement age, including competing in classic road race events throughout Europe and all around the world including Australia and New Zealand.

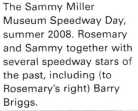

The Sammy Miller Museum Speedway Day, summer 2008. Rosemary and Sammy together with several speedway stars of the past, including (to Rosemary's right) Barry Briggs.

Dedication and the need to succeed meant that Sammy saw practice as the way forward in his trials career. Also fitness was equally important. While others might be propping up the bar on the night before an important

Bultaco's 50th anniversary celebrations, October 2008, at which Sammy was very much a central figure.

event, Sammy certainly did not. In fact, alcohol and smoking were strictly off limits.

All this helps explain why Sammy's riding career lasted so long and why, today, in his mid-70s, he is able to spend an amazing 12 hours a day, seven-days-a-week working, promoting or restoring motorcycles, to say nothing of still competing on the machinery from his museum. In fact, the museum also says a lot about the man. Not only are the machines in pristine condition, but they also run just as well as they look.

During one of my visits while writing this book, Sammy and Bob Stanley were in the process of restoring, among other machines, a 1953 three-cylinder two-stroke DKW racer. To anyone else this restoration would have been nigh on impossible, but not for Sammy and Bob; the pair simply got down to the task in hand in a totally professional manner, even though they had to manufacture many of the required parts with their own hands.

Another facet of Sammy's life has been an ongoing love of animals; something which began when the family was forced to leave Belfast for the countryside during World War Two. Here he is with his alpaca called Bruno.

Actually it was in the matter of seeing a job through where Sammy and I really were on the same wavelength. We both have the same principle – get on and complete the job! Not only that, but to the very highest standard possible.

Although his riding skills are what have grabbed the headlines, to me what is of equal importance – perhaps even more so – is Sammy's role as designer/development engineer.

Going right through from his first attempt, the home-built SHS in 1953/54, his now legendary Ariel HT5, the creation of the Bultaco 250 Sherpa, the Honda project, the SWM, the Hiro engine, the Aprilia, Sammy's own Miller, to, finally, the Armstrong, all have carried his DNA – his personal stamp of creative flair. In fact, it is true to say that Sammy's work in this area changed design of the trials bike itself.

So what are Sammy's dislikes? In his own words: 'Red tape, paperwork, computers who know about trials motorcycles, time wasters and utility companies with computerised telephone systems.'

His favourite rider of all time? Geoff Duke.

Today, Sammy, together with his second wife Rosemary, lives in the old farmhouse at Bashley Manor which was rebuilt when the other farm buildings were restored and converted into the museum – as Sammy says: 'We walk to work in the morning.'

Sammy has two children, Stuart (born 3 September 1970) and Jane (born 8 March 1972), and they, together with Rosemary, accompanied him to Buckingham Palace on Friday 27 February 2009 to collect the MBE awarded in the New Year's Honours List, which was presented by Prince Charles. The award was in recognition of Sammy's services to motorcycle heritage.

As detailed in Chapter 8, the museum was originally founded in 1983, from what had begun as a private collection. It has now been placed into a trust to leave behind a legacy for future generations. It houses one of the finest collections of fully restored motorcycles in the world, including factory racers, exotic prototypes and memorabilia spanning seven decades of motorcycling. Sammy's famous Ariel GOV 132 holds pride of place, which he not only designed, but also went on to win most trials competitions on. Historically important exhibits include the only working World Championship-winning AJS Porcupine (1949), the 1939 supercharged V-four AJS (the first machine to lap a Grand Prix circuit in excess of 100mph) and a 1905 Norton, the oldest known Norton in the world.

Now sporting over 400 machines, the collection is being constantly added to, each new addition being given a full workshop restoration, personally overseen by Sammy himself. At least one machine has been displayed at every Classic Bike show since 1983. Through his efforts, Sammy has personally ensured the survival of many rare British motorcycles, which he shares with the public by touring and through demonstrations.

In closing, I must pay tribute to a man who has tirelessly devoted his entire life to the sport and demonstrated a lifelong commitment. The Sammy Miller Museum is a living testament to the fact that he is not simply an outstanding competitor, but also a very skilled engineer, restorer, ambassador and custodian of motorcycle history.

A proud moment: Sammy receiving the MBE at Buckingham Palace in early 2009. Sammy and Rosemary, together with Sammy's two children Stuart and Jane.

A Sammy Miller postage stamp from the Isle of Man, 1997.

Postscript

BY SAMMY MILLER

I have been very fortunate to have been involved with morocycling all of my life, since leaving school at 15 with no qualifications, only a big dream and a lot of passion. It is a great pity that my teachers did not tell me to study harder, especially in languages and maths, as these subjects would have been an immense help in my motorcycling career, but then again my teachers did not give much hope for my career at all.

I have been lucky enough to meet and even ride with some of the world's great riders during my career, including Stanley Woods, Freddie Frith, Ernie Lyons, Harold Daniell, Artie Bell, Geoff Duke, Bob McIntyre, Bob Brown, Mike Hailwood, Barry Sheene and Giacomo Agostini to name but a few, and also to have been guided in my early days by Terry Hill and Artie Bell. Looking back, without question if I had had a strict manager/father like John Surtees and Mike Hailwood I would not have wasted so much time in my early days building bikes like the SHS, as my time would have been put to much better use in more competitions.

From my boyhood many things stand out, including the Germans bombing Belfast, escaping from the bunkers in the middle of the night and seeing a Junkers 88 a few feet above, seeing the Flying Fortress that crashed on the side of Cave Hill and walking around the Antrim Road after the German bombing.

Sammy with the Terry Hill Sportmax taking part in a typical Irish roads event, c.1956.

At Onchan on the Works
Ducati 125 Desmo, 1958
Ultra Lightweight (125cc) TT.

Other little things I look back on from later in my career are being the first person to ride over a car with a motorcycle (on purpose!) and scaling the north face of Cave Hill, from where you can see over Belfast, feet up on my Ariel – this took many weeks and many crashes!

I have enjoyed bikes all of my life and have been to practically every country in the world, with either the Ariel, Bultaco or Honda factories. I also still remember the long, boring days at the Honda works, where everything was so slow and programmed and not the way I work at all. I recall one development trip of 10 days which included four rest days! I soon knocked those on the head.

I have had quite a few close shaves in my day, probably the most memorable being during the Leinster 200-mile road race at Wicklow in 1956. Bob Brown, on another NSU Sportmax, and I were having quite a ding dong and I was following him into a very, very fast right-hander with an 8ft stone wall on the perimeter. I managed to select neutral – which is not the thing to do – and the bike and I slid into the bottom of the stone wall, the fairing scraping on the road on one side and this stone wall being crashed into on the other. Luckily, the bike and I escaped from the base of the wall and carried on to catch Bob up and win! At the finish Terry and Artie wondered why I was so white and why both sides of the fairing were damaged!

I also recall the Ducati parade lap at the 2008 TT on a 1970s bevel 900SS V-twin, when I was blinded by the sun and had to take abortive action and use my trials experience to ride the Ducati over the wall. Luckily, there were ample gorse bushes in which to park the bike on the other side.

Sammy with the NSU
Sportmax he had recently
restored, 1981.

Sammy and his beloved
alpacas, a recent
photograph.

People often ask me why I stopped road racing to concentrate on trials; my answer is that this was a combination of events. After 1957, Mondial, Gilera and Moto Guzzi decided to stop road racing, which meant that I was redundant and a bit disillusioned, so in 1958 I decided that I could build, develop and win in the trials field instead. Also, the fatalities in road racing were quite horrific and I had lost

Sammy with the 1958 Mototrans (Spanish) Ducati 200 Elite, which he had just restored, spring 2009.

many good friends and did not want to join them. However, if I had carried on, with Honda, Suzuki and Yamaha coming into road racing, who knows what might have happened.

When I announced my retirement from World Championship trials and did not renew my contract with Bultaco I was then approached by Yamaha with a very lucrative contract to design, develop and compete in World Championship events with them. Although I was very, very interested, I did not want to do World Championship events at the highest level, so I diplomatically declined the offer. Yamaha then went on to approach Mick Andrews, who jumped at the opportunity.

Afterwards, Honda came along with an equally excellent offer with what I wanted to do, namely design, develop and run the Honda trials team. As you now know, I did sign up and produced a world-beater for Honda.

Today, I look around the museum to see the 1956 Truimph 200cc Twin two-stroke, Norton P93 and the four-cylinder Villiers. Then there is the special tubular duplex-framed Arrow. I had come up with the concept and fitted it with BSA forks, smaller wheels equipped with knobbly tyres and an Arrow engine with upswept exhaust system and chrome-plated mudguards, and the completed motorcycle was the centre of attraction wherever it went. In many ways it was a forerunner to the Street Scrambler trial bike which was to become so popular from the late 1960s onwards, particularly in North America. The Japanese sold literally millions of the same concept.

More recently there have been disappointments with the museum, when people do not have the passion, and will sell a British treasure overseas for an extra £50. Mercenaries without passion! I feel content, however, that the

Frontal view of the museum in the summer of 2009, together with a varied assortment of its collection on display.

Another view of the museum square, this time showing the offices/ workshops on the right and tea rooms and craft centre on the left.

museum is a trust that will live on long after my session. I get immense pleasure from people's reaction to the museum; many would like me to talk forever, but there is always work to be done in the workshop and bikes to be finished. I always get satisfaction returning to the workshop in the morning after a hard day's work the day before and seeing the results we have achieved.

Unfortunately, in the commercial world of today we have people who are investing in our motorcycling heritage who are only using this to benefit their financial position, and these precious bikes are hidden away forever, which is such a shame.

I have been very fortunate that when I retired from serious competition I was able to enjoy many more years in the Classic scene, which fortunately has blossomed from then, and this extended my riding career for another 30 years.

I sometimes find it quite difficult to look at my long and successful career; it is almost as if I am looking at another person. I won my first competitive event in 1952 and my last serious one in 2007; 55 years of being the man to beat. Surely this must be the longest-ever successful period in our sport?

With a 499cc Gilera Saturno Sport, at the Colombres Rally, 10 October 2009.

Appendices

Sammy Miller Museum Motorcycle Collection

R/B = Road Bike; T/B = Trial Bike; Ohv = Over head valve; 2/s = Two Stroke; S/V = Side Valve; R/P = Restoration Project

Racing Gallery

Make	Year	cc	Model
Packer	1914	1000	Board Racer
Verdel	1912	750	Board Racer
Bultaco TSS	1963	125	Production Racer
EMC	1985	250	Grand Prix Racer
EMC	1952	125	Road Racer
NSU	1955	250	Grand Prix Racer
Spondon	1968	500	Prototype Racer
Yamaha TZ	1978	250	Production Racer
Bultaco TSS	1968	125	Production Racer
Excelsior	1930	1000	Record Breaker
Greeves	1966	250	Production Racer
Royal Enfield	1966	250	GP5 Racer
DMW	1966	250	Hornet Racer
Cotton Telstar	1965	250	Telstar Production Racer
Aermacchi	1969	350	Ala d'Oro Production Racer
Moto Parilla	1957	250	Road Racer
BSA	1968	750	Rocket Road Racer
Triumph GP	1949	499	Factory Racer
CZ	1956	350	Road Racer
Jawa	1967	340	Production Racer
Jawa	1952	500	Road Racer
Kawasaki	1969	500	Grand Prix Racer
Kawasaki	1980	500	Grand Prix Racer
Suzuki	1980	500	Grand Prix Racer
Yamaha	1980	500	Grand Prix Racer
Yamaha TZ	1973	250	Production Racer
Yamaha TD1C	1967	250	Production Racer
Yamaha	1978	125	Production Racer
Suzuki V4	1965	125	Works Racer
Yamaha TA	1968	125	Production Racer
Yamaha TD2	1969	250	Production Racer
Yamaha TR2	1971	350	Production Racer
Gilera	1957	500	Works Racer
MV Agusta	1953	125	Production Racer
Moto Guzzi	1951	250	Production Racer

Make	Year	cc	Model
Moto Guzzi	1946	500	Production Racer
Aermacchi	1963	250	Production Racer
EMC	1948	350	Grand Prix Racer
DKW	1937	250	Grand Prix Racer
New Imperial	1934	246	Grand Prix Racer
Rudge	1934	250	Road Racer
Sunbeam	1933	500	Road Racer
Chater Lea	1930	350	Sports Racer
Matchless G50	1963	496	Production Racer
Matchless G45	1954	498	Production Racer
AJS 7R	1949	348	Production Racer
Velocette KTT	1948	348	Production Racer
AJS R7	1938	348	Works Racer
Husqvarna	1935	500	Works Racer
Douglas + 90	1951	348	Works Racer
OK Supreme	1937	250	Works Racer
Excelsior	1935	247	Works Racer
Excelsior Manxman	1939	349	Road Racer
Excelsior Mechanical Marvel	1934	250	Works Racer
Ariel GOV 132	195?	498	Trials Bike
AJS V4	1939	500	Works Racer
AJS Porcupine	1949	498	Works Racer
BSA MCI	1954	250	Works Racer
Earles BSA	1951	500	Prototype Racer
Mondial	1954	125	Road Racer
Mondial	1957	250	Works Racer
Honda	1967	499	RC181
DKW	1953	350	Three-Cylinder
Moto Guzzi	1946	500	Dondonlino
Moto Guzzi	1951	250	Gambalungino
REG	1959	250	Racer

Upper North Hall

Make	Year	cc	Model
Scott	1921	500	Twin RB
Scott SA	1925	500	Twin RB
Scott	1957	596	Twin RB
Rudge	1938	500	Sports SPC
OEC	1928	350	Dupley Model RB
Francis-Barnett	1929	196	Model 14 RB
Francis-Barnett	1937	250	Cruiser G45 RB
Cotton	1936	250	JAP RB
Cotton	1922	250	S Valve RB
Quadrant	1898	1.5hp	De Dion RB
Minerva	1910	1000	V-twin RB
Dunelt	1926	250	Model K RB
Coventry Eagle	1934	250	K6 RB
Rudge Multi	1914	500	RB
Levis	1937	500	Model D RB
Raleigh	1927	350	OHV RB
Sunbeam	1922	3.5hp	Sports Bike
Matchless	1930	400	Silver Arrow
Matchless	1931	393	Silver Hawk

Henderson	1916		F2 RB
FN	1909		4cy In Line RB
Dunelt	1929	250	3cy 1 RB
Redrup	1948	248	3cy RB
OK Bradshaw	1926	350	
Neander		100	V-Twin
Radco	1922		Ladies Model

Upper South Hall

Make	*Year*	*cc*	*Model*
Penny Farthing			Bicycle
Zenith	1948	950	Jap SV
Brough		680	In Line
Excelsior	1923	175	T/S
Wolf	1914	2.5hp	T/D
Pacer	1926	1100	MAG
AJW	1946	500	SV Twin
New Imperial	1935	500	M 70
Royal Enfield	1932	148	CY-CAR Z2
BMW	1928	700	R11
Velocette	1929	350	KTT MK1
Velocette	1923	250	Model G
Velocette	1930	350	KSS
Velocette	1934	350	Mk1V KTT
Velocette	1962	200	Valiant
BSA Bantam	1953	123	D3
Excelsior	1923	150	T/S
ABC	1920	400	H/O/Twin
Omega	1921	346	3sp SV
Tri Ricardo	1927	500	Radia SV
Coventry Eagle	1924	250	3sp
Triumph	1925	550	SD Model
Douglas	1920	349	DT (Speedway)
Invicta	1920	500	King Dick
Duncan	1921	980	V-Twin
Ner Car	1923	221	Model A
Royal Ruby	1918	350	Side Valve
All Day Matchless	1914	3.5hp	2 Speed
Stanger	1923	538	V-Twin T/S
Douglas Speedway	1929		DT5 Speedway
P and M	1928	250	V-Twin
Francis-Barnett	1929	344	Pull Man
Velocette	1920	250	Ladies Model

Trials Section

Make	*Year*	*cc*	*Model*
AJS	1964	350	16C T/B
Ariel	1957	500	HTS T/B
Ariel	1955	500	HS Scramble Bike
Jawa	1977	402	Enduro
Jawa	L/T	500	Long Track
FB Mondial	1955	200	Sports Model

Gilera	1974	150	RB
Suzuki	1982	1100	GSX 1100
Honda CB 77	1964	305	CB77
Honda CL 72	1967	250	CL 72
Honda CBX	1979	1047	CBX
Benelli	1980	231	M 254 RB
Cotton	1976	250	Trials Bike
CCM	1977	350	Trials Bike
Miller	1978	350	Trials Bike
DOT	1953	125	Trials Bike
Greeves	1952	200	24 DB
Greeves	1963	250	TES
SHS	1954	197	Special
Bultaco	1964	244	Sherpa
Honda	1977	305	Hi Boy
Eskine	1955	500	Speed Way
Honda	1965	50	Monkey Bike
Honda	1964	124	CB 92
Honda	1992	125	Grand Prix Racer
Honda	1962	125	CB 77
Honda 4	1963	250	Grand Prix Racer
Honda	1963	50	CR 110
FB Mondial	1953	175	175 TV

Norton Gallery

Make	Year	cc	Model
Norton	1947		International Road Bike
Norton	1905	500	Flat Tank
Norton SV	1953	497	Prototype Army Bike
Norton FT	1924	490	16 H-Road Bike
Norton CSI	1928	490	Sports Bike
Norton INT	1938	490	Model 30 Sports Bike
Norton 30M	1947	490	Racing Bike
Norton 500T	1949	490	Trial Bike
DKW Rotary	1978	294	Rotary Valve
Suzuki Rotary	1975	500	Rotary Valve
Norton Rotary	1989	1000	Rotary Valve
Norton Pro	1951	497	Prototype Road Bike
Norton Low Boy	1960	350	Racing Bike
Norton Kneeler	1953	350	Racing Bike
Norton Model F	1956	350	Racing Bike
Norton	1974	490	P92 Prototype Road Bike
Norton	1961	250	Jubilee
Norton	1965	400	Electra

Main Gallery South Wing

Make	Year	cc	Model
BSA Gold Star	1958	500	DBD 34 S/B
BSA Rocket Gold Star	1961	650	RGS S/B
BSA A10	1961	650	Twin R/B
BSA B33	1955	500	Single R/B
BSA A7	1952	500	Twin R/B

BSA A10 Golden Flash	1952	650	Twin R/B
Triumph Trophy	1952	500	Twin R/B
Sunbeam S7	1948	487	Inline Twin
Triumph Bandit	1970	349	Prototype Twin
Triumph T100	1958	500	Twin R/B
Triumph 3TA	1962	350	Twin R/B
Triumph Side Valve	1908	500	Flat Tank R/B
Grindlay Peerless	1926	500	Sleeve Valve Engine R/B
Grindlay Peerless	1925		STI
SOS	1937	250	R/B
Brough Superior	1929	680	Jap Engine
Brough Superior	1928	1000	SS100
Villiers V4	1962	500	Ptototype R/B
Scott 3	1935	1000	Prototype R/B
Long Track Jap	1958	500	Speedway
Norton 16 H	1944	490	Army Bike
Triumph WD	1942	500	Army Bike
Triumph Cub Two-Stroke	1956	200	Prototype R/B

Main Gallery North Wing

Make	Year	cc	Model
Corgi S/C	1949	98	Side Car Type
Haythorn	1939	500	Prototype R/B
Vincent	1952	500	Road Bike
Vincent SP	1950	1000	Racer
Vincent B/S	1950	998	Sports Bike
Royal Enfield	1950	125	2/S
BSA AA Sidecar Outfit	1959	600	M21
Ariel Leader	1959	250	Twin T/S
Ariel Arrow	1962	250	Twin T/S
Ariel Square 4	1959	1000	4cy R Bike
Ariel Square 4	1936	600	4cy R Bike
Ariel	1927	500	Single Cylinder
Ariel	1916	500	Flat Tank
BSA Sidecar Outfit	1919	559	Flat Tank
BSA	1929	500	Sloper ohv
OEC	1932	600	4 cylinder
Ascot Pullin	1929	500	Road Bike
HRD	1935	500	Ohv Single
HRD	1939	1000	Ohv Twin
Ducati Mototrans	1958	200	Elite

Flat Tank Gallery

Make	Year	cc	Model
Hoffman	1953	250	Road Bike
TWN	1956	200	2/S Road Bike
Harley	1988	1200	Sportster R/B
Indian	1935	1265	In Line R/B
Indian	1921	998	V-Twin R/B
EMC	1948	500	Split Single 2/S
Monet Goyon	1932	350	SV Single
Nimbus	1947	746	4 Cyl

Victoria	1954	345	V-Twin
Royal Enfield	1926	350	Ohv R/B
Royal Enfield	1926		Wooden Model By G. Elkins
FN	1947	350	SV Single

Three Wheel Gallery

Make	Year	cc	Model
BSA Sidecar	1927	770	R/P
Morgan	1929	1096	Three Wheeler Sports
James Delivery Van	1934	680	Three Wheeler Van
Excelsior	1958	328	T/Cyl R/B
Velocette LE	1958	192	Police Bike
Quadrant	1902	80	Bicycle Type
Power Pak	1954	49	Auto Cycle
Velocette Thruxton	1966	499	Sports Bike
Parilla	1950	98	R/P
Itom	1955	50	Sports Bike
Douglas	1950	348	MK5 R/B
Douglas Dragonfly	1955	350	Road Bike
Raleigh P/Pak	1953	48	Auto Cycle
Cycle Master	1952	257	Auto Cycle
Kingbury	1921	150	Scooter
Royal Enfield Flea	1948	125	T/S Road Bike
Levis	1914	2.25hp	Flat Tank
Humber Cyclo	1925	49	Auto Cycle
Brown Auto Cyclo	1954	98	Auto Cycle
Cykelaid	1923	100	Auto Cycle
Cyclo Master	1954	25	Auto Cycle
Vincent Firefly	1953	50	Auto Cycle
BSA W/Wheel	1953	254	Auto Cycle
Packman + Poppe	1924	1000	Sprint

Bikes in Workshop

Make	Year	cc	Model
AJS V-Twin	1930	596	Restoration
Rex Acme E9	1929	700	Restoration

Bikes on Loan

Make	Year	cc	Owner
Holcroft	1902	260	Ken Blake
Raleigh	1923	350	N. Waring
Sunbeam	1937	350	K. Blake
Sunbeam	1937	250	K. Blake
BSA T/Ban	1953	175	B. Pottor
Levis	1936	350	N. Waring
Jawa	Long Track	500	S. Wigg
Ratier	1959	600	I. Munro
Manx Norton	1957	348	K. Blake
Norton Dominator	1953	500	K.V. Gard
Norton Dominator	1966	650	D. Joyce
Fan Norton	1952	500	J. Whitehouse

Model	Year	Capacity	Owner
Norton Sidecar		500	J. Mennell
EMC	1948	350	K. Blake
FN	1947	350	K. Cobbing
Peugeot	1938	350	A. Turner
Martin Side	1923	676	K. Blake
Nut	1925	700	K. Blake
Bat	1913	1270	K. Blake
Sunbeam	1938	500	S. Blake
IFA	1957	350	I. Munro
Arno	1912	500	K. Blake
Gerard	1914	269	K. Blake
G Rhone	1922	400	K. Blake
Wooden Royal Enfield			G. Elkins
Royal Enfield	1926	350	G. Elkins
Nut	1920	998	K. Blake
Western Star	1911	500	K. Blake
Gold Star FT	1957	500	W. Gardner
Triumph T100	1963	500	Mr Probert
Triumph CTT	1931	498	N. Waring
Wooler	1955	500	C. Trust
Zenith Gradua	1921	500	C. Trust
Bansee	1922	269	C. Trust
All Day Matchless	1915	169	C. Trust
Kerry	1904	3.5hp	C. Trust
Whippet	1919	150	C. Trust
Douglas	1945	602	K. Blake
Royal Enfield	1926	250	Unknown
Douglas	1935	500	K. Blake
Humber	1912	2.75hp	K. Blake
Rex Acme TT	1926	350	J. Squirrell
Cotton	1934	350	J. Squirrell
Seeley	1971	500	C. Seeley
Bultaco TSS	1968	250	Mario Garno

Index

ND - #0341 - 270225 - C0 - 260/195/21 - PB - 9781780912134 - Gloss Lamination